IMAGES
of America

CALIFORNIA'S WHALING COAST

On the Cover: Fields Landing Whaling Station, most likely pictured between 1940 and 1942, was the only whaling station in the United States from 1940 when it began operations until 1952 when it seized operations. The station was situated at Fields Landing, 10 miles south of Eureka, Humboldt County, Northern California. The station had several whaleships that went up and down the coast in search of whales and brought them back to the plant for flensing.

IMAGES
of America

CALIFORNIA'S WHALING COAST

Dale Vinnedge

ARCADIA
PUBLISHING

ISBN 978-1-4671-3171-1

Published by Arcadia Publishing
Charleston, South Carolina

Printed in the United States of America

Library of Congress Control Number:

For all general information, please contact Arcadia Publishing:
Telephone 843-853-2070
Fax 843-853-0044
E-mail sales@arcadiapublishing.com
For customer service and orders:
Toll-Free 1-888-313-2665

Visit us on the Internet at www.arcadiapublishing.com

This book is dedicated to the whalers and their efforts to sustain a once-romantic industry. Among them are Frederick K. Dedrick, John D. Loop, Hermann Foland, "Gibb" Hunter, John Davenport, and Jose Machado, heads of whaling companies struggling to keep their companies going during good times and difficult times for whaling.

Contents

ACKNOWLEDGMENTS

The author wishes to acknowledge a few of the sources whose collections formed a large part of this book. The San Francisco Maritime Museum Library was a valuable source, in particular accessibility to the Alta California Newspaper collection, covering the 1850s to the 1890s. The Oakland Public Library and access to the *Oakland Tribune* provided information on whaling from the 1800s and 1900s. The San Francisco Public Library and its *San Francisco Chronicle* collection provided important information. Also, collections of newspapers all over the state on microfilm form a part of the book. Information for parts of the book was available thanks to the public libraries of Santa Cruz, Monterey, San Diego, Watsonville, Salinas, and many others. Universities, including Humboldt State, San Jose State University, and the University of California, Berkeley are reflected in the material. Also included in the list are the archives of the State of California, San Francisco Maritime Museum, and the Kendall Whaling Museum, now part of the New Bedford Whaling Museum.

The photographs are all part of the collection of the author. Many of the photographs were purchased through postcard bourses. However, the bulk of the photographs and postcard images have been collected through online auction houses that have started up in the last 10 years. Never could all of this material have been collected through used-book stores and antique shops.

Books form a very small part of this work, because few volumes have been written on the subject of California whaling after 1900. There have been a number of magazine articles that contributed to various areas of whaling over the years. A few of these books and magazines are mentioned in the bibliography.

INTRODUCTION

Whaling came to California in the Mexican period, when Henry Dana Jr. was on the coast with the hide and tallow trade. The Boston ships left, but the whalers stayed on. They were here in the time of the California's, and they were involved, coming to the aid of the Americans when San Diego was under siege. The whalers were here when California became independent, and they were here when California became a state. They stayed here until the end of whaling.

Whalers provided products to lighthouses before petroleum. They provided lubrication that sped the wheels of the industrial revolution. They supplied baleen that served the needs until plastic was invented. During the war years, whalers provided oil for the manufacture of margarine, and meat when beef and pork were not available.

But, time moves on, and most of the products that whalers provided have seen their need diminished or replaced. So, naturally, the whalers have seen their business fade into the horizon. Whaling in California was active in the mid-19th century, but the industry as a whole was already disappearing as California was getting involved. After 1900, the industry was relegated to a few whalers. Technology improvements kept California in the whaling business, until whaling was discontinued in 1972.

The story of whaling in California is the story of small business, and of the dreams of many people developing their trade of locating various species—how best to track them, and how best to take them. It is the history of developing new methods to capture different species of whales.

One

Yankee Whaling

In the early days of the nation's history, New Bedford and Nantucket took the lead in the hunt for the whale. Ships roamed the seas of the world, hunting whales for their oil and bone. From the Arctic to the South Seas and into the South Pole, the whalers gained a complete knowledge of the great oceans. For more than a century, American seamen dominated the whale oil industry.

When attention was directed toward California, the whaleships of New England were among the first to arrive. They were not interested in hides and tallow, however. It was learned that valuable sea otter skins could be obtained there, skins that in China would bring high prices. Whaling was temporarily discontinued while the captains became fur traders. The Spanish, and later Mexican officials, prohibited this trade, but the Yankee captains found ways of circumventing the laws and had a thriving trade in collecting furs. This trade, however, soon attracted Boston ships, which were laden with trade goods, forcing the whalers to return to their craft.

Scammon's Lagoon, on the coast of Lower California, bears the name of Charles Melville Scammon, one of the more famous of the whalers operating in West Coast waters. He was known to set out from San Francisco and return with a full cargo of oil after only a short few months. His ship was not weather-beaten, as were ships that had been out from two to five years to fill their holds. Old whalers knew that Captain Scammon had discovered a spot where whales were plentiful and easy to get. How easy they never suspected.

The truth was that Captain Scammon learned that the gray whales lay hidden in shallow lagoons, along the coast of Baja California Del Sur, where the females gave birth to their young. One of these places was a large landlocked bay resembling San Francisco Bay, but smaller. Scammon would sail his ship into the bay and set up his try-works on shore. His men would then go after the whales from the smaller whaling boats in the landlocked harbor. It was not long before there was company in the lagoon, and the whalers spread out from Scammon's Lagoon all the way south to Magdelena Bay. The first arrivals to the lagoons found a huge pile of discarded bones that had no commercial value. Captain Scammon did well financially, and the lagoon still bears his name.

New Bedford being far away from the whales, and with greater railroad access after 1869, ship owners decided to make San Francisco their whaling base. The business grew to tremendous proportions, and even New Bedford and Nantucket were eclipsed as operating centers. Along with San Francisco, a fleet went out of Honolulu, operating under the flag of the Kingdom of Hawaii. During the off-season, the old San Francisco whaleships would anchor in Oakland Creek, as the estuary was then called.

Several great disasters struck the whaling fleet, which was on the verge of collapse. The first of these disasters occurred in September 1862, when 33 ships of the San Francisco and Hawaiian fleet got trapped in the ice in the Bering Sea and were crushed into matchwood by the quickly advancing freeze. Leading up to the disaster, the season had been a good one, and the whalers were unusually plentiful in the far north. The whaling fleet worked its way into the North Pacific and began moving slowly back as the season advanced. The weather turned cold, and the ice and a cold snap came ahead of its usual time. The ice closed in so quickly on the doomed ships that they did not have a chance to escape. They were completely crushed and lost, along with their valuable cargoes of oil and bone.

The men managed to make their way over the ice and along the shore to three of the ships that had taken up anchorage beyond the islands and out of the ice danger. These craft, greatly overloaded, bore the survivors back to the Hawaiian Islands. San Francisco was especially hard hit by this disaster.

But more trouble was in store. The Civil War was raging, and the *Shenandoah*, one of the Confederate raiders, managed to get into the Pacific. The whalers had no knowledge of the warship's presence in the North Pacific, and 25 of the whalers were sunk and lost to the California fleet. Most of the ships were burned, with the men being taken off.

The final blow came in 1897–1898. Once again, the northern seas had been particularly open, and the whaling fleet had gone right into the Arctic after the whales. Some of the ships lay at anchor on the east side of Point Barrow, and the remainder on the west side. Then, the wind shifted, and the ice closed in. Within a few hours, what was left of the California whaling fleet was a tangled mass of wreckage. A little over 1,200 men managed to make their way across the ice to the trading station at Point Barrow, a distance of some 40 miles.

At that time, George Bower and a handful of Eskimos were the only inhabitants of Point Barrow, and there was a limited amount of food to sustain the stranded men until the arrival of the first rescue ships in the next year. Word was sent to the outside world of the plight of the whalers.

The Coast Guard cutter *Bear* had just reached Seattle, its crew anticipating a long winter vacation, when the telegraph brought word from the north that around 1,000 men were stranded at Point Barrow and short of food. Unless aid could reach them quickly, death by starvation would be the lot of many of them.

To the credit of the Coast Guard, every man aboard the *Bear* volunteered to load the ship with supplies and sail north to rescue the whalers. Capt. Francis Tuttle, with considerable experience in the revenue service, knew the area well. However, the ice by that time had become so thick that the *Bear* could only force its way as far north and Nelson Island, far from Point Barrow. Lt. David H. Jarvis; Lt. Ellsworth P. Berthorf; the ship's doctor, Samuel P. Call; and Mr. Kolichoff volunteered to land and force their way through the racing snow storms to the site of the disaster. They also planned to drive a herd of 400 reindeer ahead of them to serve as an emergency food supply. Natives accustomed to living in the throes of hard northern winters swore that the three white men could never get through.

They began a battle overland, through snow-filled canyons and across frozen arms of the sea, over the ice-filled lakes in the face of howling winds until, eventually, they reached Point Barrow after 1,500 miles.

As a result of the efforts of the Coast Guardsmen, every one of the whalers cast ashore were saved. But the weather was too much for the whaling fleet to overcome. A few of the old ships continued to run from the Oakland mudflats until about 1910. By then, they also quit. After this time, whaling was carried out from shore stations, the hunting being done by steam tugs. Whales were shot from bomb guns and small cannons.

In 1871, the whalers lost ships valued at $1 million. Almost all of the ships sailed from San Francisco, with the bulk of them owned on the East Coast. New Bedford was home to 21 ships; New London, 2 ships; San Francisco, 3; Edgartown, 2; and Honolulu, 4 ships.

Vessels were lost to the ice almost every year. Many whalers were lost in a single season, but several times ships were lost just a few at a time or individually.

Today, only memories remain of a once-exciting and adventurous period of American and Pacific Coast sea life. While it lasted, fortunes were made and many interesting pages of romance and history were written. The sea is now vacant of American flag whalers.

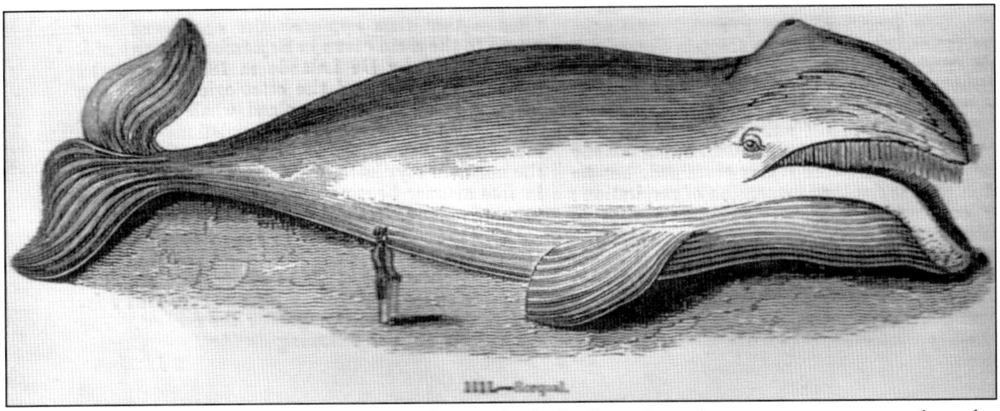

Before the invention of cameras, artists depicted whales based on descriptions given to them by whalers. Artists did not have the ability to view live, or even dead, whales, for the most part. This print appeared in *Penny* magazine of April 30–May 31, 1833.

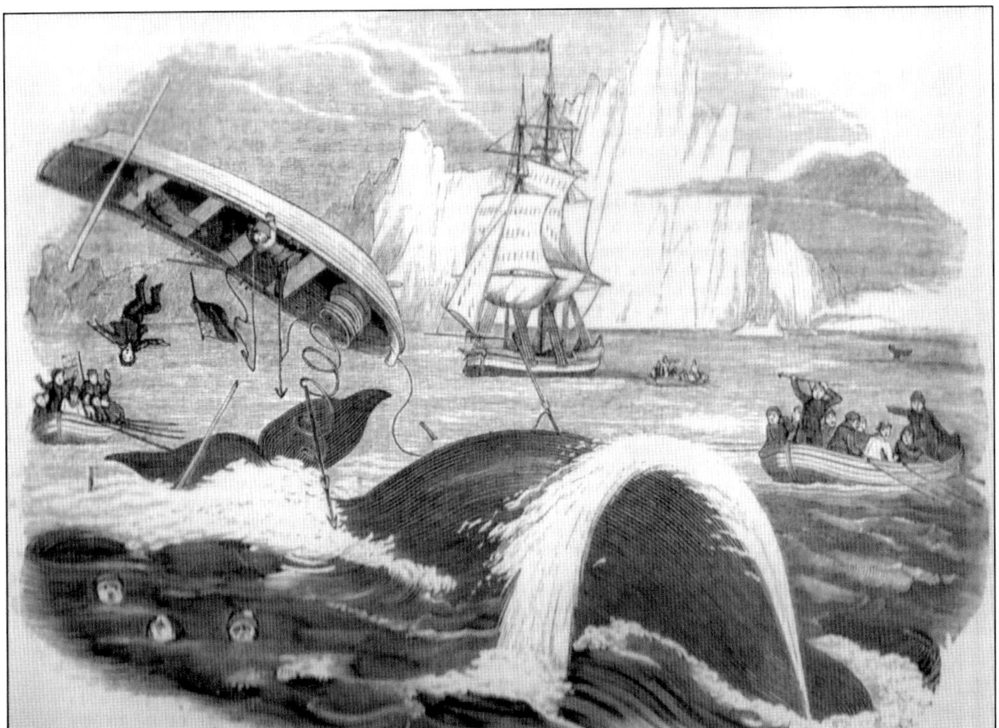

In the 1800s, artists were getting a better idea of what whales looked like. Sometimes, though, errors were made. This is another image from *Penny* Magazine of April 30–May 31, 1833.

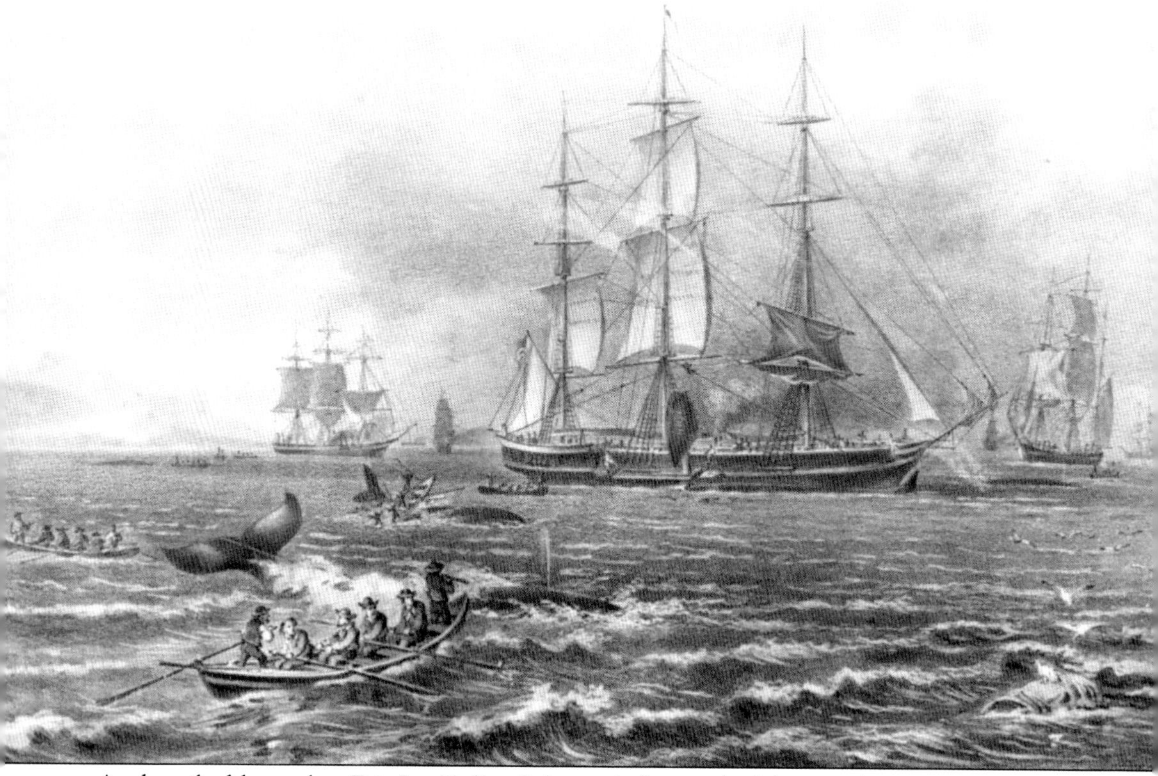

As described by author Eric Jay Dolin, "Many whalemen died from violent encounters with whales and from terrible miscalculations about the unforgiving nature of nature itself." This print appeared as the frontispiece in the 1874 book *The Marine Mammals of the North-Western Coast of North America*, by Charles Melville Scammon.

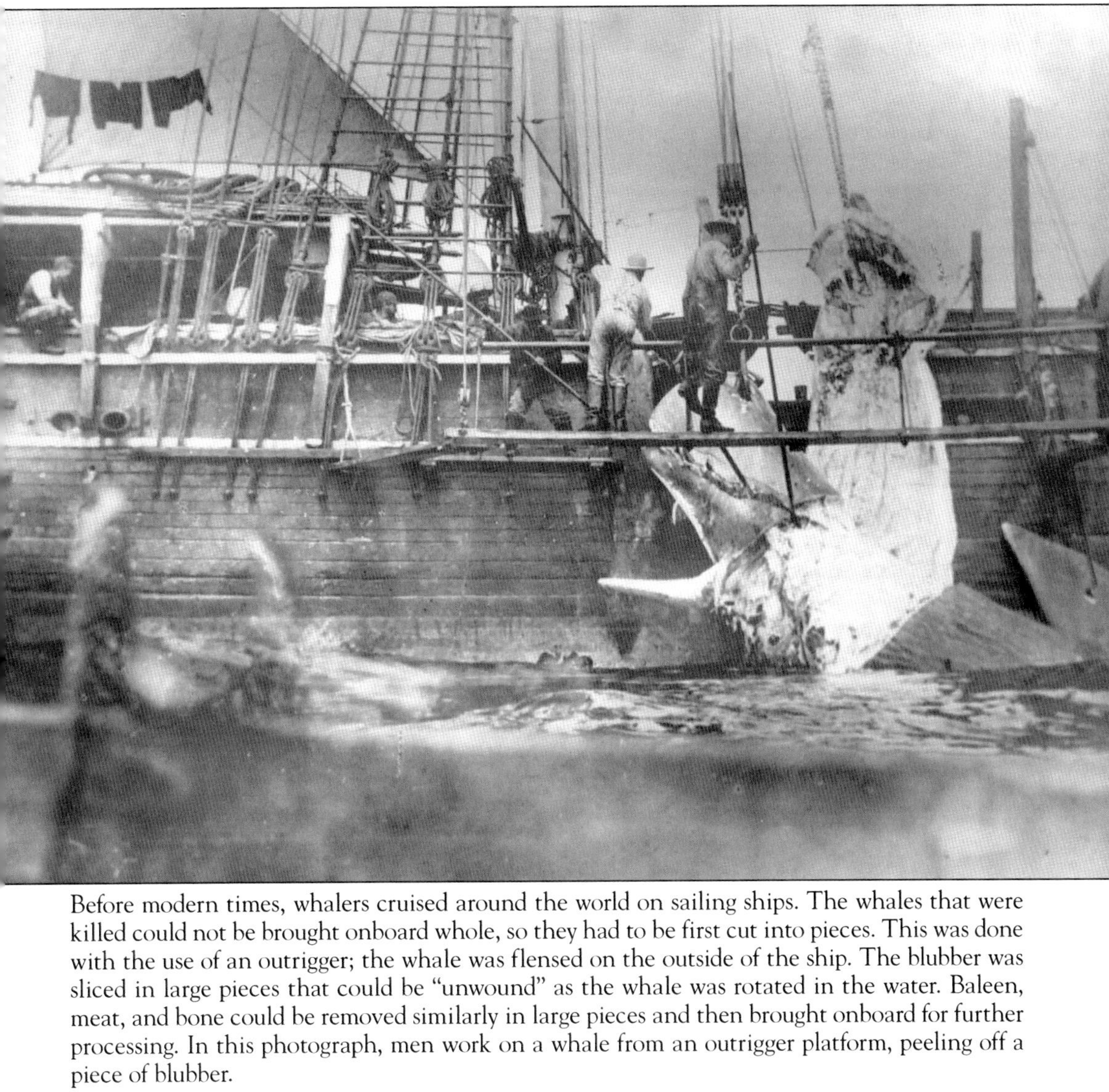

Before modern times, whalers cruised around the world on sailing ships. The whales that were killed could not be brought onboard whole, so they had to be first cut into pieces. This was done with the use of an outrigger; the whale was flensed on the outside of the ship. The blubber was sliced in large pieces that could be "unwound" as the whale was rotated in the water. Baleen, meat, and bone could be removed similarly in large pieces and then brought onboard for further processing. In this photograph, men work on a whale from an outrigger platform, peeling off a piece of blubber.

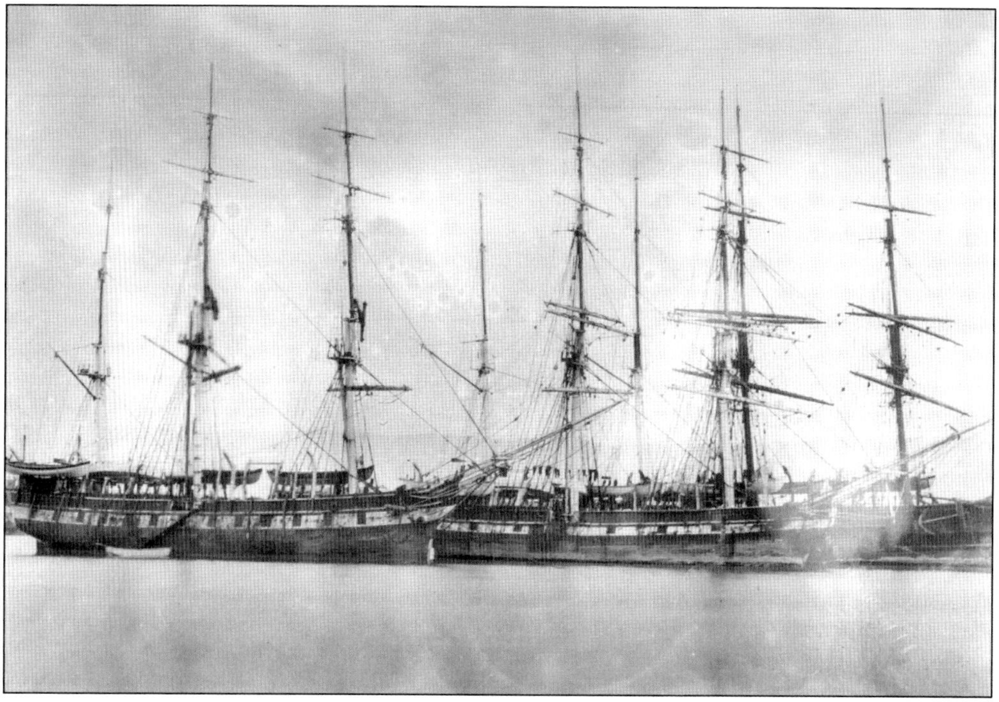

These whalers have either returned from a voyage and are unloading, or they are preparing to sail north for the new season. The ships would overwinter in Oakland mud flats (the present-day Oakland Estuary). Whalers would do the same in Hawaii, as half or more of the whaling fleet returned to Honolulu each fall.

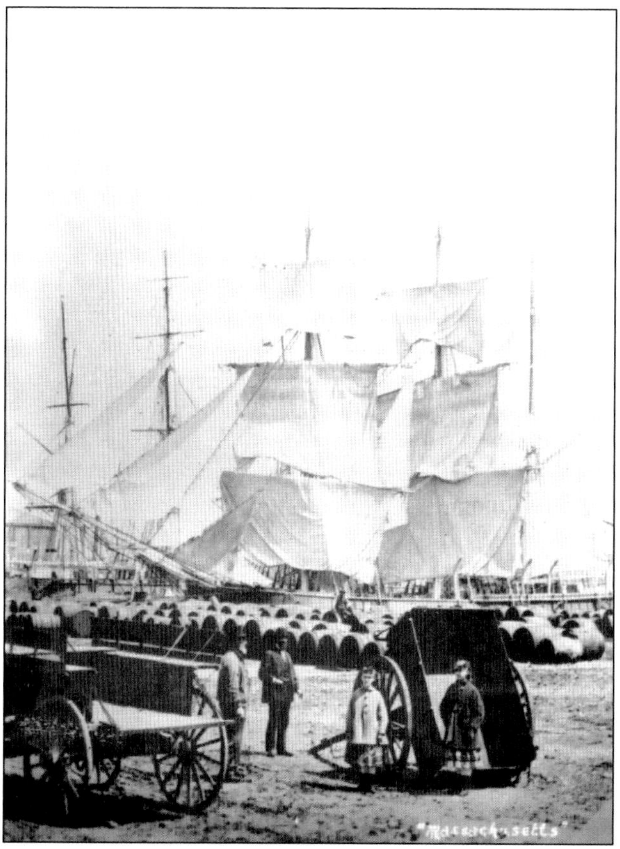

Shown here is the Arctic Whaler & Trading vessel *Belvedere*, built in Bath, Maine, in 1880. For 33 years, the old whaler ploughed the waters of the Pacific. It was understood that $12,000 was paid for three-quarters interest. Capt. S.F. Cottle, a veteran whaling master, retained one-fourth interest and would command the vessel on its next run for the Arctic.

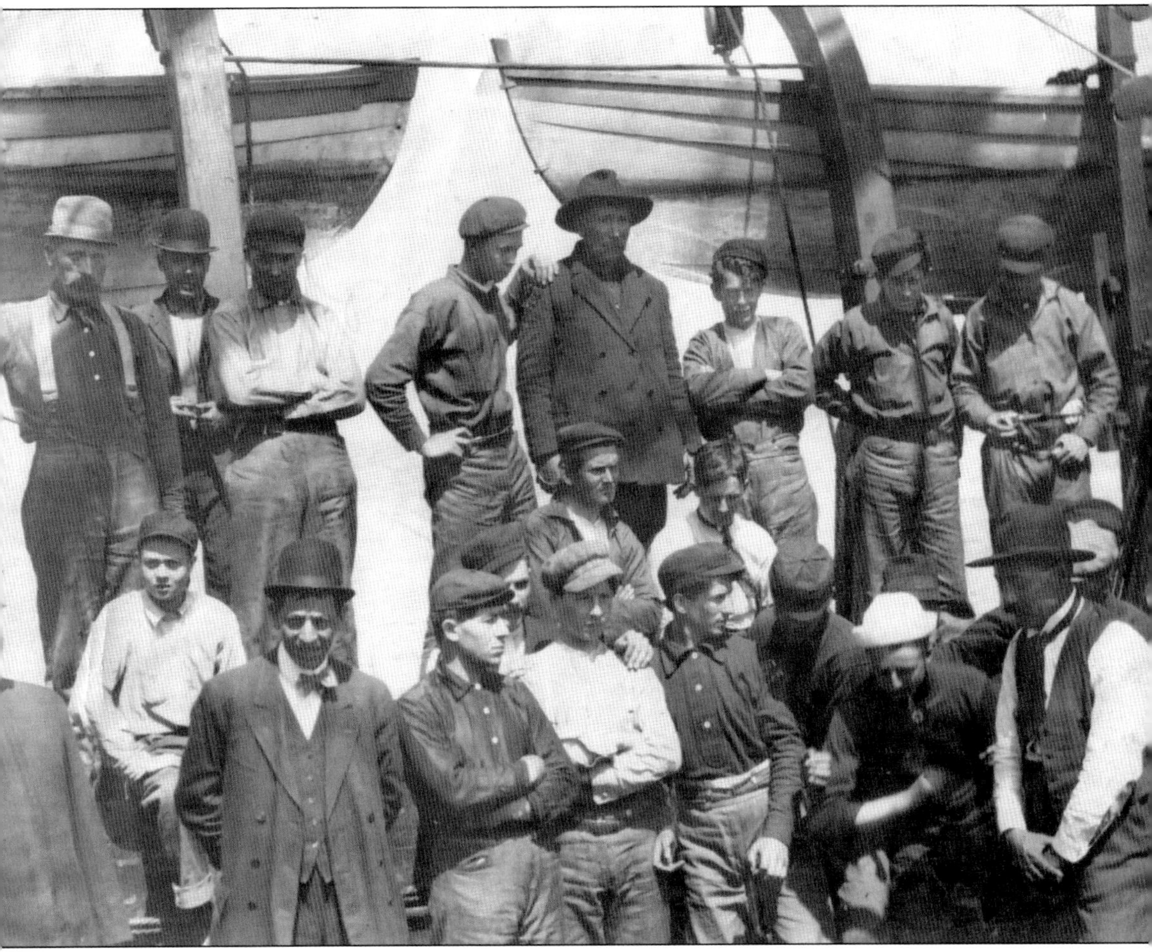

This photograph shows a crew of the whaler *Belvedere*. On one voyage, the ship departed Nome on August 13, 1919, en route to the Siberian coast. The ship was abandoned on Tuesday, September 16, 1919, at 7:45 in the morning by her crew of 30 and her three passengers. She had been trapped in the ice 12 miles northeast of Cape Jinretlen on the coast of Siberia. The financial loss included the vessel's value, $100,000, and her cargo of 110 tons of general merchandise, furs, ivory, whalebone, walrus oil, and hides worth $90,000.

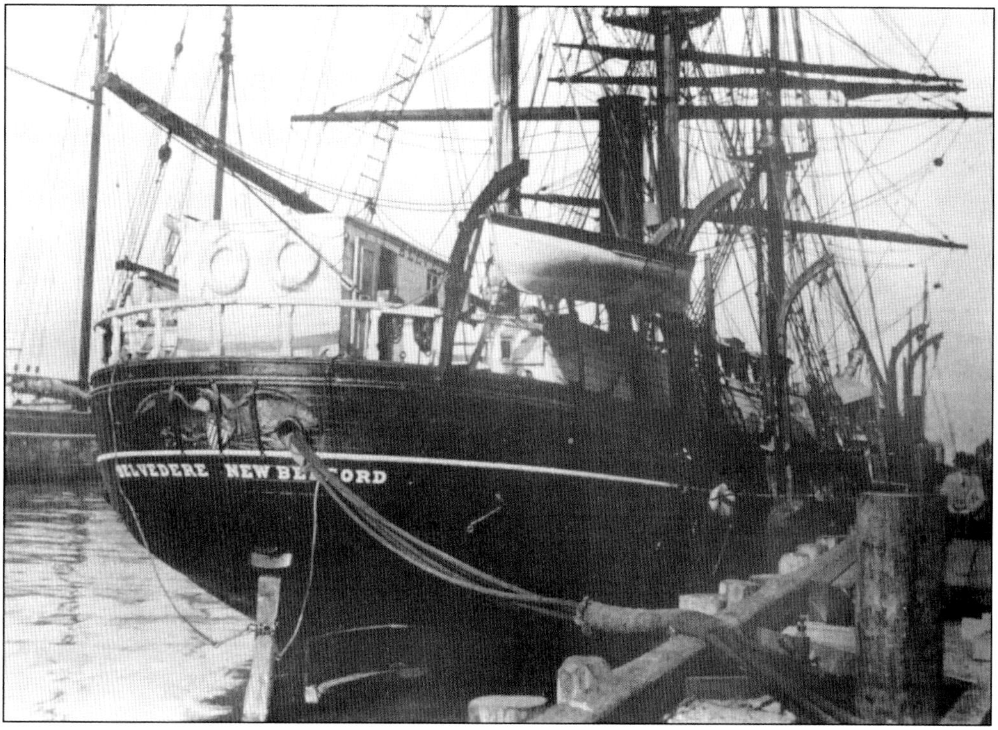

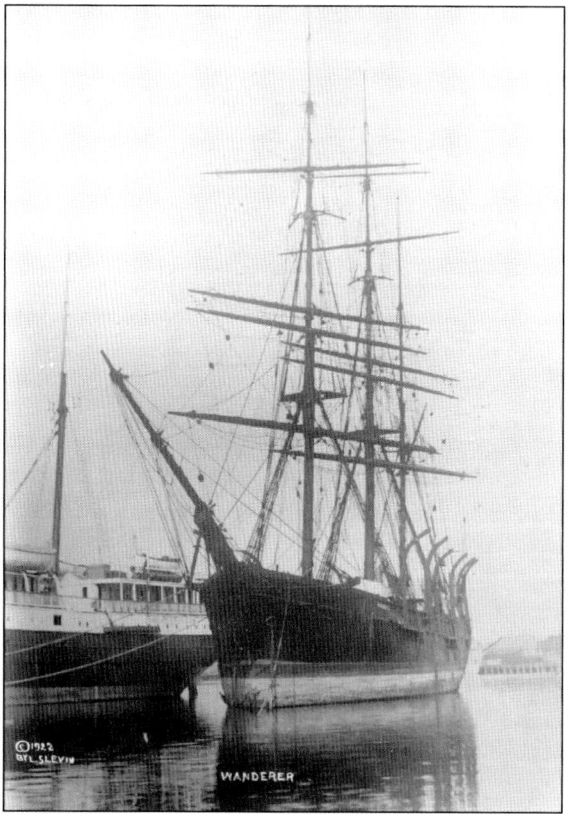

Shown in this undated photograph is the crew of the *Belvedere*, wearing the general clothing of the turn of the century. The crew is probably in port in San Francisco. Based on the comfortable clothing the men are wearing, the ship is not in the Arctic.

The *Wanderer* was the last whaler to be built in the Holmes shipyard in Mattapoisett, Massachusetts, and it was the last whaler to sail from the port of New Bedford, on August 15, 1924. It never returned. She was commanded by Capt. "Thar She Blows" Porter. The *Wanderer* came to an untimely end on the rocks off Martha's Vineyard at the start of a voyage that was to have taken her to the whaling grounds in the South Atlantic.

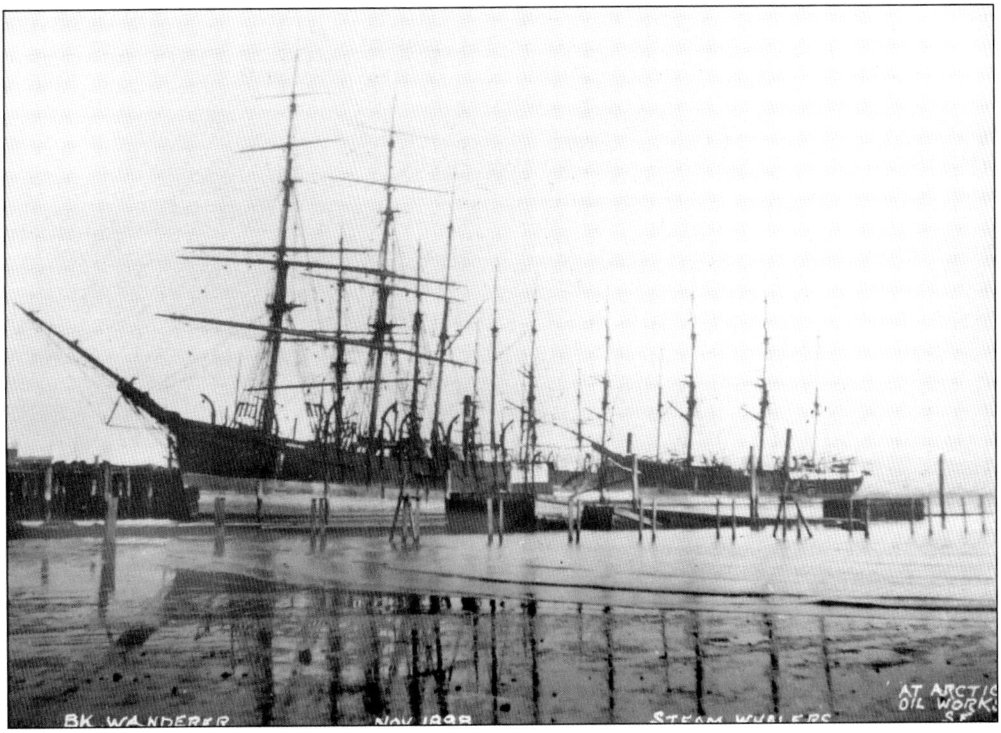

The *Wanderer* is seen here at Arctic Oil Works in November 1898. In 1924, the 46-year-old bark, built in Mattapoisett, Massachusetts, in 1878, was tied to the rocks on the west side of Cuttyhunk, Massachusetts, in preparation for a coming storm, but the anchor slipped, and the ship was smashed to bits against the rocks. The *Wanderer* had been in the movies, figuring in *Down to the Sea in Ships*, but Capt. Antone Edwards decided to pursue South Atlantic whaling when the loss occurred.

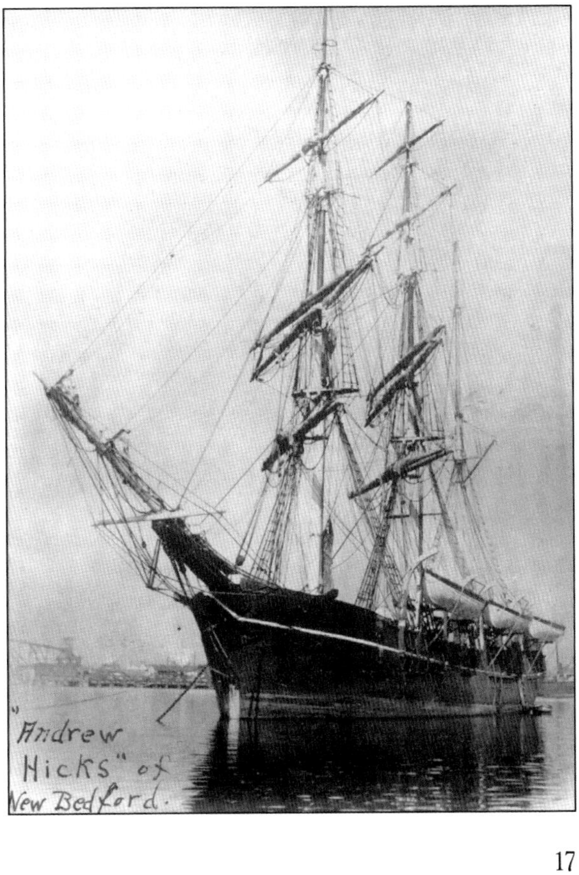

Andrew Hicks was the last famous whaler of the 19th century. Its namesake was one of the most successful and enduring entrepreneurs in the whaling industry, owning nine vessels. William T. Shorey, a famous black captain, was in charge of the *Andrew Hicks* for most of the 1890s. The last American whaler, the ship was sold to become a merchant ship in 1917 in New Caledonia.

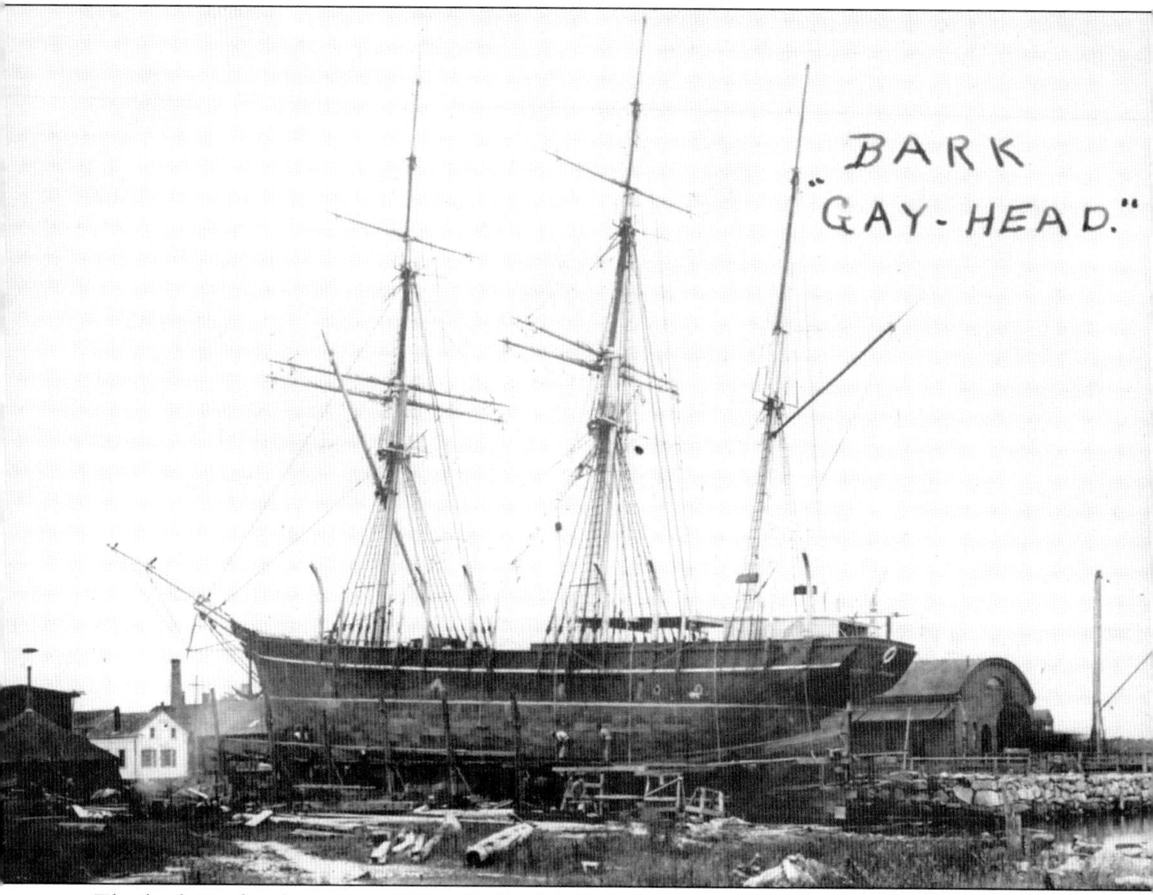

The bark *Gayhead* was out of New Bedford, Massachusetts, originally. A logbook exists in the New Bedford Whaling Museum of a voyage mastered by William Lowen, from October 20, 1856, to August 28, 1860, to the Pacific and Arctic Oceans. The owner-agent was J.B. Wood & Company. Built at Mattapoisett, Massachusetts, in 1852, the *Gayhead* was lost in the Arctic in the Whaling Disaster of 1871, when a fleet of 33 American whaling ships were trapped in the ice and subsequently abandoned. It dealt a serious blow to the nation's whaling industry, which was already in decline.

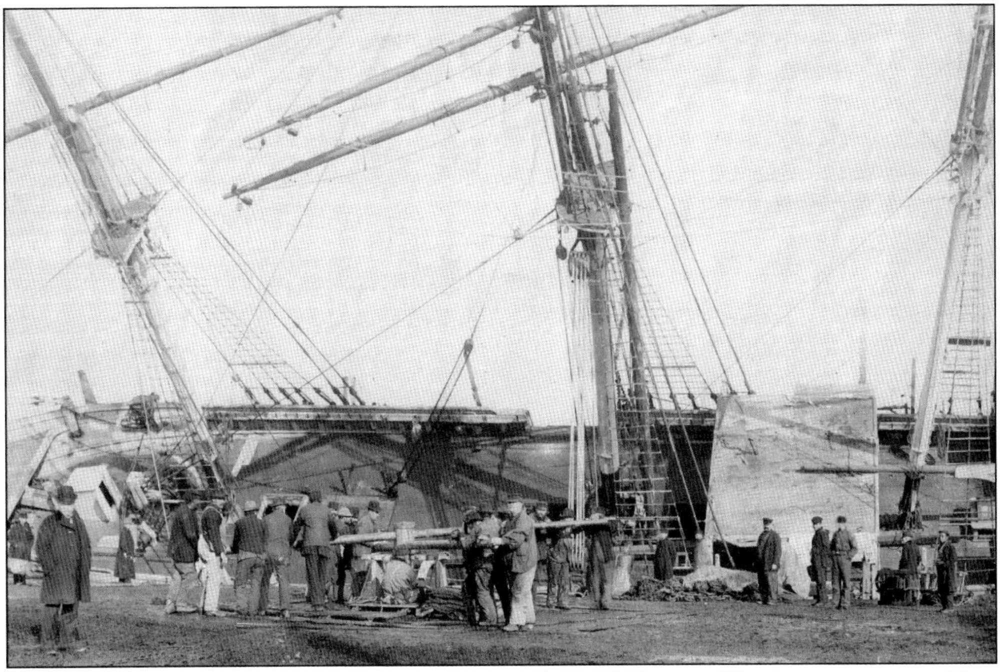

Josephine was built at Bath, Maine, in 1877 and was 385 tons. Her home port was New Bedford, Massachusetts.

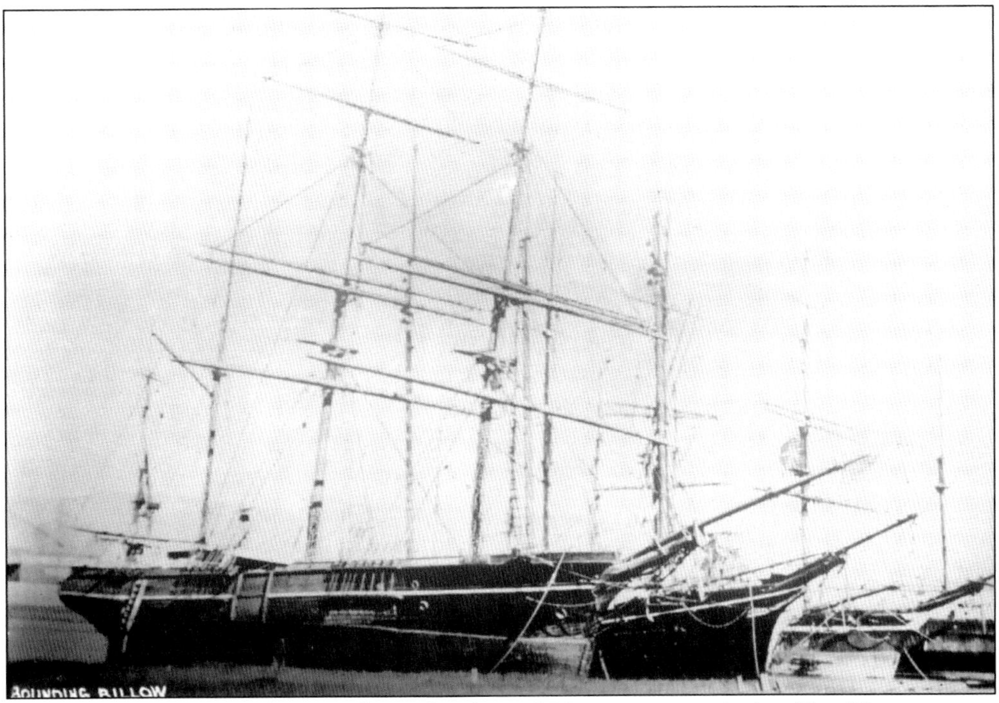

For 42 years, the old whaler *Bounding Billow* braved "the stormy winds that blow." It was sitting in Oakland Creek in 1896 and was dismantled there. Everything that could be taken out of her was removed, and the hulk was sold to the highest bidder. It was then taken to California City and burned to save the copper and iron.

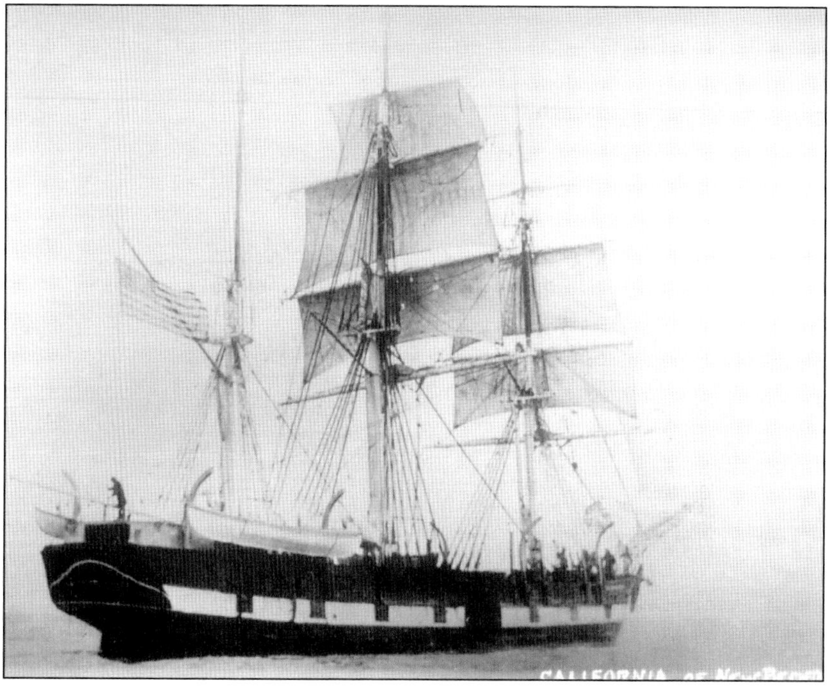

In 1904, the whaling bark *California* returned with a gruesome story dealing with the capture of 11 Japanese poachers by Russians off the Siberian coast. All 11 had been executed by their captors.

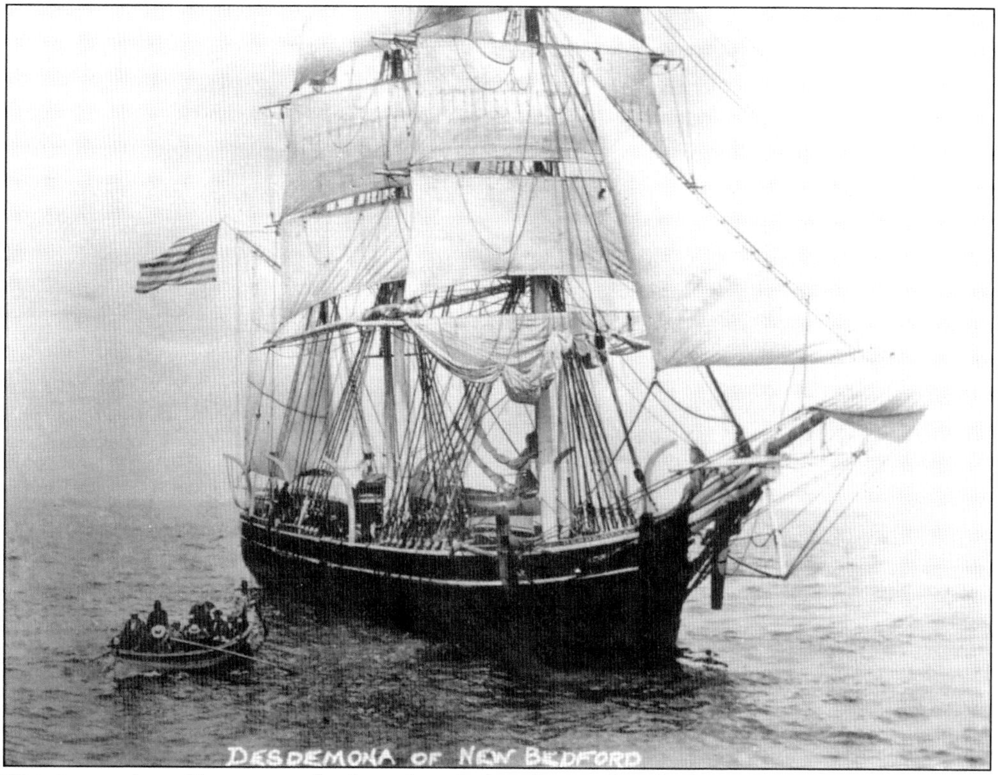

This is a starboard bow view of a ship identified as the whaling bark *Desdemona* at sea. Her sails are set, and a US flag is flying aft. A whaleboat filled with men and women is pulling away from the starboard side. The topmasts are partially cut out of the photograph.

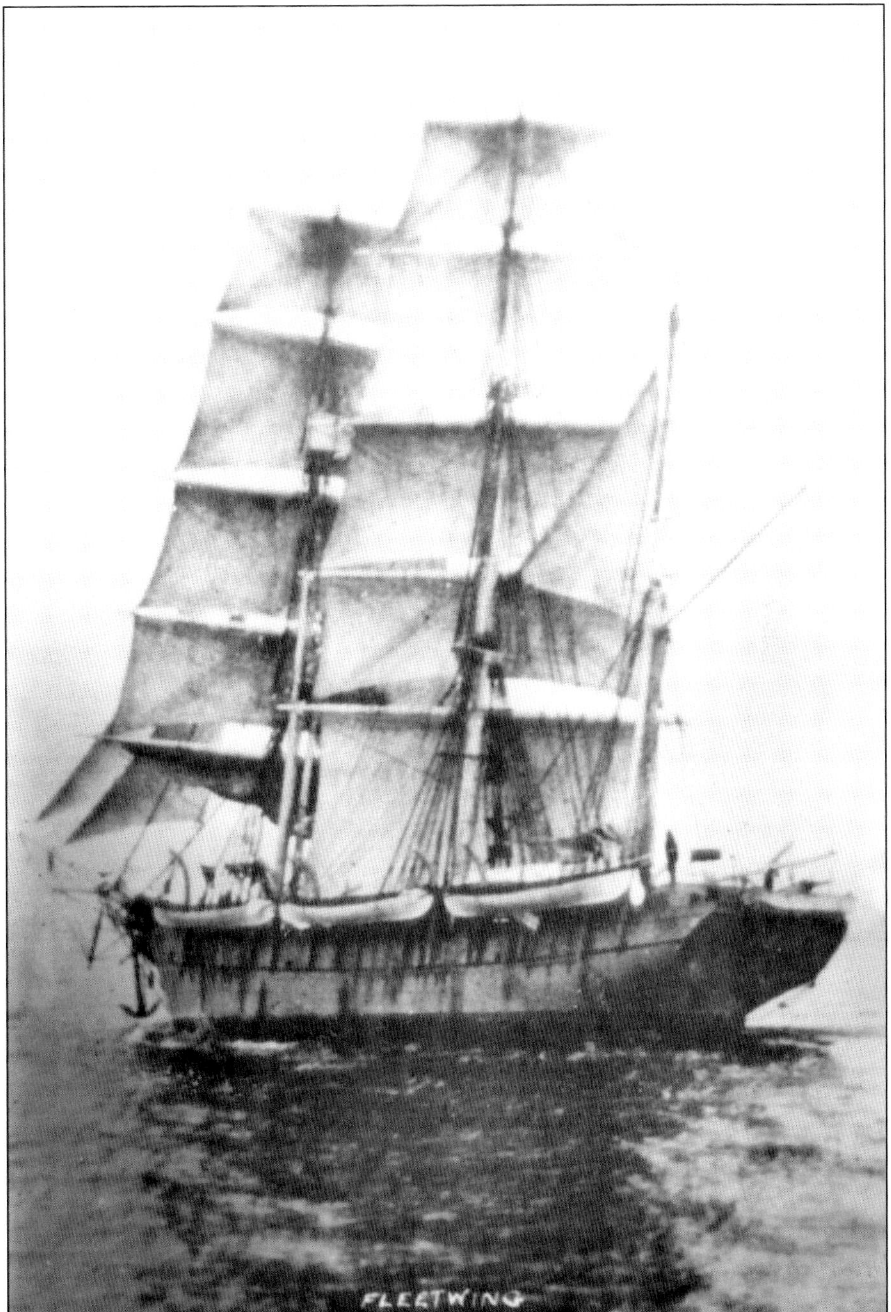

The 114-foot wooden whaling bark *Fleetwing* went ashore on a reef one mile northeast of Point Barrow on August 3, 1888, and was lost. The following are excerpts from the wreck report filed by agents J. & W.R. Wing in New Bedford, Massachusetts. "Heavy gale of wind and heavy sea. Night time and stormy. . . . Parted chain cable and went ashore on a reef off Point Barrow, Arctic Ocean. Second anchor not holding in time. . . . No assistance could be rendered at the time and the vessel pounded until cable cut the *Fleetwing* went over bar. The crew was rescued after the gale abated by other ships of the whaling fleet. The vessel sank and went to pieces."

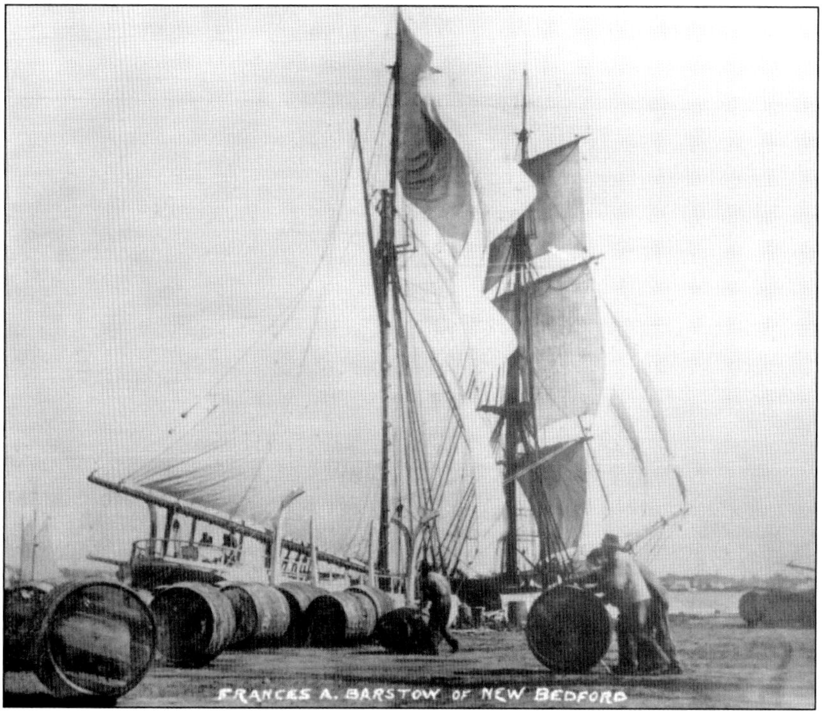

The *Frances A. Barstow* of New Bedford was built in 1877. The ship whaled from 1877 to 1899, and was sold to Bermuda in 1900.

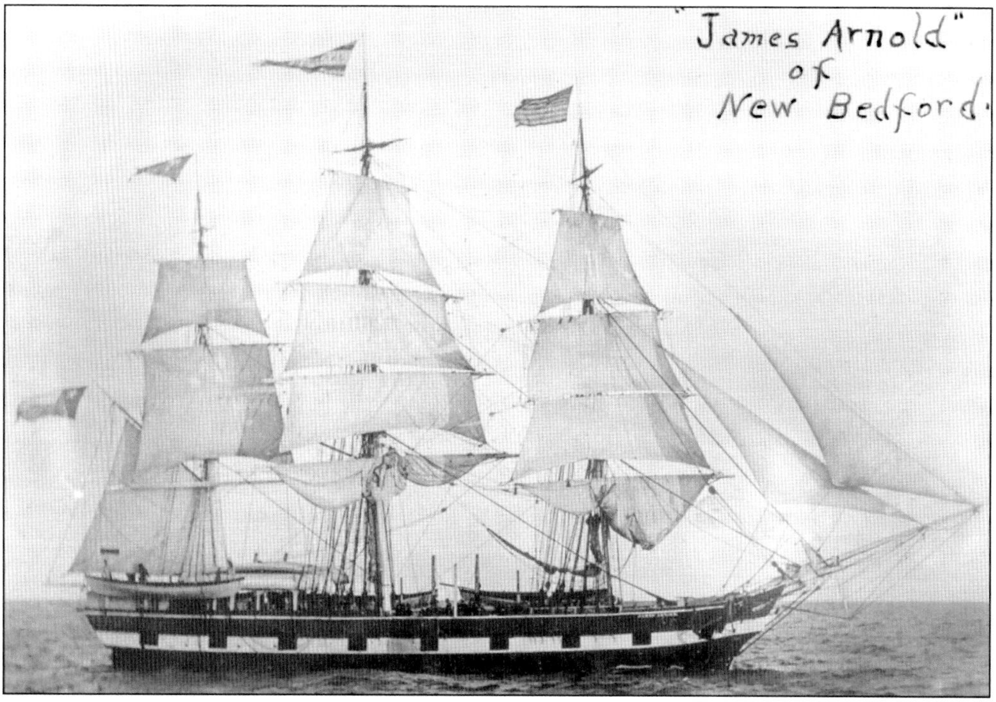

The whaler *James Arnold* was built in New Bedford in 1852 and was active until 1892. She was named after the whaling merchant James Arnold, whose estate is now known as the Wamsutta Club in New Bedford. He donated his fortune to create the Arnold Arboretum in Boston.

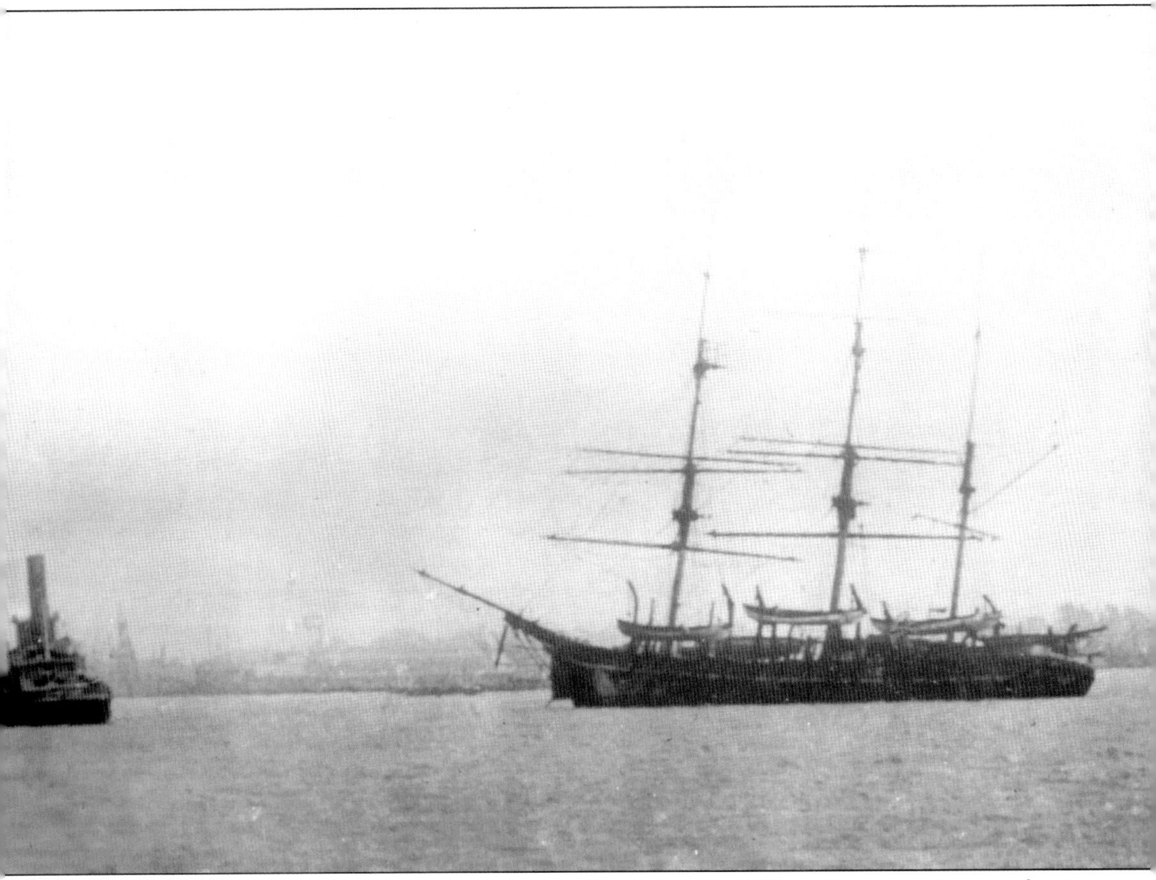

The whaler *John & Winthrop* arrived in port on November 39, 1897, with a strange story of an attempt by some members of the crew to burn the vessel and escape to the Klondike. On August 19, around midnight, two fires were discovered. Though they were put out without much damage, subsequent investigations proved that three sailors, J.H. Krueger, Harry Jones, and Osborn Digman, had started the fires with the purpose of escaping in one of the small boats to the mainland and then striking out for the Klondike. A few days before the fires, the whaler spoke to a fellow whaling vessel, the *Gayhead*, and heard the first news of the gold strikes near Dawson, Alaska.

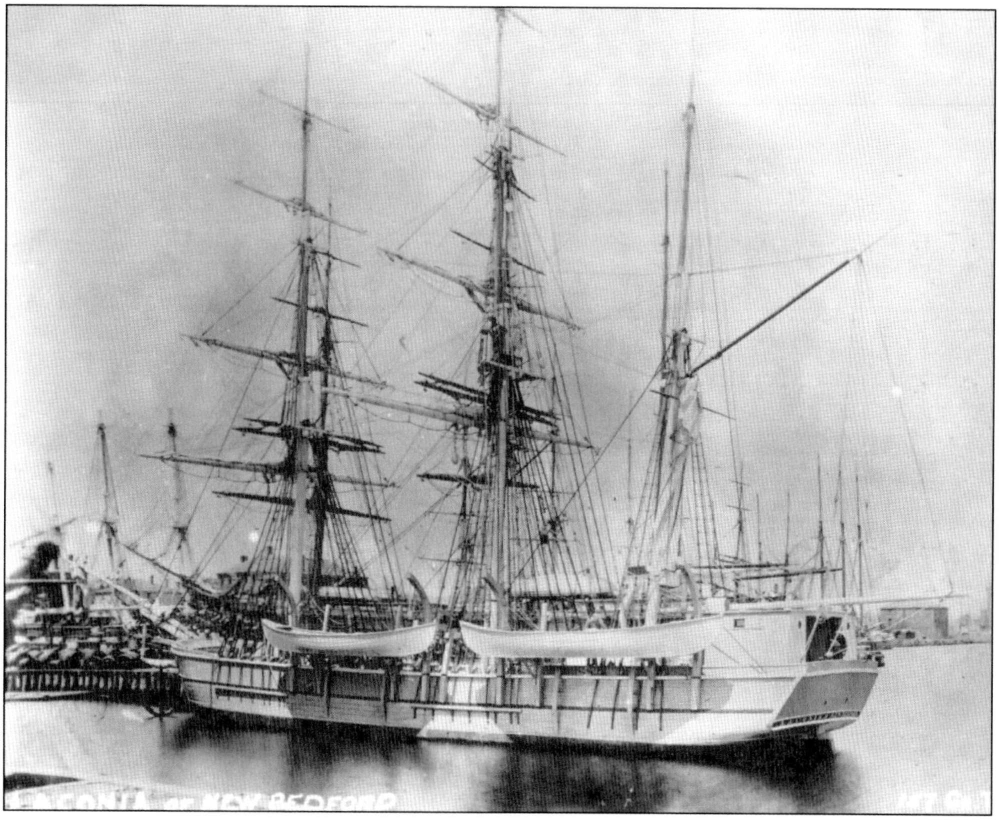

The *Laconia* was owned by William Lewis, who was in the whaling industry at New Bedford, Massachusetts, and San Francisco, California, and went whaling to the Arctic in 1876. Lemuel Eldridge of the *Laconia* fell from the main topmast and was instantly killed. He was 18.

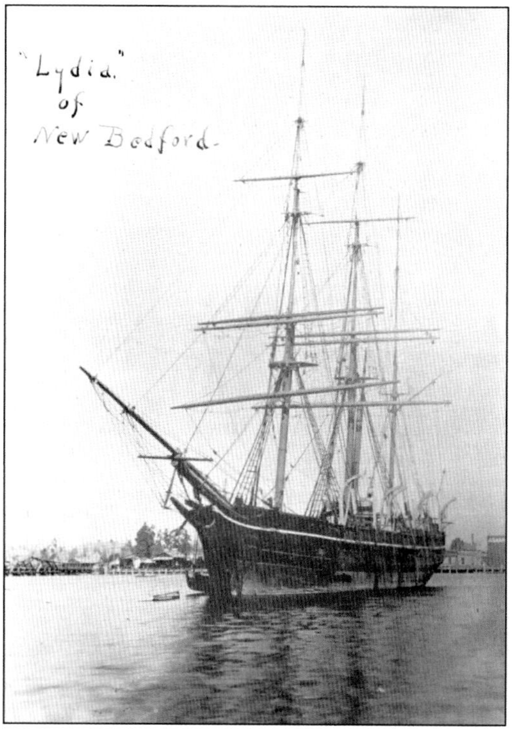

The *Lydia*, a wooden-hulled whaler built in 1840, was laid up in 1907. Her remains are buried at the foot of King Street in San Francisco. In 1980, the whaler was discovered during sewer construction at the foot of King Street near Pier 42. Historians believe she was placed there in 1907. Discovered in the buried hull was a case of 24 bottles of "high class" ginger beer, brewed between about 1860 and 1906 by A.S. Watson and Company, Ltd., of Hong Kong and Manila.

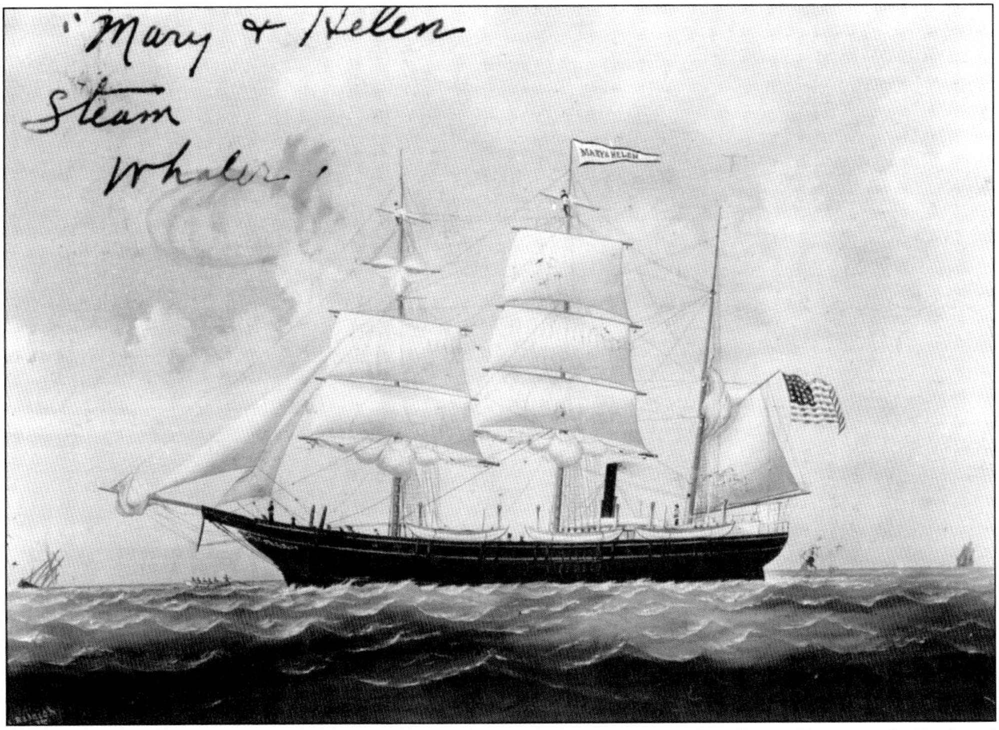

The *Mary and Helen* was specifically built for Arctic navigation by Goss, Sawyer, & Packard of Bath, Maine. Launched on July 17, 1879, she was the first steam whaler built as such for American registry. During her first and only season, she not only justified the faith of her owner, Capt. William Lewis of New Bedford, but revolutionized the American whaling industry. The *Mary and Helen* was acquired by the Navy at San Francisco and renamed the USS *Rogers* and commissioned on May 30, 1881.

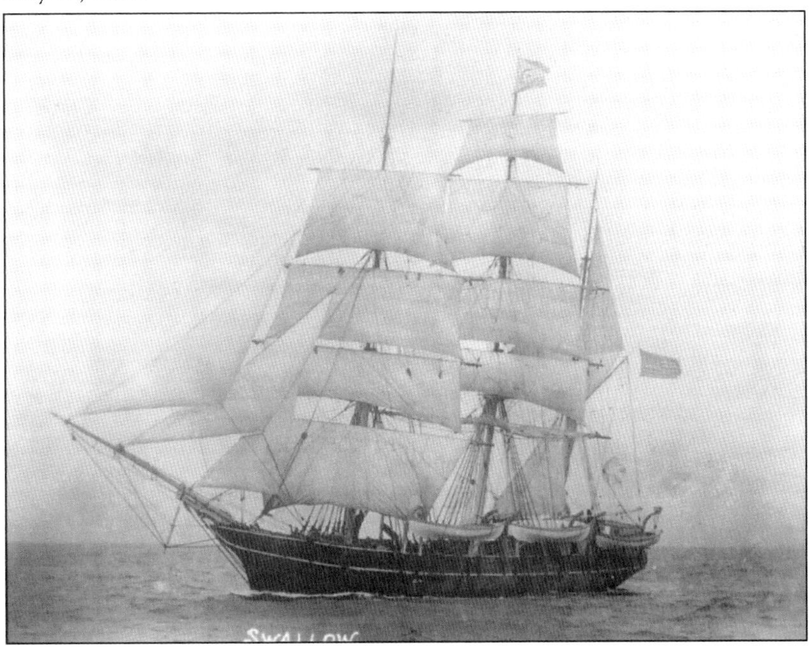

The bark *Swallow*, seen here with sails set, was a whaler and later on a merchantman. It was lost at sea about 1901.

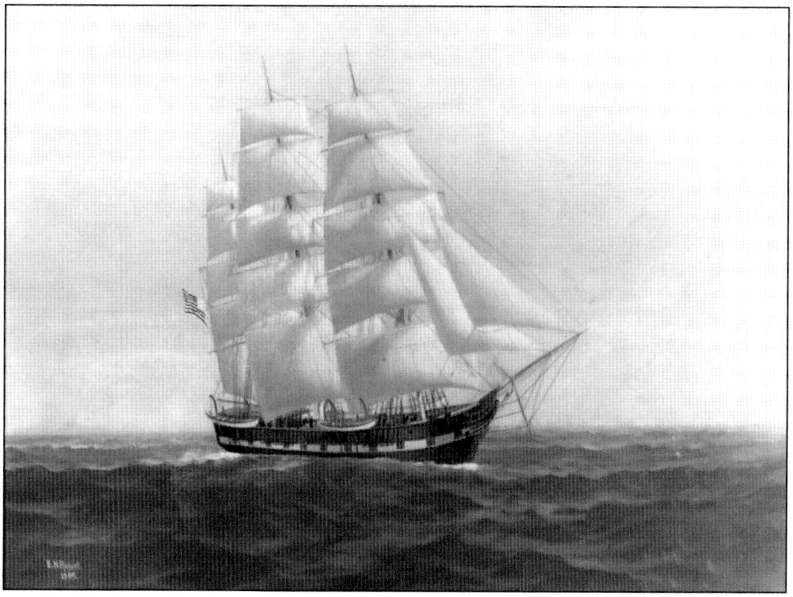

The name of this ship is not known. The painting by E.N. Russell is dated 1905.

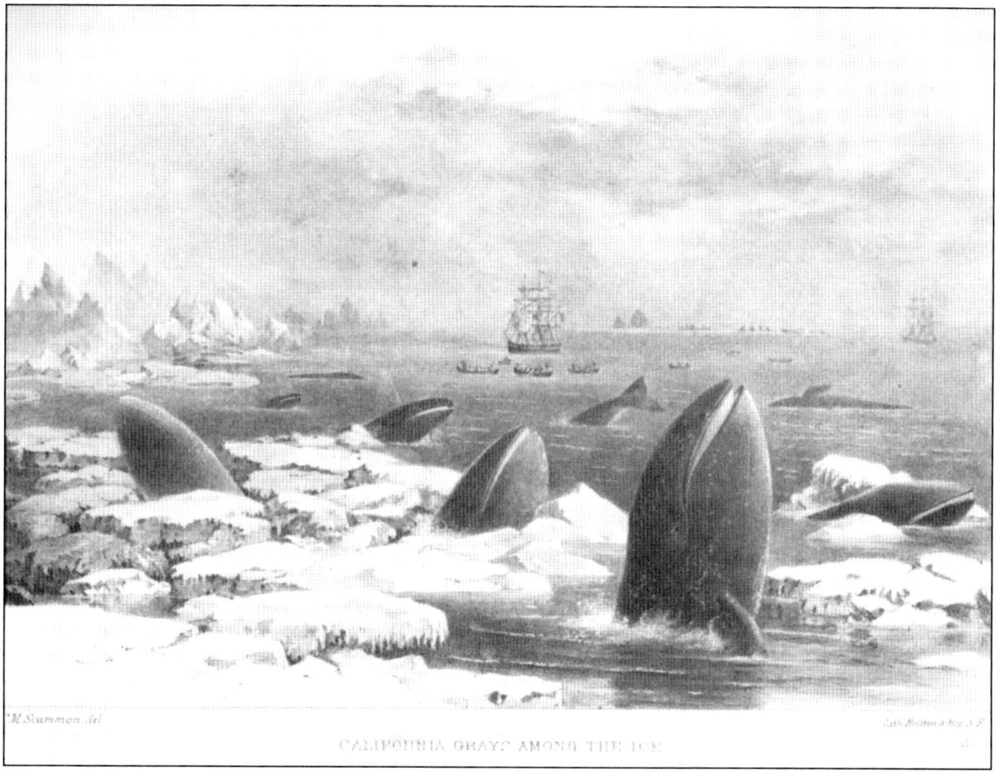

Many of the habits of the California gray whale are widely different from those of any of any other species of balaena. The whale makes regular migrations from the hot southern latitudes to beyond the Arctic Circle. In its passages between the extremes of climate, it follows the general trend of an irregular coast. It travels so near land that it was exposed to attack from the native tribes inhabiting the seashores, prior to 1900, who passed much of their time in the canoe, and considered the capture of the whale worthy of the highest distinction.

A sperm whale has valuable spermaceti oil in the head, in a cavity called the case. The first stage in working on a sperm whale is to make a hole in the cavity and bale the case of this precious oil. This image is from *Marine Mammalia and American Whale Fishery*, by Charles Scammon.

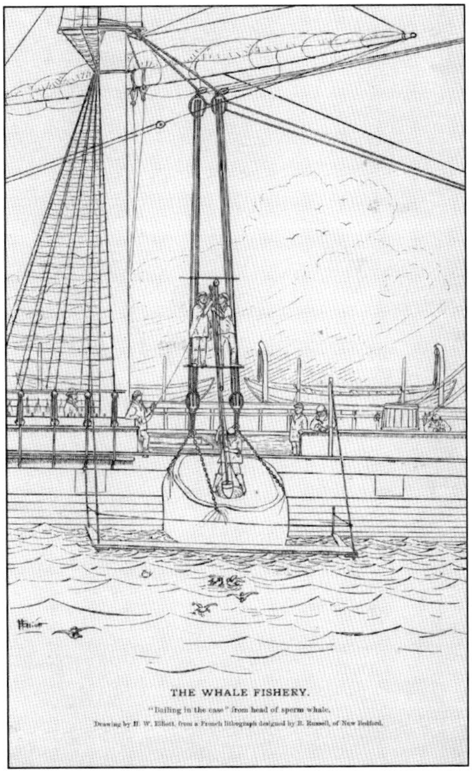

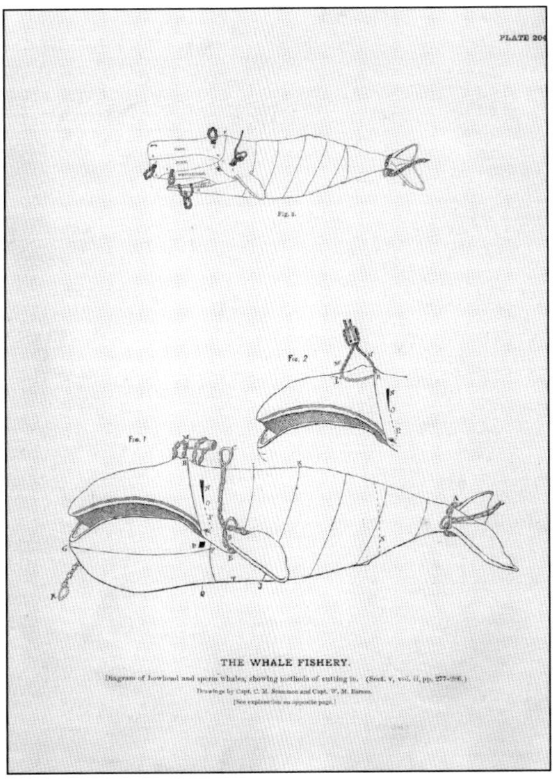

This drawing, from *Marine Mammalia and American Whale Fishery*, by Charles Scammon, shows the method of cutting in the sperm whale and the bowhead.

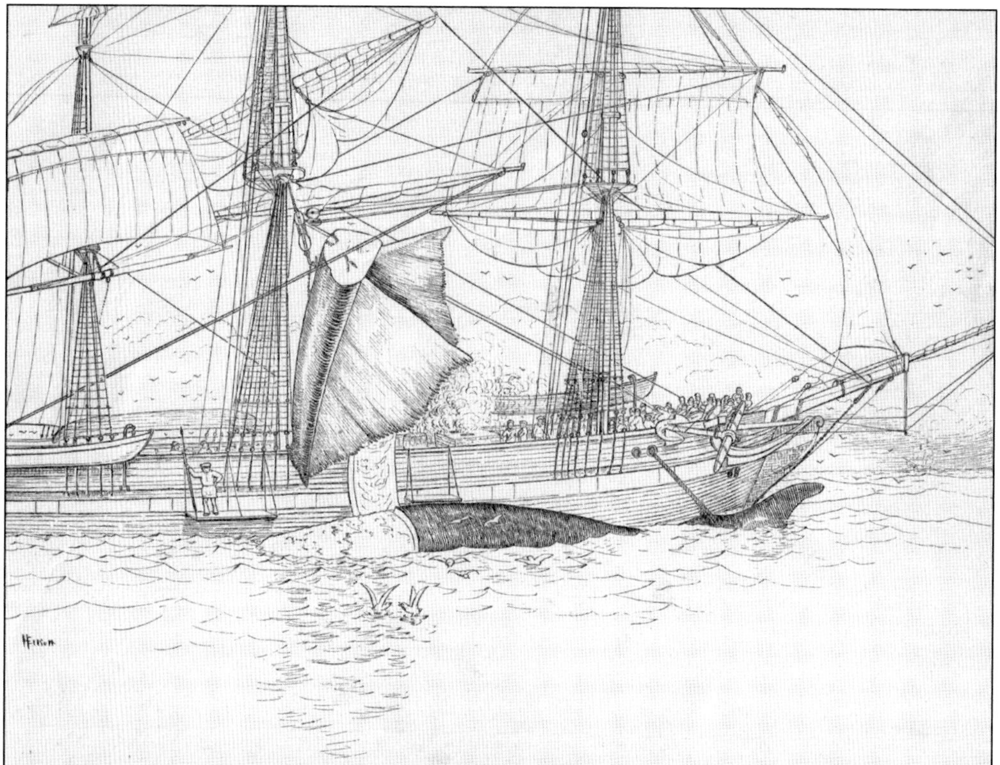

THE WHALE FISHERY.

"A ship on the Northwest coast of America cutting in her last right whale." (Sect. v, vol. ii, p. 277.)

Drawing by H. W. Elliott, from a French lithograph designed by B. Russell, of New Bedford.

This drawing by H.W. Elliott depicts "a ship on the Northwest coast of America cutting in her last right whale." A platform is lowered over the side of the ship, and the whale is taken apart and hoisted onto the ship in pieces.

THE AMERICAN WHALE-FISHERY.

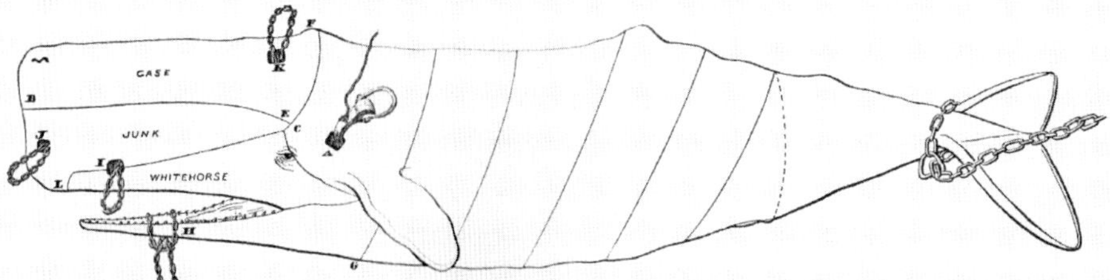

OUTLINE OF A SPERM WHALE, SHOWING THE MANNER OF CUTTING-IN.

This diagram of a sperm whale shows how it is cut up.

This drawing shows a typical shoulder gun that was used from the whaling boats during hunts. The gun shoots an explosive projectile that is designed to kill the whale. Sometimes, it may take more than one projectile to kill the whale.

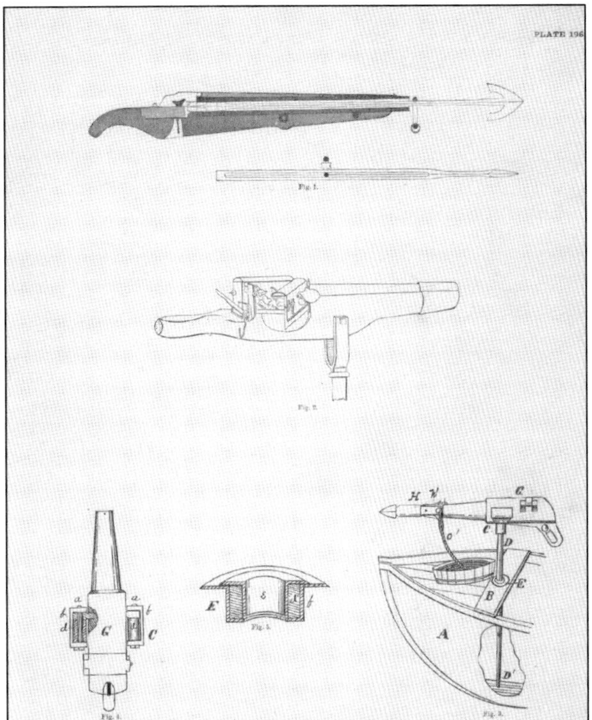

THE WHALE FISHERY.

English and American swivel guns. (Sect. v, vol. ii, p. [illegible].)

[See explanation on opposite page.]

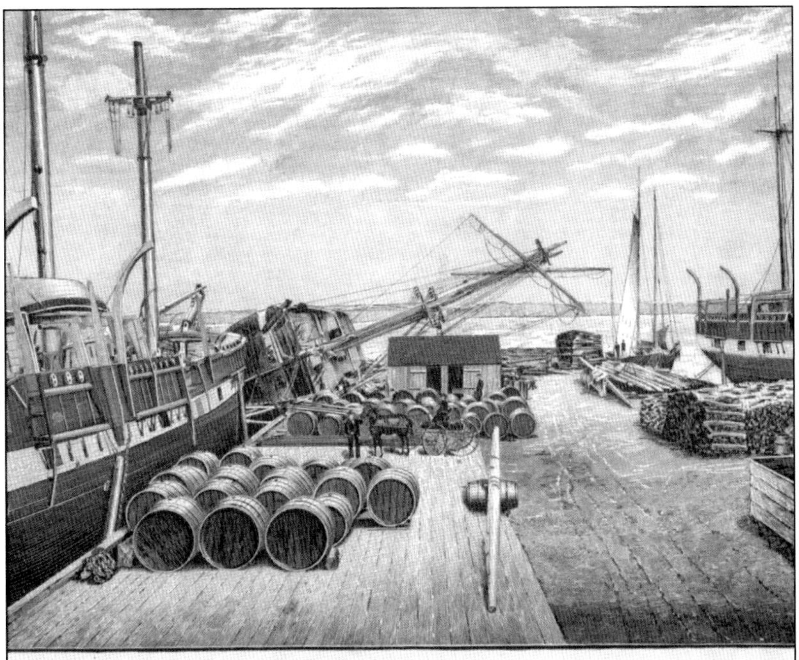

THE WHALE FISHERY.

Whale-ships at New Bedford wharves; ship hove down for repairs; oil-casks. (Sect. v, vol. ii, pp. 289, 290.)

From a photograph by U. S. Fish Commission.

Upon returning to New Bedford, ships are unloaded on the docks. The oil is sold and shipped from there. There are several types of whale oil, with the sperm whale case oil being the best. Some oils are suited to particular uses, such as illumination.

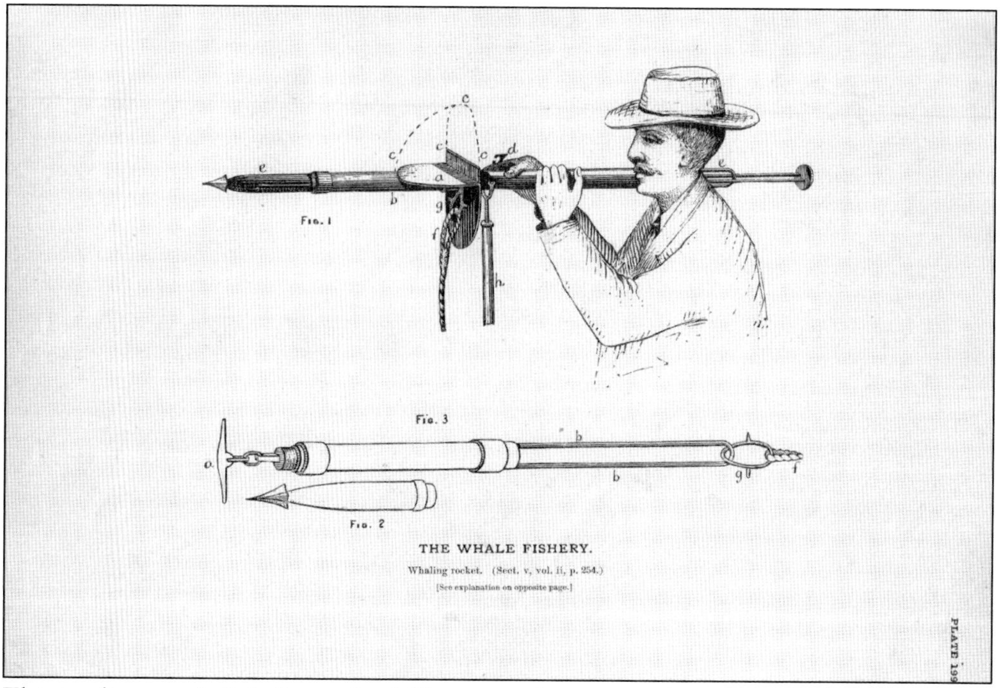

This is a diagram of a "whaling rocket." The projectile consists of a cast-iron shell, and the rocket has a loop extension. The bomb is filled with material that will explode after impact, with the shrapnel causing internal damage, sufficient to kill the whale if lodged in a critical area.

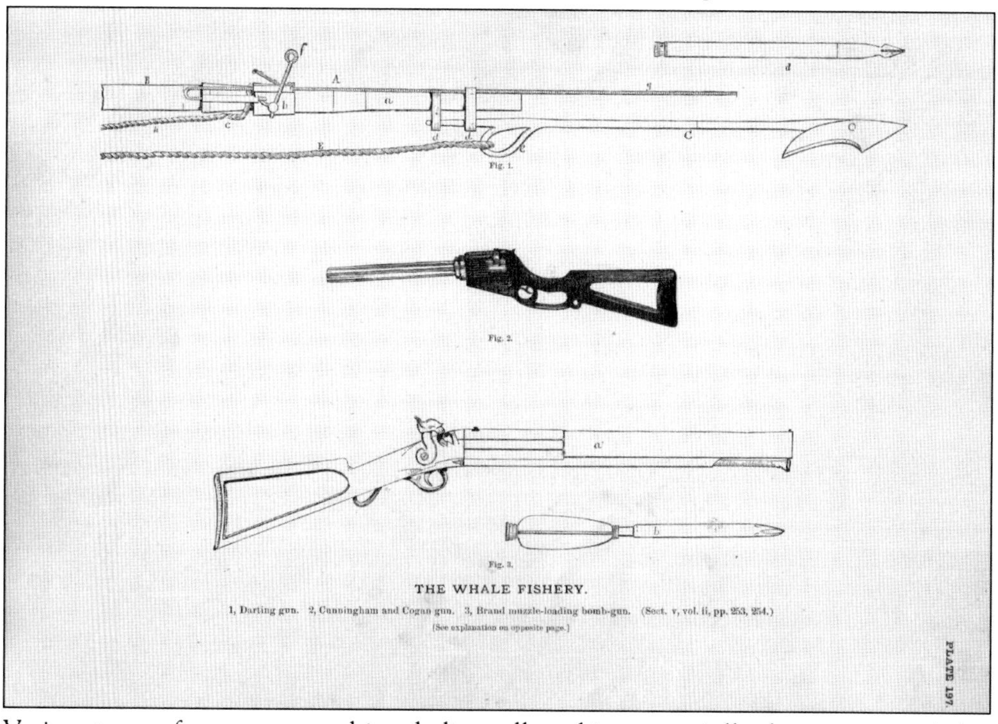

Various types of guns were used in whaling, all working essentially the same way. A few representations are shown here.

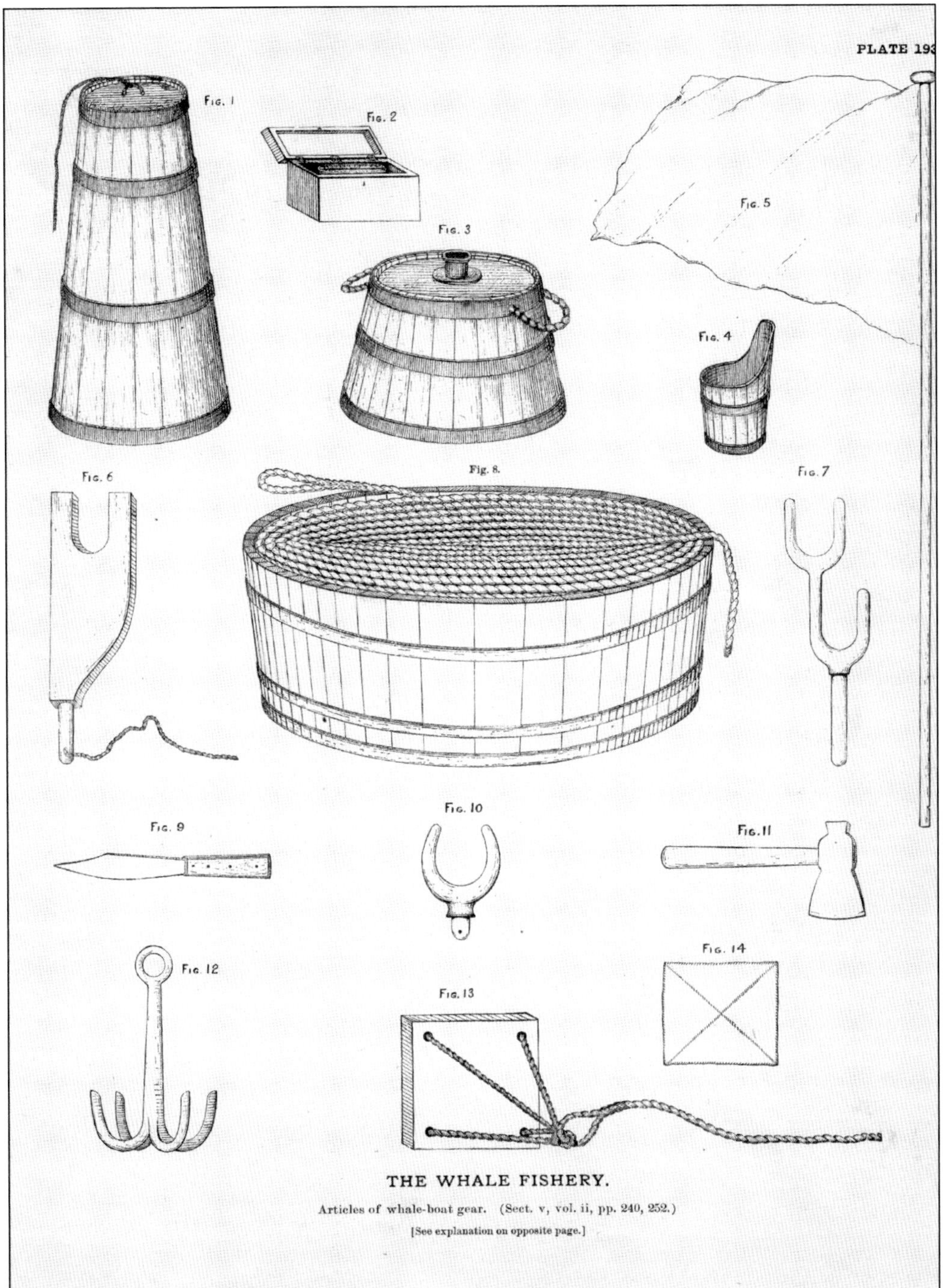

This drawing shows various pieces of whaleboat equipment, including coiled rope. It was essential that, after the whale was captured, the rope went out cleanly. A loop can snag on the boat, causing the boat to be pulled under. If a man gets snagged in the rope, it will take him underwater to his death.

PLATE 198

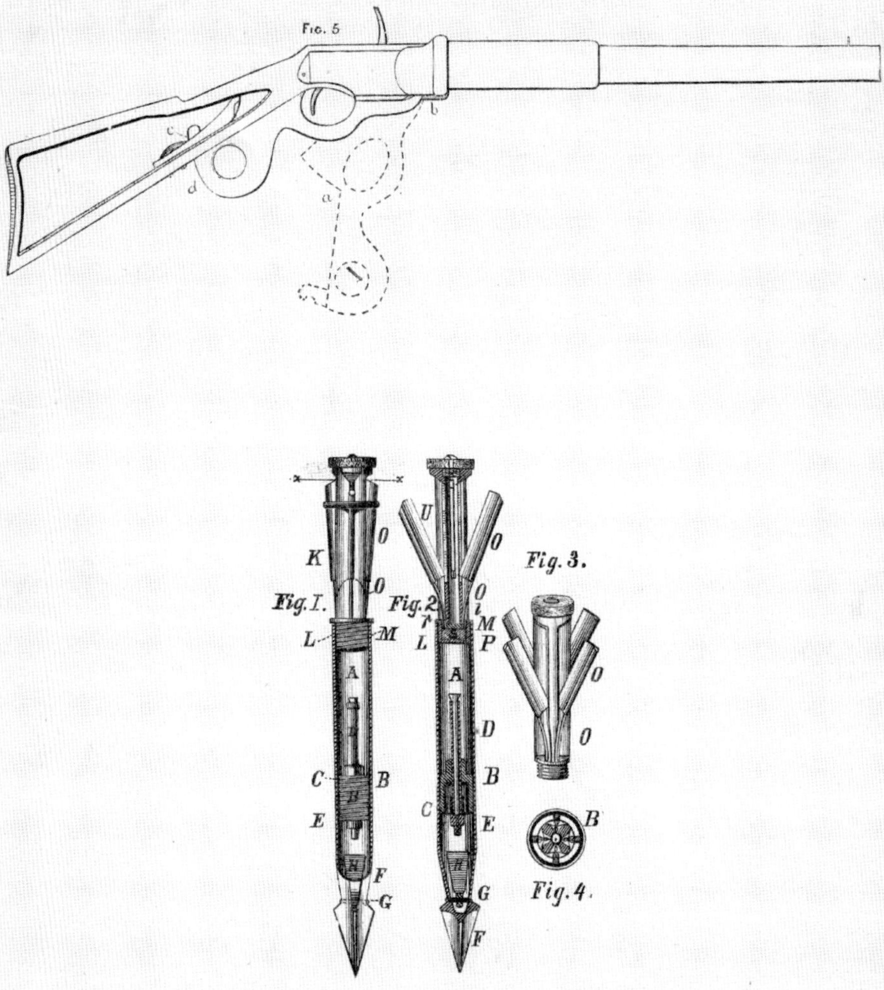

THE WHALE FISHERY.

Pierce and Egger's breech-loading bomb-gun and Pierce bomb-lance. (Sect. v, vol. ii, p. 253.)

[See explanation on opposite page.]

This drawing shows the Pierce and Egger's breech-loading bomb-gun (top) and Pierce bomb lance. Similar designs are in use today by Eskimos in Alaska. It explodes inside the whale, causing damage to the animal and hopefully killing it quickly.

Two

California Shore Whaling

With the California Gold Rush in full swing, it was not hard to book passage on a steamer to Panama for the crossing to the Pacific side, and then north by steamer to California. So, John Davenport, his wife, brother, and an inventory of whaling supplies started the trip to California, only to be shipwrecked along the Nicaragua coastline. They had to walk south to get to the debarkation point to the Pacific Ocean, which they eventually reached. But, unfortunately, their supplies did not. From the eastern coast of Panama, they managed to cross the isthmus to the western side, finding a mass of people trying to book passage to San Francisco and then on to the gold fields.

The party of five, along with the other passengers, booked passage on a steamer, but this vessel was shipwrecked on the coast of Central California. Notice of the shipwreck appeared in the daily papers, and a number of vessels left San Francisco to rescue the now-stranded passengers. It took several vessels a few days to rescue all of the passengers. The Davenport trio arrived on the last boat from the wreck. Arriving in San Francisco, they began their whaling business. Among the first steps was acquiring whaling equipment, including a try-works for rendering the whale blubber into oil.

Prior to this time, a group of men in Rhode Island formed a corporation of gold-seekers. The Bristol County Mining & Trading Company purchased supplies, but they did not book passage aboard one of the steamers. The company must have decided it was less costly and perhaps faster to buy their own vessel for their equipment and men. They bought a whaleship, which was one of many abandoned in port due to the Gold Rush in California. Whole crews had abandoned their ships in California, or booked passage from the East Coast to go whaling. So, on August 14, 1849, the bark *Otranto*, with Capt. William Howland, sailed to California. Instead of landing all of its equipment in San Francisco, they sailed to Stockton, where the company's workers would be closer to the goldfields and their pockets better off for not having to pay passage from San Francisco to Stockton for men and equipment. The men now needed to procure wagons for the overland passage to the goldfields, where they would disappear amongst the thousands of other men trying to find gold.

The *Otranto* was abandoned and sat in Stockton, like so many other vessels in San Francisco and other West Coast ports. The *Otranto* was reported in the *Alta California Newspaper* of September 12, 1850, in a list of vessels in Stockton, California.

John Davenport found the little whaler in Stockton , and either bought or leased her because the little ship was spotted near Bodega on October 9, 1852, cruising for whales, and again on October 11th and 12th off Point Reyes, finally cruising October 13th off San Francisco. The ship had some success in October, as the Alta California reported that the steamer Ohio saw her at Monterey with 50 barrels of oil. Captain Davenport was in San Francisco on November 19th and back in Monterey in November 23rd. It seems that he was whaling and trading, as he imported into San Francisco 30 barrels of oil and 1,400 sacks of potatoes on November 30th, with Captain Butts, Captain Davenport's brother-in-law, who along with his wife, came west with The Davenports. The vessel was released on June 22, 1853, with a Captain Kendrick in charge. The Otranto never went whaling again. Capt. Davenport had removed the try-works in Monterey. While the operation did not take a lot of whales, it took a few. An exact count is not available, but between October 9 and November 30, 1852, Captain Davenport was catching whales off the coast between Drakes Bay in the North and Monterey in the South. Whaling could have continued up to June 1853 when he released it Captain Kendrick. Gray whales, however, had migrated to the north by April, so he probably has stopped going out in April or before. No more whales were taken until 1854, when better-organized companies went whaling. Companies were formed by Captain Davenport and Captain Clark (Machado) in 1854, with both companies using Portuguese whalers who had settled in California after leaving whaling ships in San Francisco and California. Some were recruited in San Francisco, and others found the whaling companies on their own.

Captain Davenport preferred to use larger ships rather than the whaleboats while first using the *Otranto*. With the new company, he started using the *Caroline E. Foote*. The ship was used at sea and put in on a regular basis to Monterey and Santa Cruz. It was used on a regular basis until May 11, 1865, when Captain Hazard sailed away from San Francisco with the vessel. Captain Davenport moved from Monterey to Soquel and continued whaling, later moving to what became known as the town of Davenport, where he had a landing. While some vessels were built and launched at Davenport, there is no information available that anyone went whaling from there. However, a Portuguese whaling operation was located a few miles north.

Edwin C. Starks wrote a history of California shore whaling in 1923, published by the California Department of Fish and Game. In it, he discusses the start of shore whaling in California. "Shore whaling in California started at Monterey Bay, and it is about the only place on the coast where whaling is still continued." After the beginning it proved to be so profitable that whaling stations were established at various points along the coast, as well as some on the Lower California cost. There is some discrepancy as to the year of the beginning. Scammon says the first station was established in 1851 by Captain Davenport. G.B. Goode's "Fishery Industries" gives the same date, saying, "Captain Clark (née Machado) began whale fishing at Monterey where an American, Captain Davenport, the first California shore whale fisher was engaged before him."

In a few short years, the California shoreline was populated at various places with whaling companies. The California stations were located in the following cities: Crescent, Half Moon Bay, Pigeon Point, Santa Cruz, Monterey Bay (two stations), Carmel Bay, Point Sur, San Simeon, Port Harford (or San Luis Obispo), Cojo Viejo (Point Conception), Goleta, Portuguese Bend (San Pedro), Dead Man's Island (San Pedro), and San Diego Bay (two stations). In the 90 years since this list was compiled, all of these stations have been corroborated by newspaper reports, shipping results, or by firsthand accounts or statements from the station manager himself. Another station, at Bolinas Bay, has been added as a result of newspaper articles. The information was from a letter carried by the San Francisco newspaper the *Alta California* and subsequently referred to by some historians. It is doubtful, though, that this station ever existed, as it seemed to be an ambitious endeavor that was never corroborated. As it turns out, the letter reads very much like a stock prospectus. In the end, 15 stations were established, according to Stark.

The following locations in Baja, Lower California, have also been mentioned by researchers and corroborated in newspaper reports: Cape Colonet, San Martin Island, Punta Banda, Santo Tomas, and Magdalena Bay. There may also have been a few more stations.

While Captain Davenport may have been the first to shore whale off the California coast, it was the Portuguese who made it an industry. Portuguese whalers from the Azores, Madeira, and other islands were recruited to work in whaleships that left New England for the Pacific Ocean. Some of these whalers jumped ship in Hawaii or San Francisco and were recruited or made their way to Monterey and went to work for the shore whaling stations in Monterey or farther south. Soon, stations opened up in Carmel and other points south.

Captain Clark (nee Machado) started several stations, from Monterey to the south. Captain Davenport started another whaling company in Monterey in 1854, and Clark also started a Portuguese whaling company in Monterey in 1854. Clark worked for several whaling companies on the coast for over four decades.

This illustration, depicting a whaling scene in the California Lagoons, is from the frontispiece of *Marine Mammalia and American Whaleman*, by Charles Melville Scammon. This is a lagoon in lower California. Captain Scammon discovered the "playgrounds" of the California gray whale, where the females went to give birth and land raise their young before the season changed, when they migrated north.

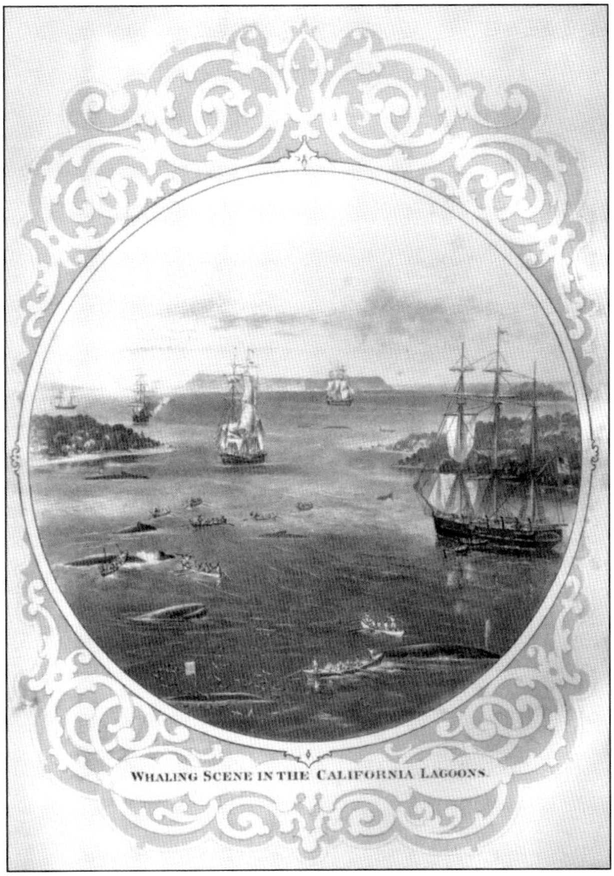

This adobe structure was built in 1847 by David Wight as a family home. However, by 1855, the Old Monterey Whaling Company began shore-whaling operations and used adobe as a headquarters and employee residence. The man standing in front of this photograph is holding a whaling shoulder gun. (From California Department of Parks and Recreation, Old Whaling Station.)

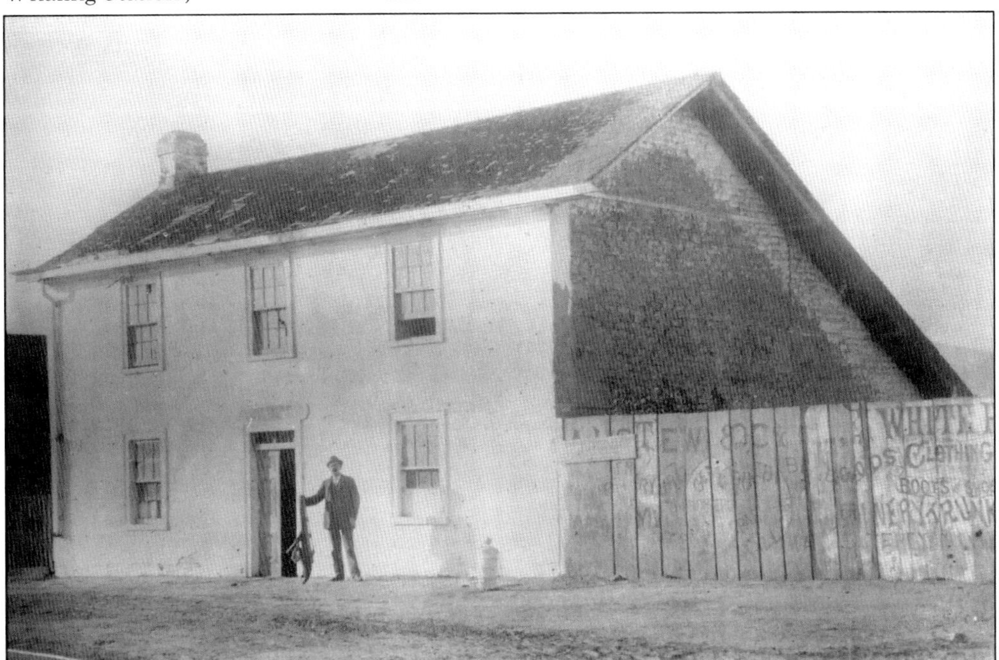

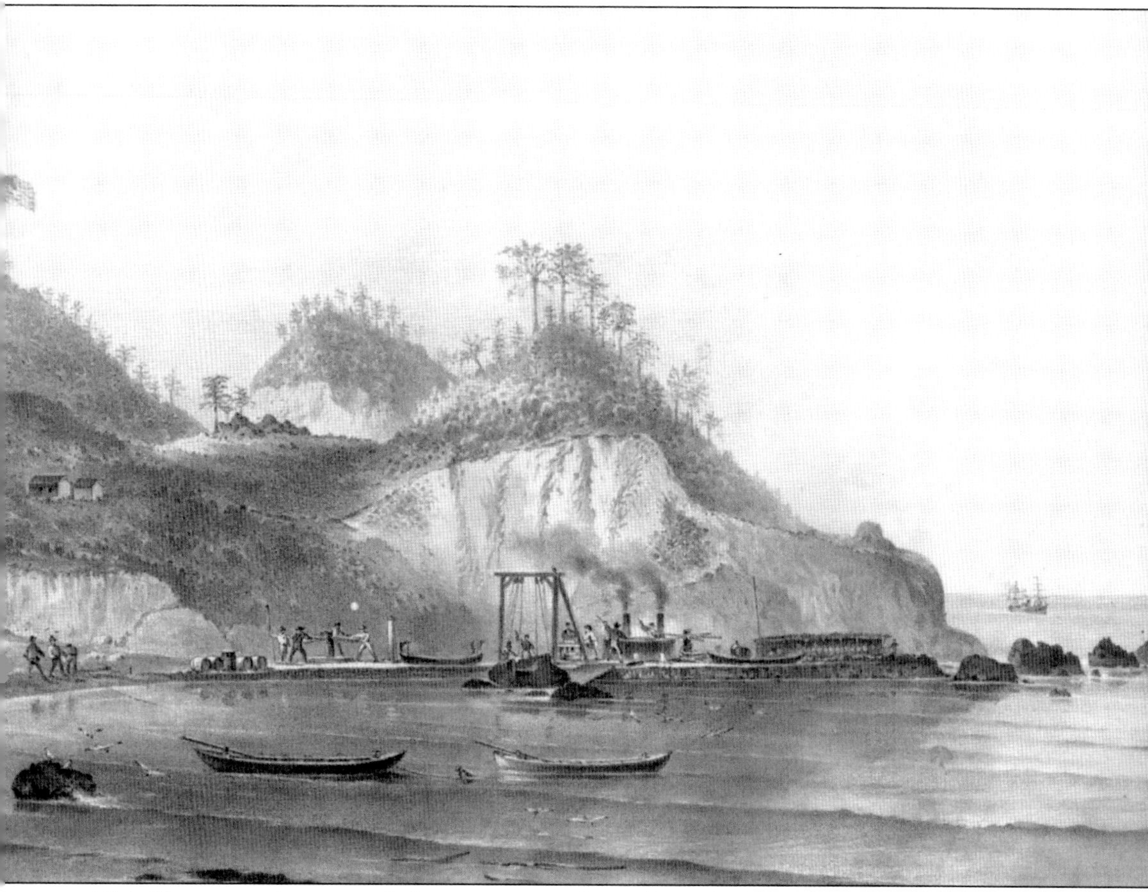

This illustration depicts a whaling station on Carmel Bay. In *Marine Mammalia and American Whaleman*, Charles Melville Scammon writes, "Under a precipitous bluff, close to the water's edge, is the station; where, upon a stone-laid quay, is erected the whole establishment for cutting-in and trying-out the blubber of the whales. Instead of rolling them upon the beach, as is usually done, the cutting tackles are suspended from an elevated beam, whereby the carcass is rolled over in the water—when undergoing the process of flensing—in a manner similar to that alongside a ship."

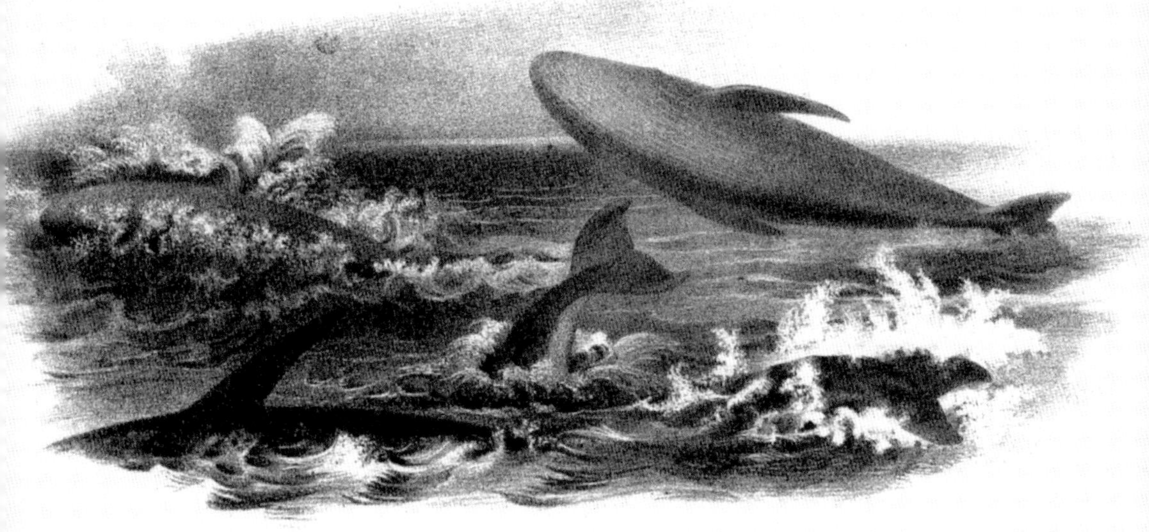

C. Scammon del. Britton & Rey

HUMPBACKS LOBTAILING, BOLTING, BREACHING AND FINNING.

Scammon describes humpback whales in his 1872 book *Marine Mammalia and American Whaleman*: "The Humpback is one of the species of rorqual that room through every ocean, generally preferring to feed and perform its uncouth gambols near exclusive coasts, or about the shores of islands, in all latitudes between the equator and the frozen oceans, both north and south. It is irregular in its movements seldom going a straight course for any considerable distance; at one time moving about in large numbers, scattered over the sea as far as the eye can discern from the mast-head; at other times singly, seeming as much at home as if it were surrounded by hundreds of its kind; performing at will the varied actions of 'breaching,' 'rolling,' 'finning,' 'lobtailing,' or 'scooping,' or, on a calm, sunny day, perhaps lying motionless on the medium-looking surface, as though life were extinct."

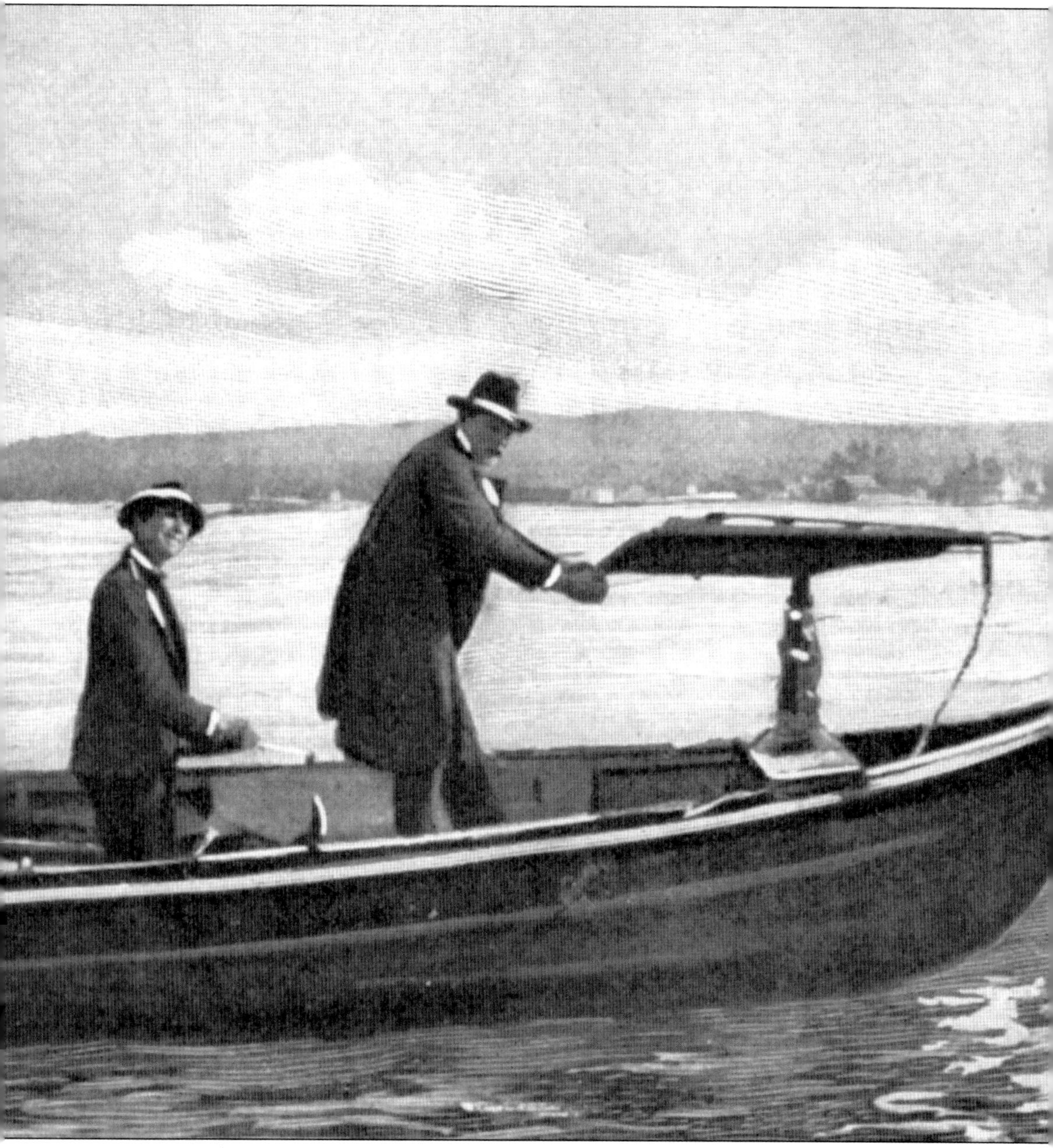

Capt. Jose Pedro stands ready to fire the harpoon in an illustration from "Offshore Whaling in the Bay of Monterey," by Edward Berwick, in *The Cosmopolitan* magazine of October 1900. "Jose Pedro a born, whale killer with eye trained to divine the devious deep sea meanderings of vagrant humpbacks between blowing-times; right-hand on the trigger wire, left on the butt of his Greener swivel-gun, there he stands, alert to fire the moment those glossy back monsters can be approached within gunning distance."

The whaling weapon known as the Pierce harpoon bomb-lance gun is described by Scammon in *Marine Mammals and the American Whaleman*. Pierce's harpoon bomb-lance gun is made of brass, has a 14-inch barrel, and is 1.5 feet long including the harpoon.

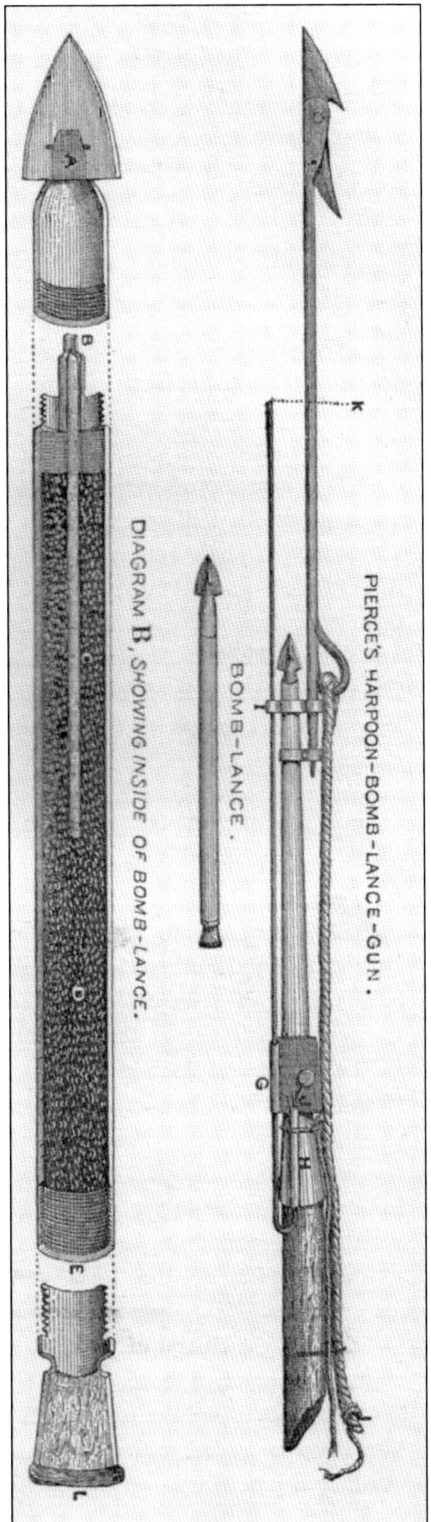

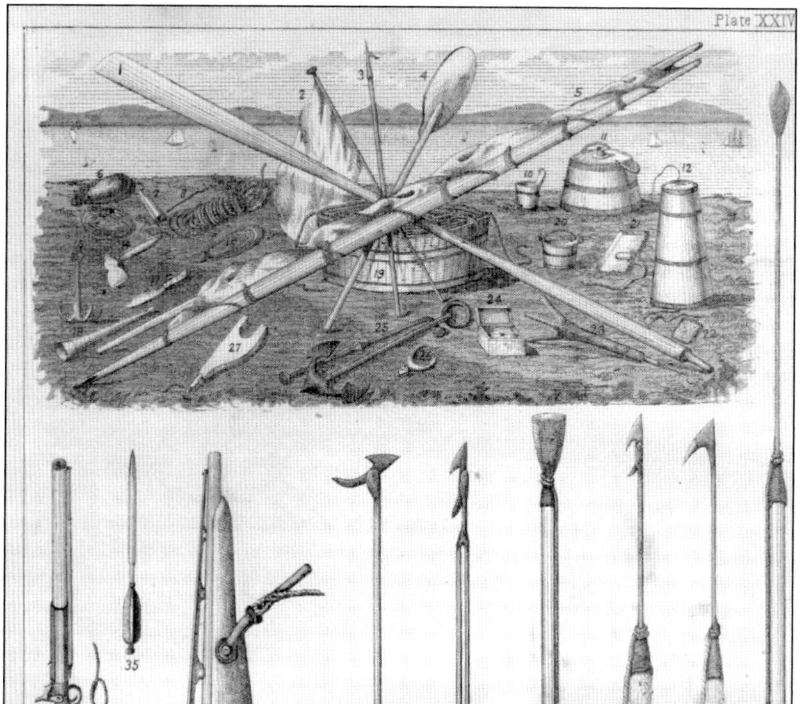

In *Marine Mammalia and American Whaleman*, Charles Scammon details the implements of a whaleboat: "The equipment belonging to a modern whale-boat consists of one mast and yard, or sprit, one to three sails (but usually a jib and a mainsail), five pulling oars, one steering-oar, five paddles, five rowlocks, five harpoons, one to three line tubs (into which the line is coiled), three hand-lances, three short-warps, one boat-spade, three lance-warps, one boat-warp, one boat-hatchet, two boat-knives, one boat-waif, one boat-compass, one boat-hook, one drag, one grapnel, one boat-anchor, one sweeping-line, lead, buoy, etc., one boat-keg, one boat-bucket, one piggin, one lantern-keg (containing flint, steel, box of tinder, lantern, candles, bread, tobacco, and pipes), one boat-crotch, one tub oar-crotch, half a dozen chock-pins, a roll of canvas, a paper of tacks, two nippers to which may be added a bomb-gun, and four bomb lances; in all forty-eight articles, and at least eighty-two pieces."

This illustration is titled "Whaleboat with Greener's Gun Mounted," from *Marine Mammalia and American Whaleman*. Scammon writes, "At dawn of day, the boats may be seen, careening under a press of sail, or propelled over the undulating ground-swell by the long, measured strokes or oars, until they reach the usual whaling-ground, where the day is passed moving to and fro unless the objects of pursuit are met with."

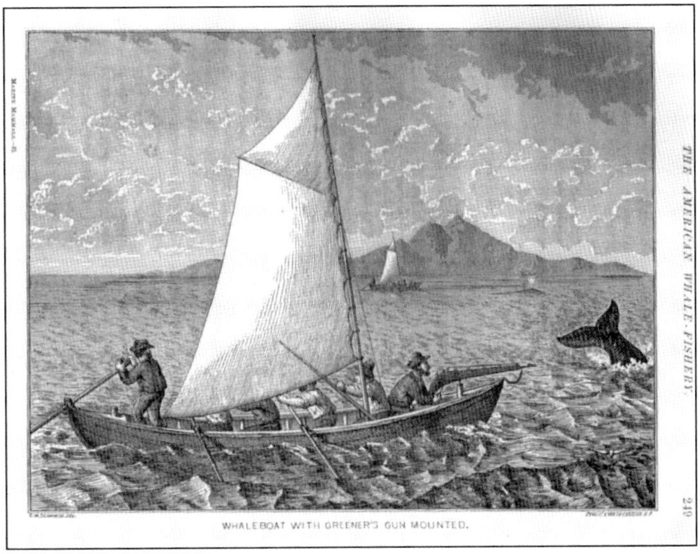

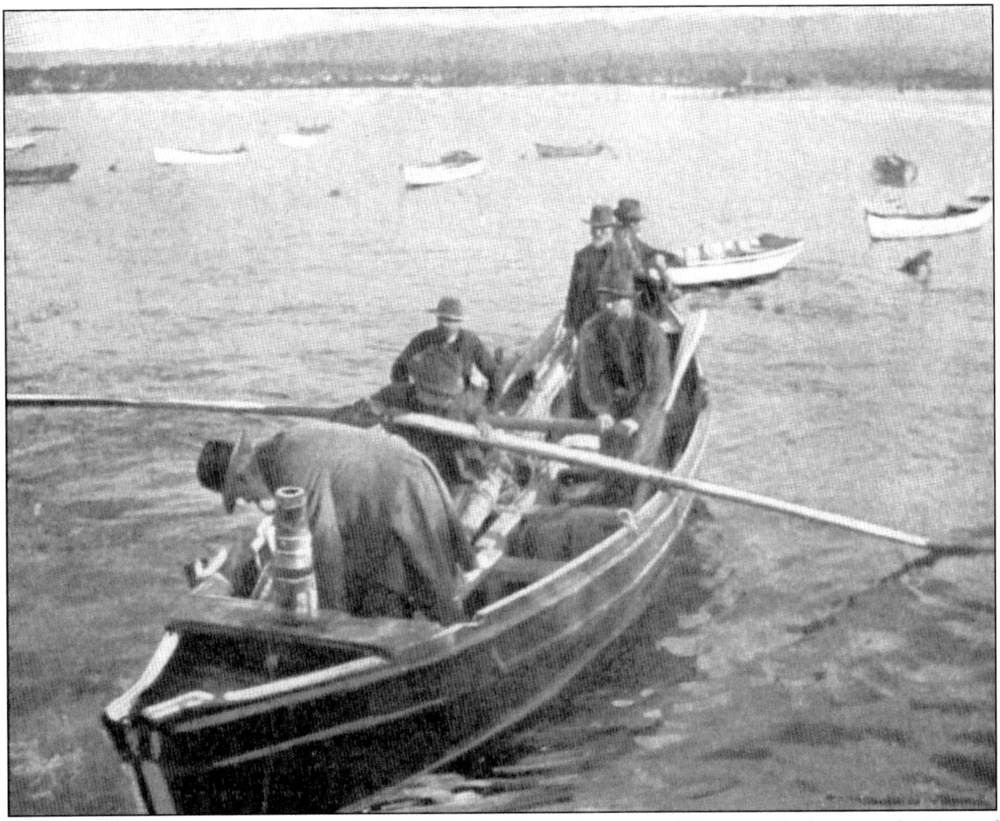

This image, "The Return of the Whaleboat," appeared in "Offshore Whaling in the Bay of Monterey," by Edward Berwick, in *The Cosmopolitan* magazine, October 1900. "On the third day, the gases which are generated in the whale's carcass cause the body to float, and at early morn the hardy toilers of the sea tow their harvest home. With favorable breezes, sails make the work lighthouse; otherwise, eight stout oarsmen in two boats laboriously pull the black floating island to the try-works, close to Monterey."

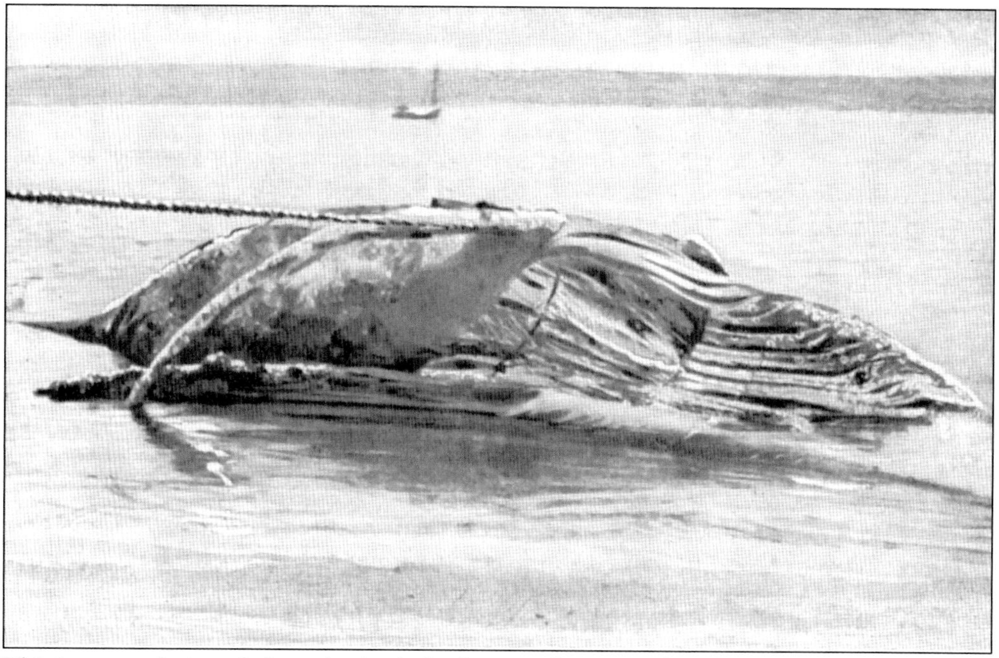

This is a ventral view of a humpback whale, showing flutings and markings. The image appeared in "Offshore Whaling in the Bay of Monterey," by Edward Berwick, in *The Cosmopolitan* magazine, October 1900.

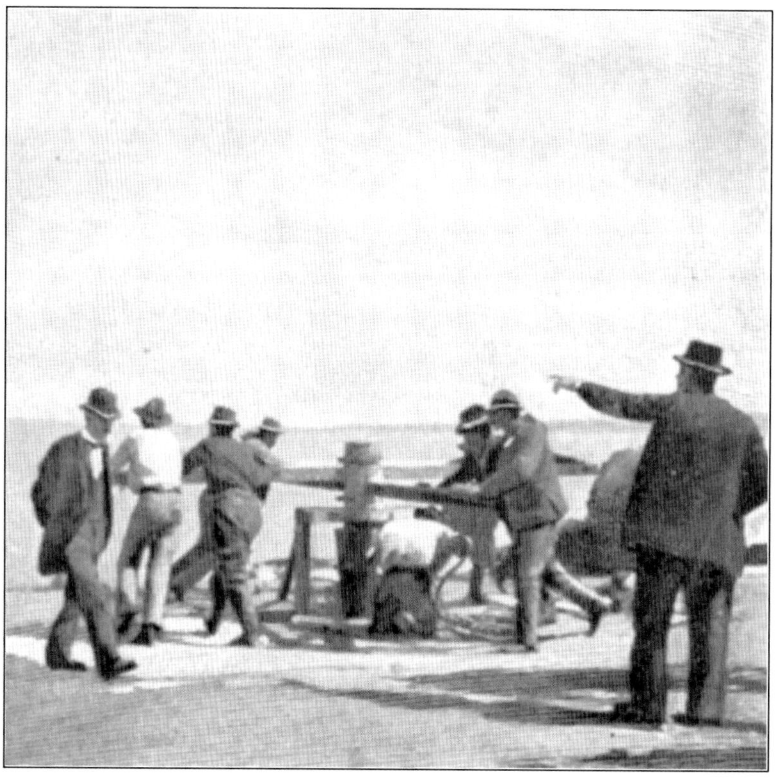

"Here it is made fast by a huge chain and cable attached to one of the flippers; the shore end of the cable being coiled on a wooden capstan on the bluff where the try-pots stand. At the next high tide the 'ship-keepers' and 'blubber-carriers' (as the shore whalers are called) man this capstan, and float the carcass as high up on the white sand beach as the water permits."

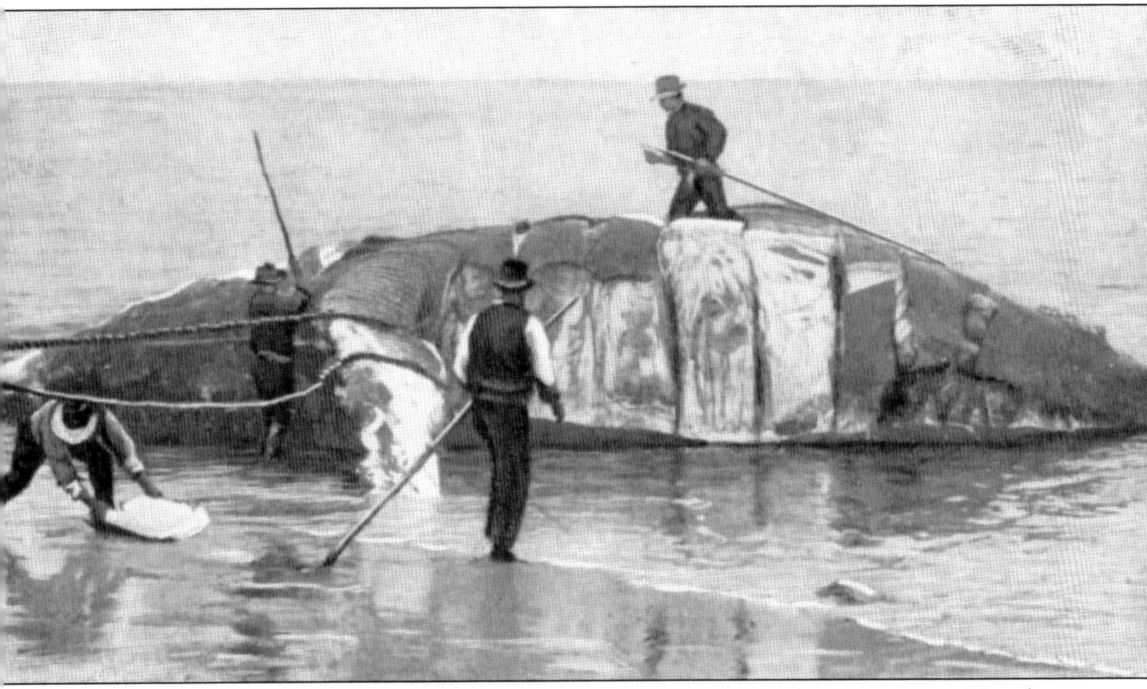

Here, workers cut blubber from a calf-whale. Writing in *The Cosmopolitan* magazine of October 1900, Berwick describes cutting blubber from a whale. "The work of stripping the blubber then commences. For this a whole armory is needed—long handled blubber spades, narrow and keen-edged, huge hooks and forks, and tremendous knives, some with two handles for 'mincing.' Stretchers are two, made wide and flat, long enough to carry as much blubber as two stout fellows can stagger under up the inclined plane from the beach to the mincing-vats on the rocks above."

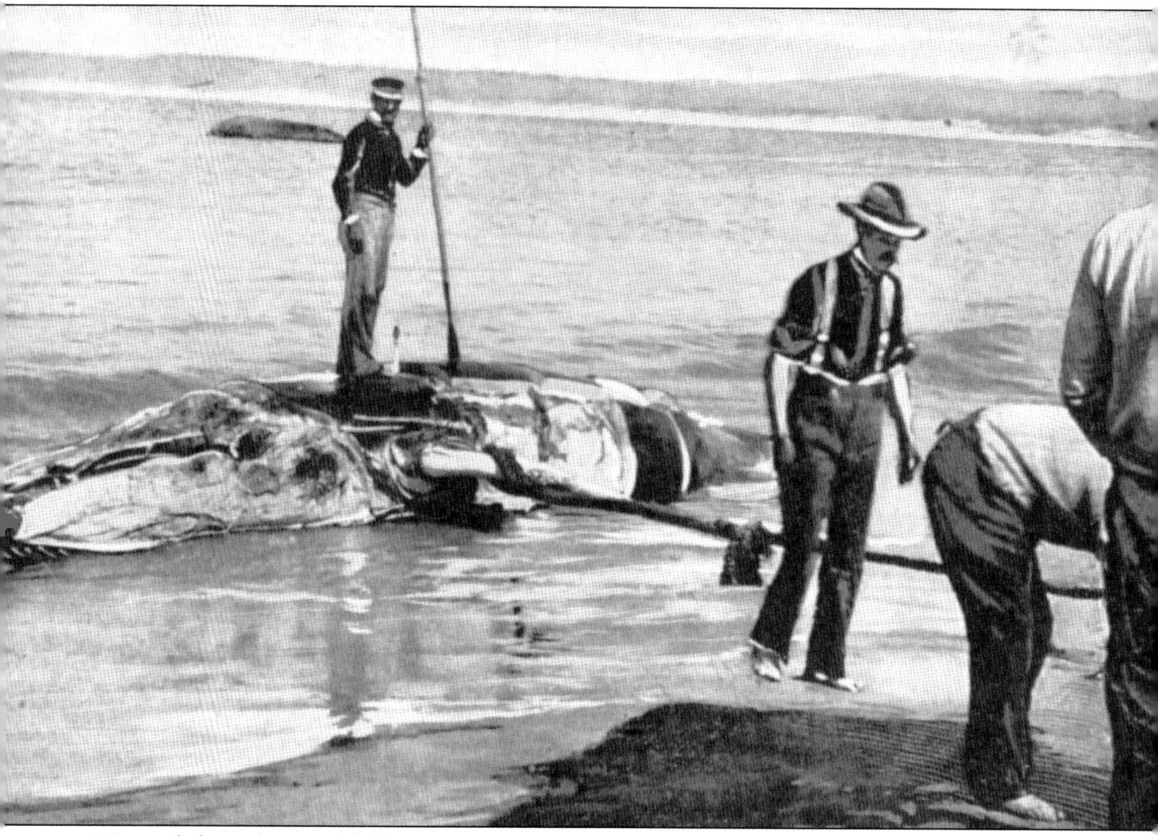

Here, while workers cut blubber from a calf, the mother is seen anchored in the distance. Berwick continues his description of the process of removing blubber from a whale: "And now the leader cuts the first 'scarf' under the flipper. As his spade makes its way through the glossy, jet black skin, the blubber, white and glistening, shows beneath, looking for all the world like the solid fat on the back of a mammoth hog. Two or three parallel cuts, a foot apart or more, follow; the resulting strips are divided transversely and dexterously separated from the underlying mountain of flesh."

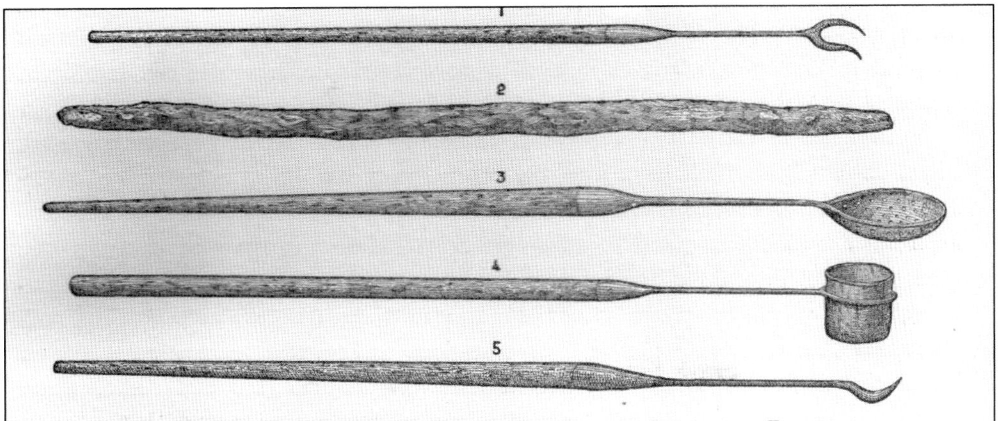

Seen here are implements used in cutting a whale, from Berwick's article, "Offshore Whaling in the Bay of Monterey," in *The Cosmopolitan* magazine. "The cutting stage, which is so constructed as to admit of the officers standing upon it immediately over the carcass when using the cutting-spades, is put over the side and lowered into position; meanwhile the rest of the cutting-gear is being got in readiness, which consists of toggles, spades, boarding and leaning knives, gaffs, pikes, blubber-hooks, head straps, fin-chain, throat toggle, head-axes, etc."

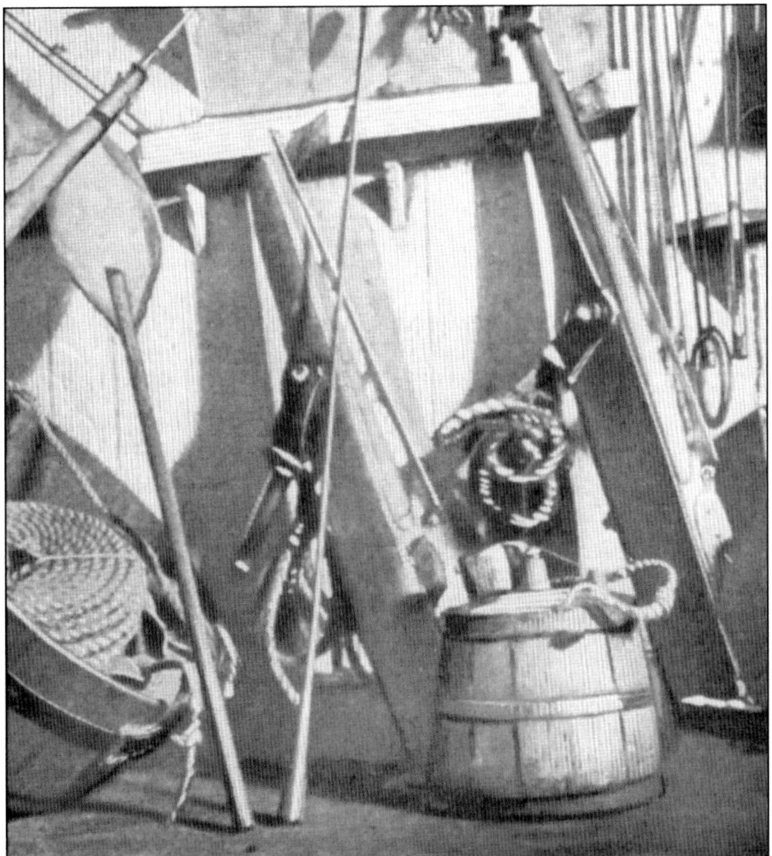

Berwick writes in *The Cosmopolitan* magazine of October 1900: "Gunning distance for harpoons is no long range, twenty fathom (whalers do their reckoning in fathoms) being an extreme shot. For though the Greener gun takes a charge of fourteen drams of powder, the harpoon is heavy, and has a long and heavy whale-line, one inch thick, attached to a loop sliding in a central slot."

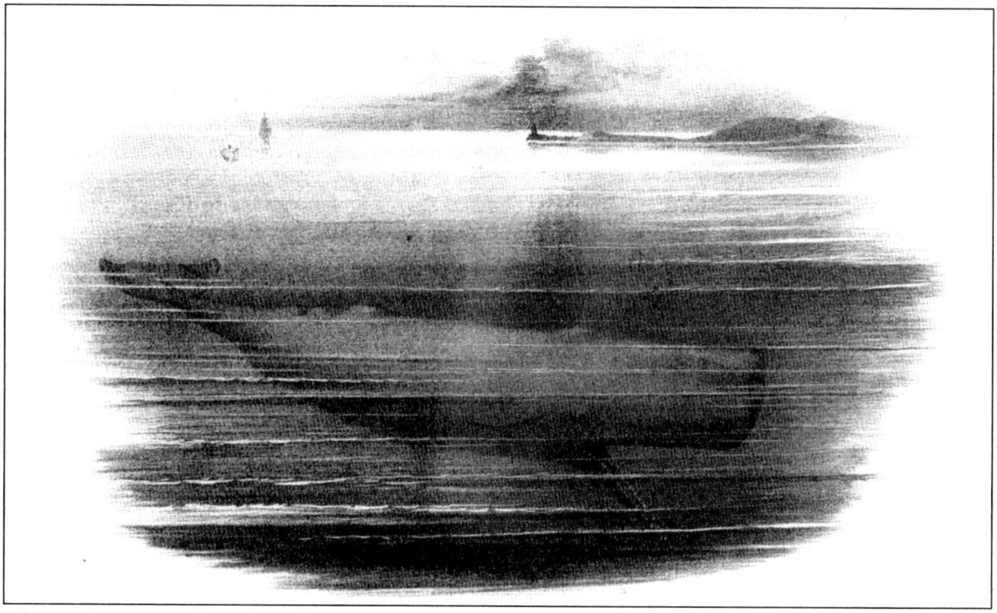

Charles Scammon describes the sperm whale in *Marine Mammalia and American Whaleman*: "This is the largest of the toothed cetaceans, is known to English and American whalemen as the Sperm Whale, to the Germans as the Pottfisch, and to the French as the Cachalot. It widely differs from all other of its order, both in figure and in habits. The fully matured animal equals, if it does not exceed, the Bowhead, or Great Polar whale, in magnitude and in commercial value."

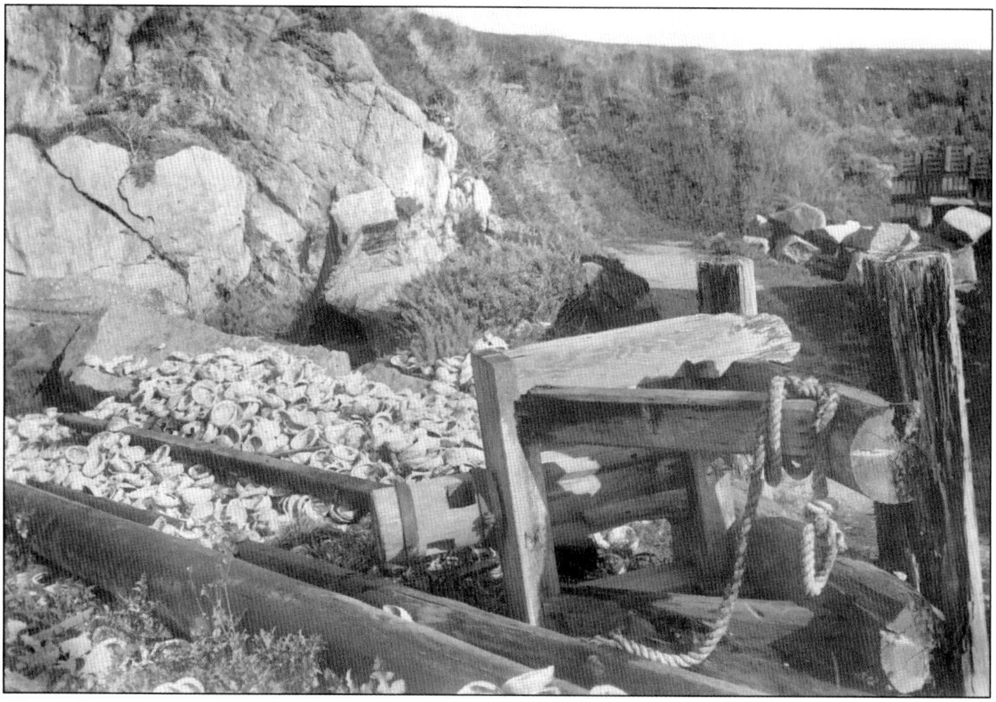

Shown here is the Old Whaling Station windless, which was active in the 1870s. This photograph was taken by Slevin. The caption with the photograph reads, "Old Whaling St., Point Lobos, windless of 1870." The purpose of the windless on shore or on a boat is to bring the whale-line.

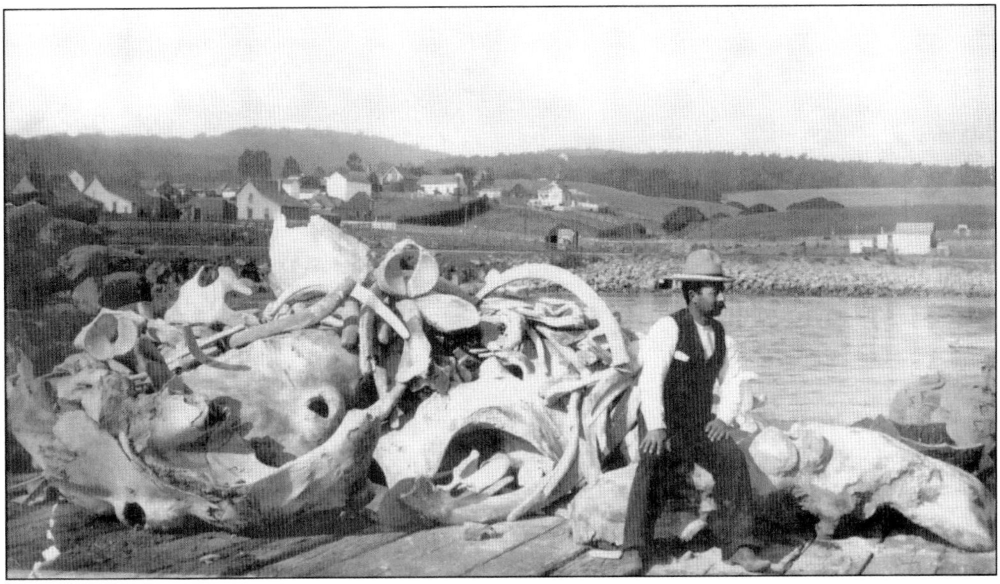

Michael Noon sits on a pile of whalebone at Monterey's wharf. This photograph shows the area of the whaling station on Decatur Street. The photograph was taken by Joseph Kurt Oliver, around 1896.

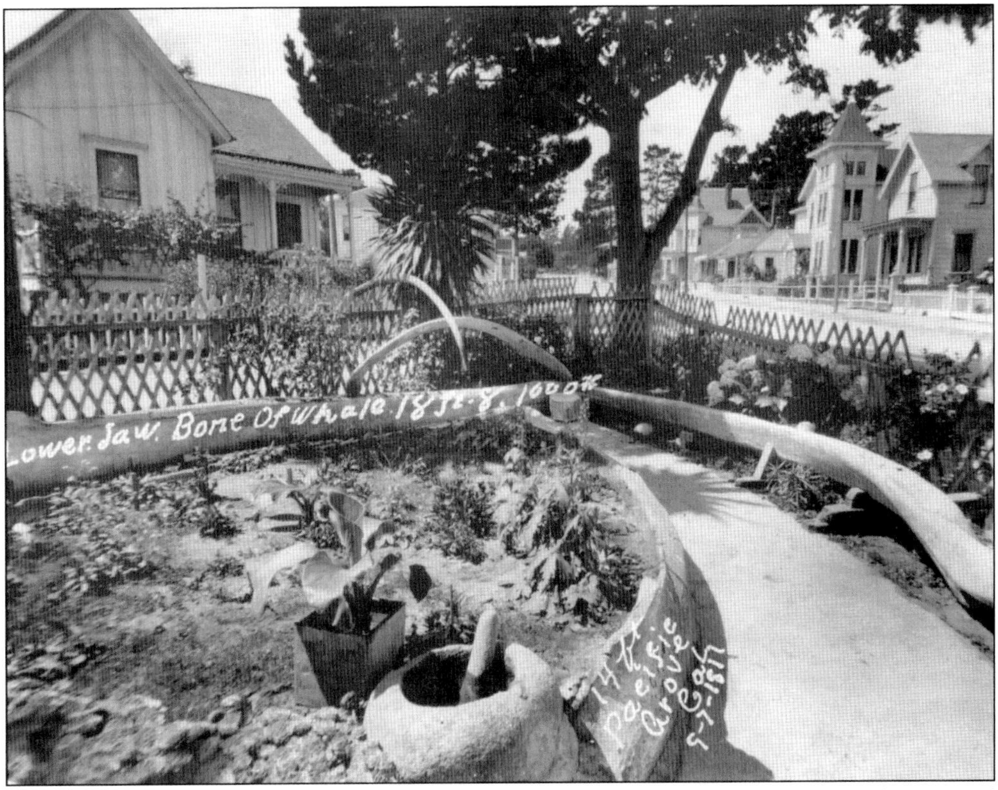

This is a photograph of five whale jawbones at a cottage in Pacific Grove, probably taken around 1900. Handwriting on the photograph at one of the bones reads, "Lower Jaw Bone of Whale, 18 Ft – 8, 1000 lb." A second label reads, "14 ft. Pacific Grove, Cal., 9-7-1811."

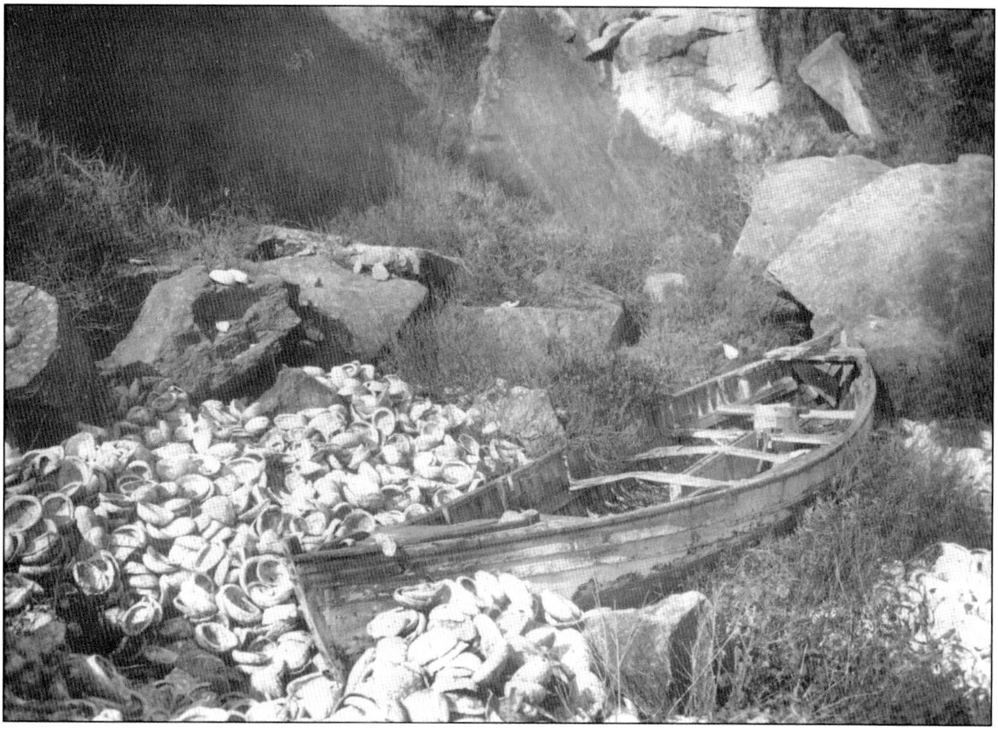

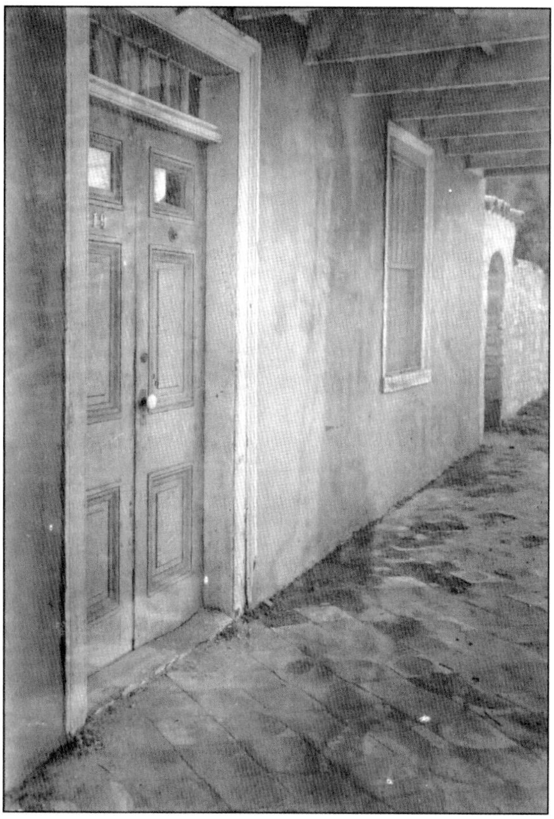

An old whaleboat is pictured here surrounded by abalone shells. This area was the location of a Japanese abalone operation that started around 1900 and operated for many years. Prior to that, this location was part of the Carmel Whaling Company.

This is the St. Anthony Church in Monterey, California. This walkway was once the site of an impressive collection of whalebones. Each time a whale was caught, Portuguese fishermen would carry bones on their backs all the way from the beach and kneel before the church to set them into the dirt walkway in honor of the saint. The bones, which got to be up to a foot thick, were removed around 1936 by the church.

Three

Long Beach Whaling

Capt. John Davenport Loop whaled in the Long Beach area from 1910 to 1919. His operation was small. His "whaler" was a modified pleasure launch with a harpoon gun mounted in the bow. His boat, the *Camiguin*, would go out from Long Beach and search for whales from Portuguese Bend, where shore whaling was prosecuted in the 1880s.

The boat's engineer, Clyde Tibbits, spotted the first whale from the old whaler's hill. Along with Loop, the crew included A.H. Mason. After some two hours, the little *Camiguin* finally was near enough to shoot the monster. Captain Loop estimated the whale was a finback, from 60 to 75 feet long, almost twice the size of his vessel. He hesitated, and his chance was lost. B Loop was left with the impression that they could get within shooting range of the leviathans.

Whaling was not a full-time occupation; only Captain Mason was said to have some "East coast whaling experience." For years, Loop was an operator of a merry-go-round in the Long Beach amusement zone. In addition to the *Camiguin*, he had another boat, the *Music*. His boats were primarily for sightseeing, not whaling. He maintained small craft and glass-bottomed boats on a rental basis for tourists. His income secure, Loop was able to attend to his whale "expeditions" on a sporadic basis.

On February 7, 1911, the hunters captured the coveted prize, fulfilling a long-cherished ambition of Captain Loop. He used his eight-bore Pierce shoulder gun, which fired explosive bombs, to take the whale.

After initial success, Loop purchased a full complement of the latest whaling guns and harpoons. As soon as a whale was killed, he brought it in and, by a sort of dry-dock method, floated it to a lighter, which was later anchored some distance offshore. He then transported sightseers out to view the whale. When decomposition set in, Loop brought his prize alongside one of the large wharf derricks, where it was hoisted onto a flatcar and shipped to a fertilizer plant near Los Angeles.

Captain Loop exhibited eight whales in the Long Beach area between 1911 and 1916, four of them on barges, but they could only be kept for a couple of days, due to the unpleasant odor. Of the eight whales, information is available for seven: six were California gray whales, and one was a humpback whale. He believed that he had taken about 36 whales, but he felt that 80 percent of the whales he struck were lost. This list, from the *Long Beach Telegram*, indicates in parenthesis the number of the exhibited whale:

2/8/1911 first whale 35 foot female California Gray, exhibited (1), odor offensive, towed out to sea and cut up.

11/28/1911 two gray whales killed, neither recovered.

12/6/1911 shot two fin whales, one died and sank and was not recovered, the other swam away with an unexploded bomb inside.

1/4/1912 Two Gray whales killed and sank with buoys, one recovered for exhibition (2) and sent to a phosphate plant near Los Angeles, the other was not recovered.

3/9/1912 California Gray shot and chased to Catalina, chase given up due to darkness.

12/31/1912 California Gray shot and not recovered.

1/12/1913 California gray whale killed and put into dry-dock for exhibition (3) 35 foot, 20 tons, exhibited near municipal wharf, 1,650 people visited the whale.

3/26/1913 Shot and captured a humpback whale, first one taken here. The whale was 50 feet long and was taken to dry-dock for exhibition (4) and loaded on the float (barge) named the John D. Loop.

2/15/1914 California Gray 35 feet long weighing about 20 tons is shot and exhibited (5), taken later to the fertilizer plant.

3/29/1915 large California Gray whale 43 feet in length, weighing 20 tons. After exhibition (6) the whale was sent to the dry-dock, and was transferred to a rail car for shipment to the fertilizer plant.

1/22/1916 35 foot California Gray whale shot and sank, it came to the surface and was towed in by a fisherman believing he killed it with a rifle shot, not exhibited. Fertilizer plant gave proceeds of catch to Capt. Loop.

3/29/1916 35 foot California Gray whale embalmed and placed on exhibit (7). Placed on a barge, anchored along the shore at the Western Motor Boat Works, at Seaside park.

A professional embalmer took charge of the huge carcass of the whale caught on March 29, embalming it so it was absolutely free from any unpleasant odor. This was the first whale successfully embalmed on the Pacific Coast. The embalming method took five years to develop.

Following the embalming of this catch, captured whales were brought in to have the blubber tried-out (boiled in oil, like bacon in a kettle of fat), tenderloins cut for human consumption, and the remainder of the meat processed for fertilizer. Captain Loop introduced whale meat to Southern California markets and, during the war, was encouraged by the US Food Administration.

Additional whales were caught for meat, oil, and fertilizer. The *Long Beach Times* is the source unless otherwise specified:

11/21/1916 California Gray cow 50 feet long, 8 feet in diameter, weight 40 tons.

1/17/1917 California Gray, 6 tons of whale tenderloin was cut out for local markets.

2/26/1918 California Gray whale, forty seven 1/2 feet long.

Winter 1918 2 more whales caught during the winter campaign, securing an average of about 20 barrels of oil from each. (*Pacific Fisherman*, June 1918.)

Winter 1919 Captain Loop and his companions, Capt. Jack Stevens and Bert Stevens, went on a winter cruise to Scammon's lagoon, during which they killed five California Gray whales. (*Nevada State Journal*, May 16, 1919.)

Captain Loop and his friends gave up whaling after the 1919 winter season. However, he made plans for years on how to improve whaling and its related products. He invented an aerial harpoon, called a "Go Devil," to be dropped upon a whale with a buoy attached. When the whale came up for air, he would be attacked with a bomb gun. The "Go-Devil" was a lance 11 feet long in the form of a cylindrical pipe one and one-fourth inches in diameter. Its penetrating end, four-sided and sharp as a razor blade, when dropped from the sky was said to penetrate the whale's blubber without difficulty. The lance carried a receptacle with three pounds of liquid carbon dioxide. The charge expanded to approximately 160 cubic feet and was expected to kill the mammal by extreme low temperature. Loop received a patent for his efforts to develop the "Go-Devil."

He made several trips over the ocean in the naval blimp *B-3*, during which about 30 whales were sighted. Before Captain Loop could make flights in Navy blimps, he had to obtain permission from the secretary of the navy. He was granted the requested permission, probably because his invention had potential to be developed into a weapon.

Other ideas Captain Loop experimented with included bombs and explosive powders; a whale dairy on Catalina Island in conjunction with millionaire William Wrigley Jr., who had recently purchased the island; whale hunting from a baby blimp (A blimp was reportedly being rigged at a Los Angeles flying field to try out Captain Loop's method); use of a hydroplane from which one could hunt for sardines and whales; and an explosive lance that Loop expected to revolutionize whaling.

Captain Loop's Mexican expedition was commercial. Its object was whale oil. His patents include the whale lance (patent no. 1498741) and the whale-harpooning apparatus (patent no. 1472223).

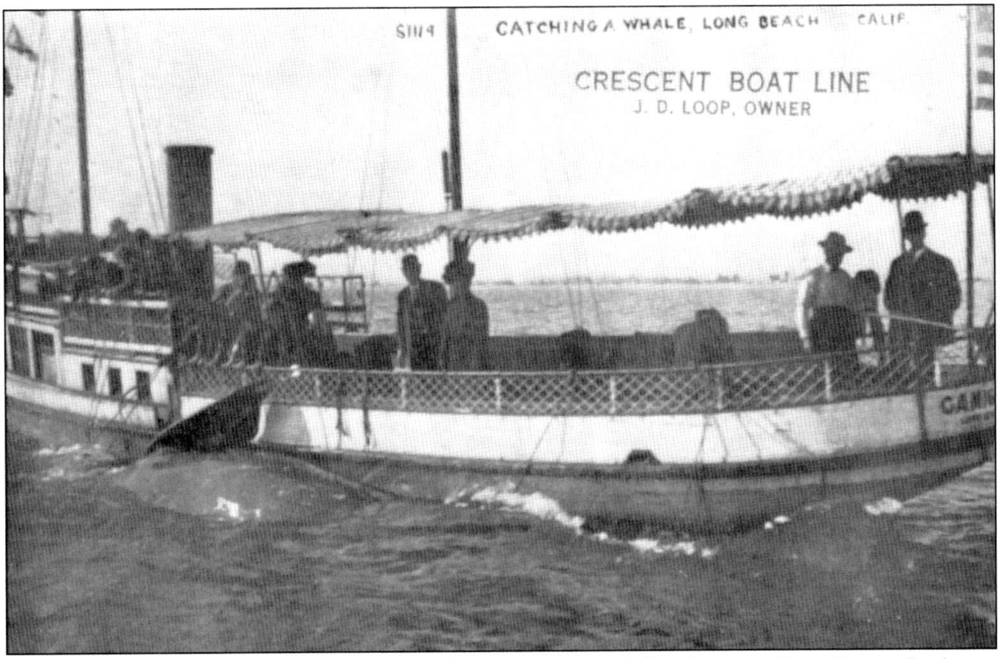

Shown here with a whale is the excursion boat *Camiguin*, of the Crescent Boat Line, which ran a daily boat to Long Beach. John Davenport Loop, the owner, went whaling from 1911 to 1916 in search of whales to exhibit.

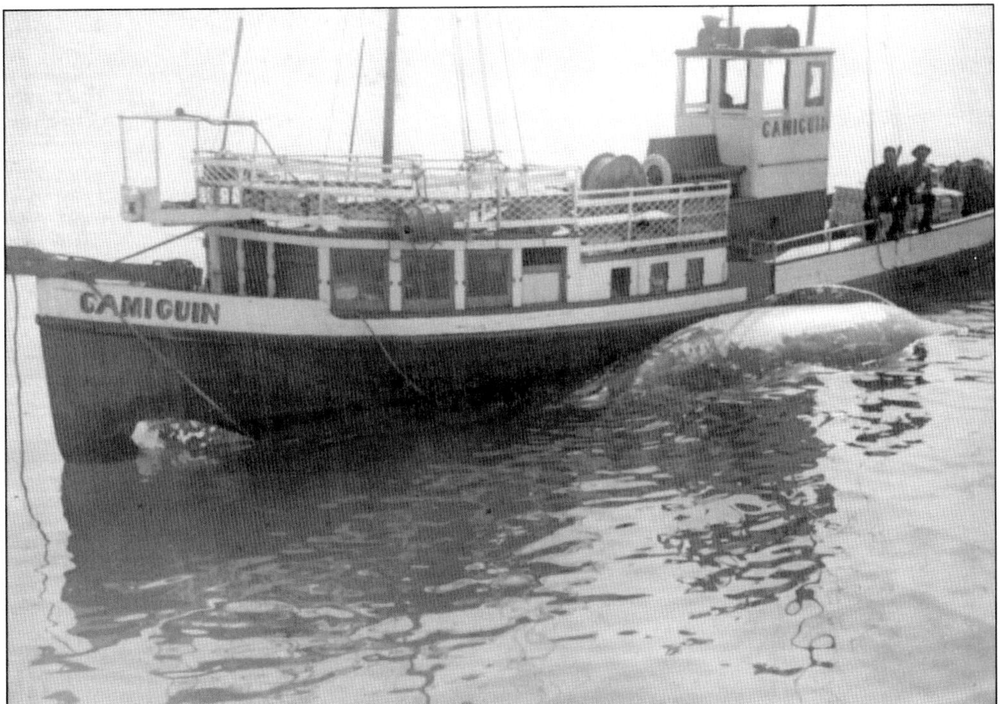

Here, another whale is seen with the *Camiguin*. After being caught, the whales would be tied up in the harbor, and tickets were sold for sightseers to go out to the whale.

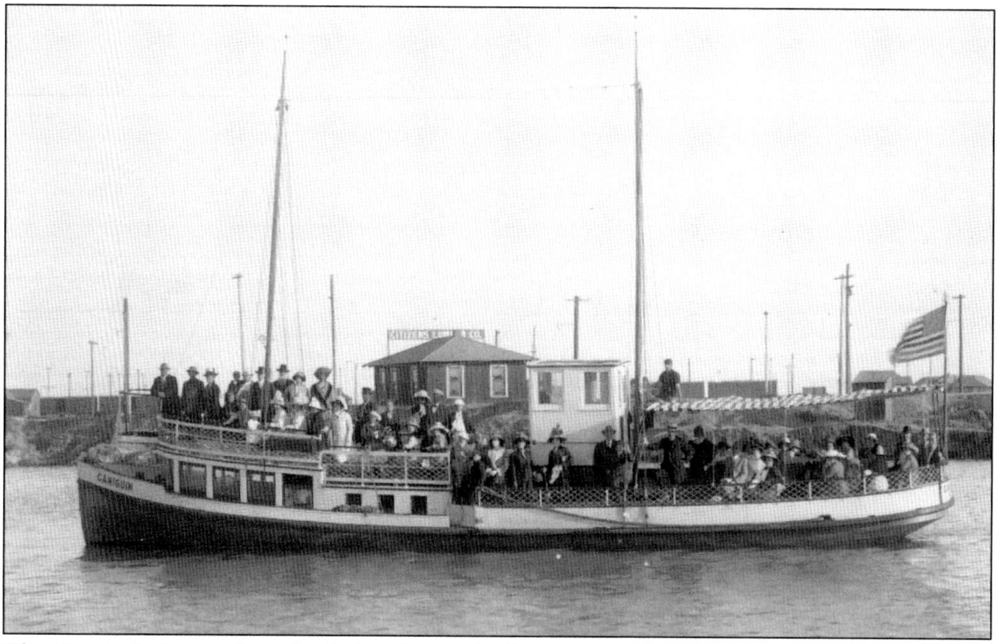

The *Camiguin* is seen here loaded with people. Loop ran a daily boat to Portuguese Bend for tourists. Portuguese Bend was the location of a whaling some 50 years previously.

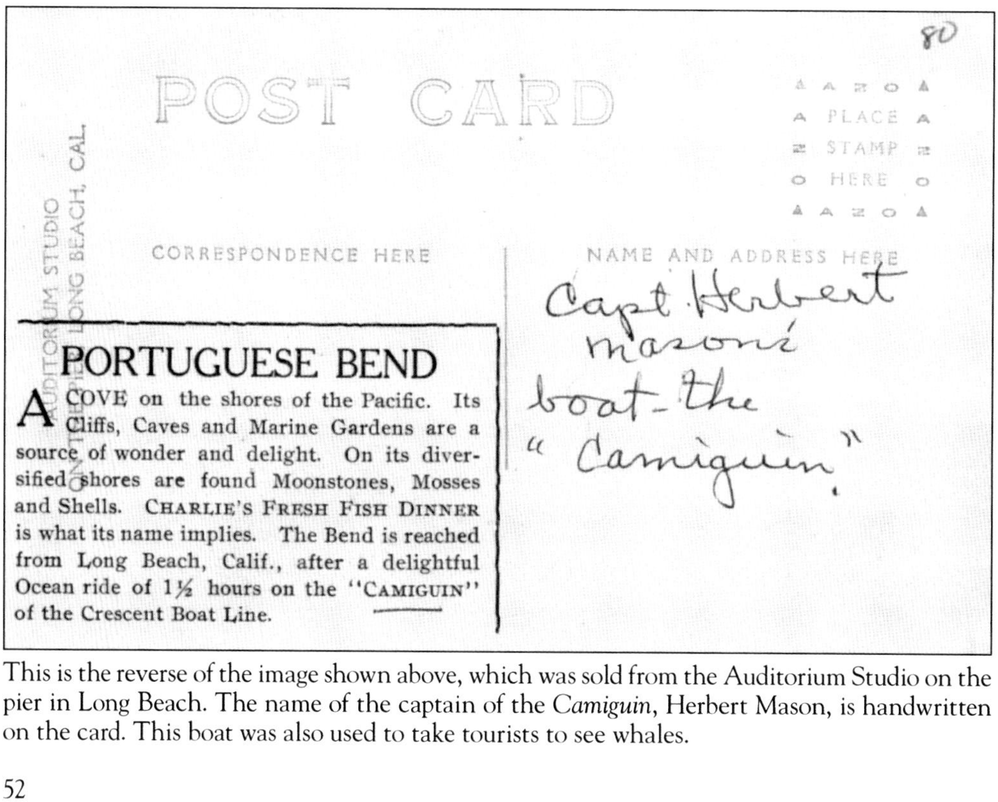

This is the reverse of the image shown above, which was sold from the Auditorium Studio on the pier in Long Beach. The name of the captain of the *Camiguin*, Herbert Mason, is handwritten on the card. This boat was also used to take tourists to see whales.

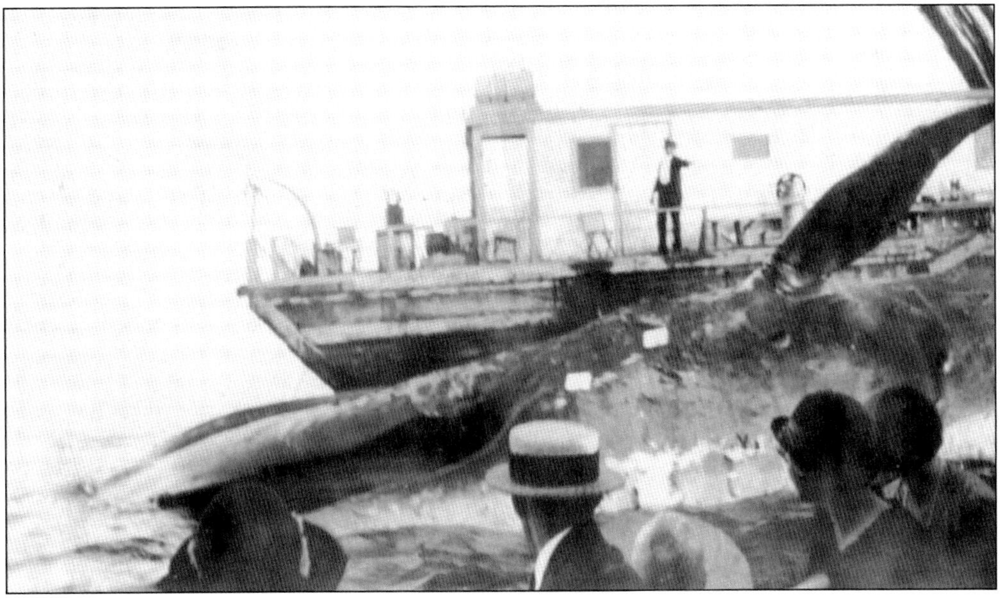

In this photograph, Captain Loop gives his lecture about the blue whale and whaling.

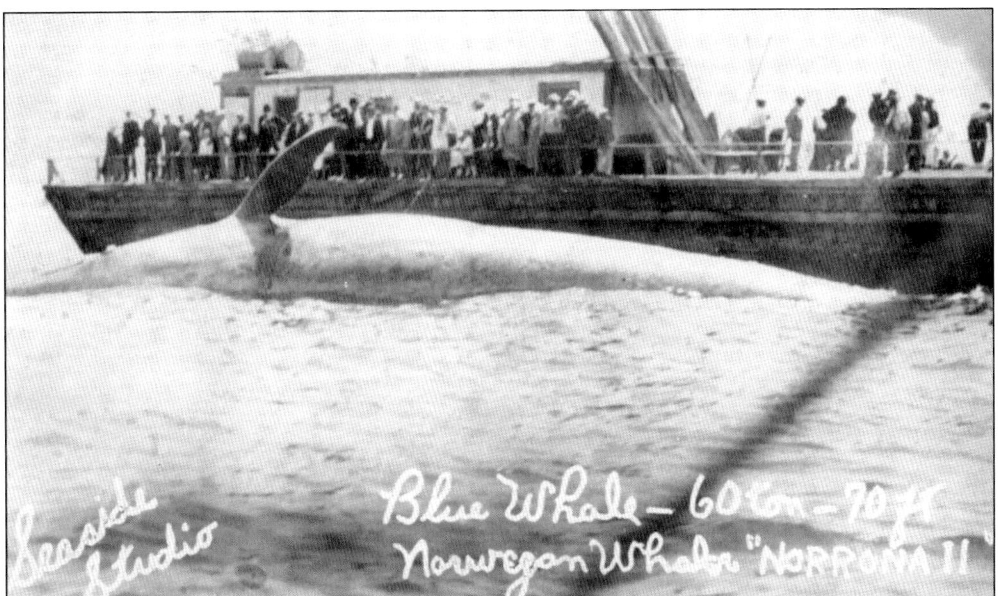

A Norwegian whaleboat also took tourists to see the blue whale. The name of this boat was the *Norrona II*.

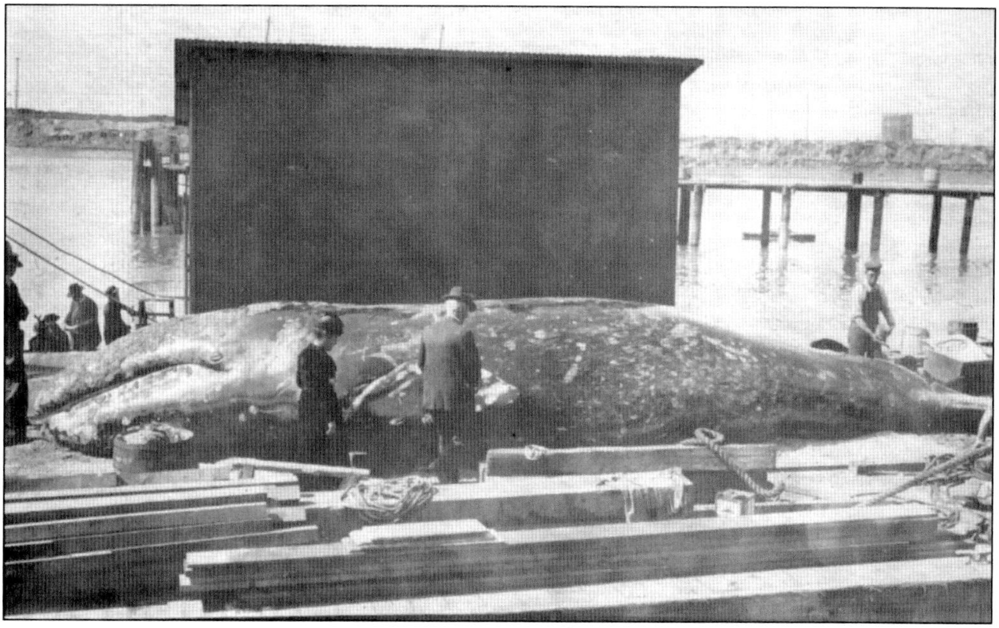

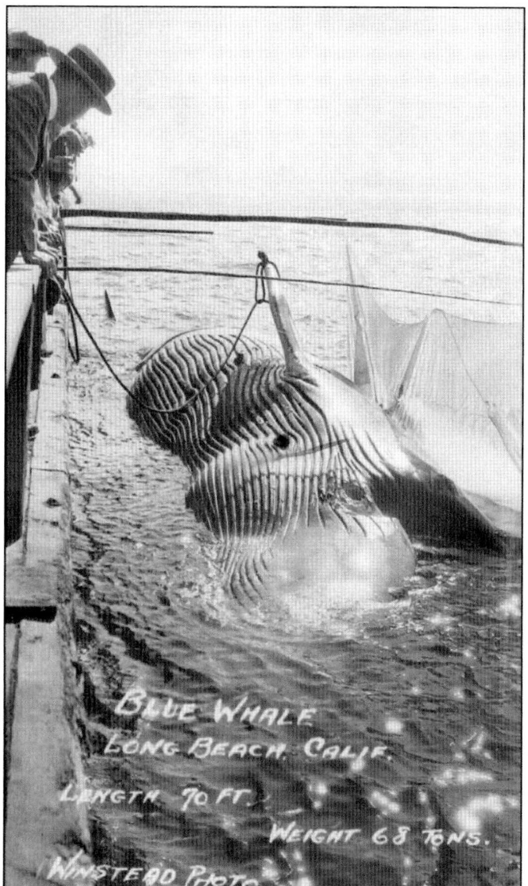

Shown here is a gray whale on a lighter (barge) in the harbor. Tourists would pay to walk out to the barge on the pier to view the whale.

This photograph was taken by the professional photographer Winstead. The black holes in the whale indicate positions where an air hose was used to inflate the whale so it would float. A wood plug was then inserted in the hole after inflation.

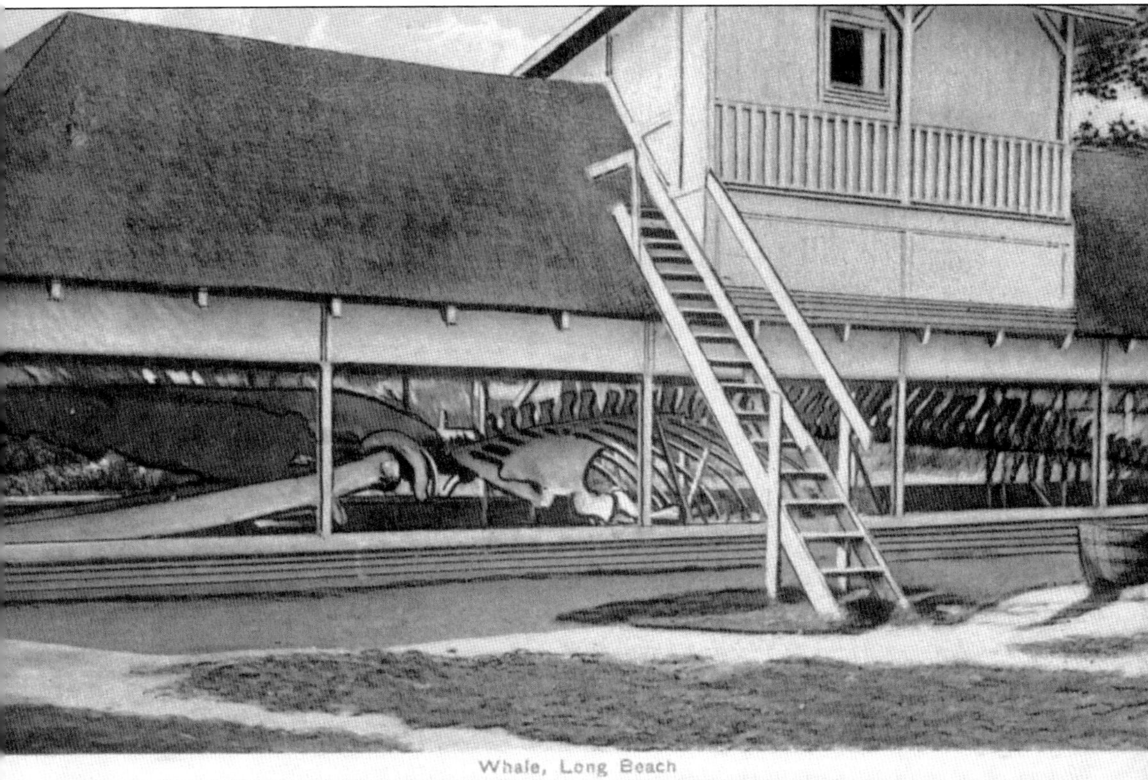

This whale skeleton in Long Beach was exhibited for many years. The whale was believed to have washed up on one of the Long Beach beaches in the 1930s. It was buried and dug up about a year later and displayed on city property. It is not known if the whale is associated with Captain Loop. The whale appears to be a blue whale and may have reached eight feet or more.

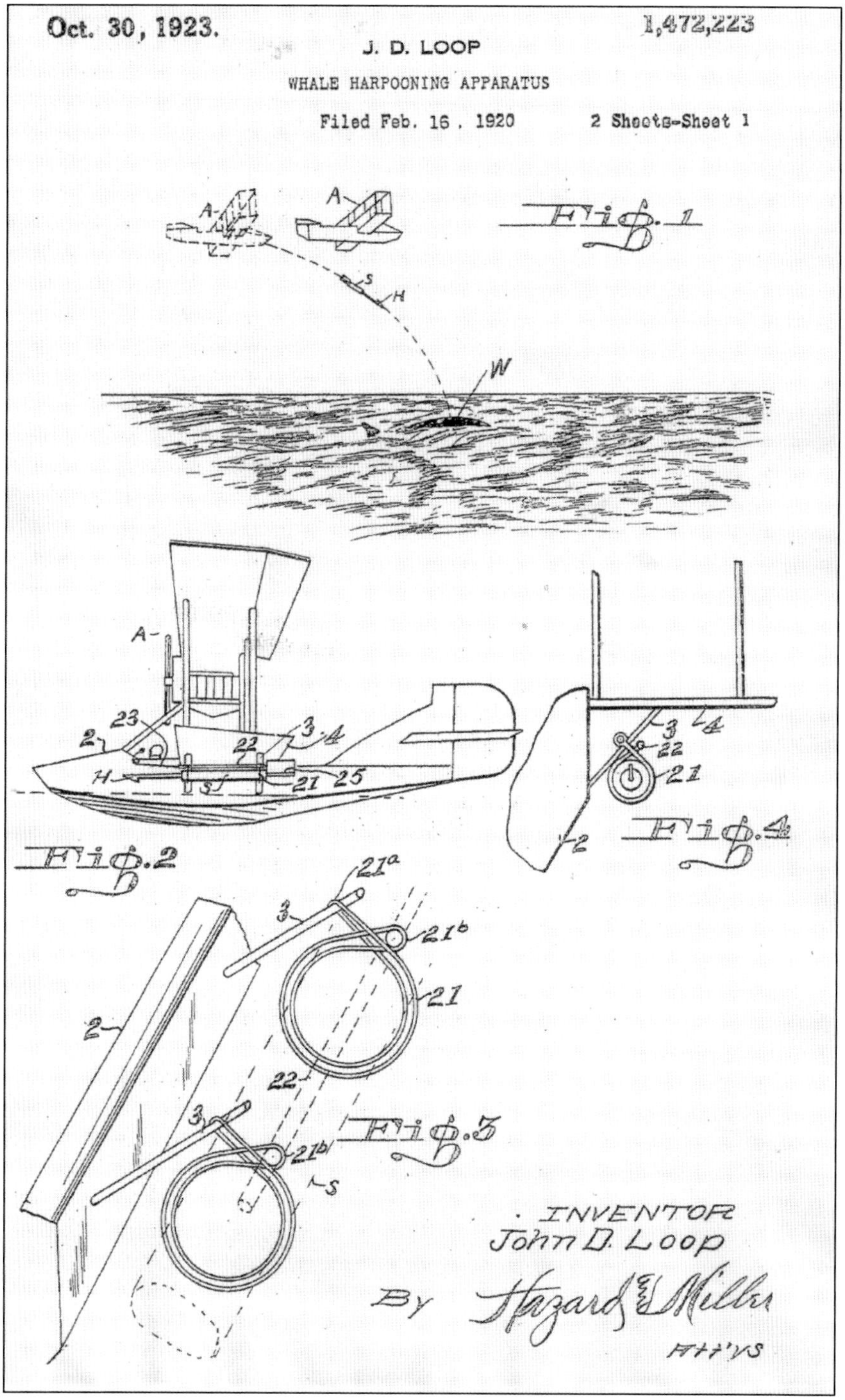

This is John Davenport Loop's drawing to accompany his patent application for his blow-devil harpoon. It was designed to be dropped from a plane or dirigible. Upon hitting a whale, it would trigger a tank of carbon dioxide to release its contents. The idea was that inflating the whale with 10 pounds of carbon dioxide would kill it. The device was never tested against a whale to see if the carbon dioxide would kill a whale or not..

Four

Exhibited Whales

In California, Capt. John D. Loop exhibited whales in Long Beach from 1911 until about 1915. He harpooned whales in the ocean between Long Beach and Catalina Island. After they were captured, he brought the whales in and anchored them in Long Beach harbor. He then sold excursion tickets and took the public to see the whales. Captain Loop may have been the first person to hunt whales for the express purpose of exhibition. The whales were processed into fertilizer after being exhibited, but the first whale was taken out to sea and released, sinking to the bottom. In 1915, Loop announced that he had finally succeeded in embalming a whale, claiming that it would last indefinitely in that condition. Captain Loop caught and exhibited eight whales over five years, including one humpback. The others were California gray whales.

Captain Loop experimented with various methods of preserving the whales, seeking to extend the amount of time they could be exhibited. The first whale, exhibited without any preservation, was towed out to sea within a couple of days, its stench having become unbearable. Loop experimented with ice and refrigeration, which also proved unsatisfactory. Then, he turned to embalming. He worked with a local mortician, who was able to stabilize the decomposition process using a couple hundred gallons of embalming fluid. After this success, Captain Loop never embalmed another whale. How long the embalmed whale lasted is anyone's guess.

The Pacific Whaling Company (PWC), whose name was similar to that of a company that had whaled for many years but had just folded, primarily sailed vessels from San Francisco to the North Pacific and the Arctic. Many of the company's ships started retiring in the 1890s, and the company liquidated around 1905 due to the scarcity of whales and the low demand and price of oil. M.C. Hutton's company was named the Pacific Whaling Company of Long Beach (PWC) but usually was called the Pacific Whaling Company. It was an unregistered exhibition company, not a whaling company, and was connected to the Ocean Products Company.

Hutton had the idea that the American people would be intensely interested in viewing a whale firsthand. The story goes that he assigned the most expert men in his employ to cruise about the Catalina Islands and catch a whale. It was Hutton's idea to send the whale on a transcontinental tour of the country, as part of the company's work in educational and biological matters. It is probable that Hutton knew Loop and consulted him.

The 100-foot railcars were specially constructed in Van Wert, Ohio, and then sent to Long Beach, where a glass enclosure was constructed. The exhibited whale required 200–300 barrels of embalming fluid. Additional fluid had to be added often. This became expensive, and many of the whales were returned to the sea or burned within a couple of years. A 60-ton whale was reported just sitting on a siding after the exhibition season. Another, dubbed "Trenton's whale" in the newspapers, was left to the City of Trenton, New Jersey, with the request to cremate it on the spot. The city was concerned with the smell and did not incinerate the whale, which was left in its tank for seven years. In 1938, the city took it by the truckload to the municipal incinerator.

The PWC provided exhibition trains from 1929 until 1945. Trains were sent around the country, from the West Coast to the East Coast, visiting hundreds of cities that were equipped with railroad sidings. The company sent advance men ahead of the trains to get everything ready for the exhibition. The exhibition was billed as an educational event and was said to be provided by the educational arm of the biological division of the company. In reality, the exhibition part of the company was the entire company. The other parts of the company, the "educational" arm and "biological" arm, were developed by marketing and never actually existed.

Among the advance men were the following: C.C. Rose, billed as manager of an educational tour, self-styled "Prince of Whales"; David Tennyson, general manager of the central states division of the PWC (1931); Capt. Frank J. Lee, publicity manager, advance agent of the exhibiting tour; Capt. Harry Lee of the Catalina Whaling Co. (1932); Roy B. Jones, contracting agent; R.F. Clarke, company representative in charge of making arrangements; Frank Peters, agent; W.M. Leslie, general representative of the Seattle Whaling Co.; Carl H. Sonitz, advance engineer (1932); John B. Murphy, company representative; Thomas Lawson, or Dawson, of Los Angeles, one of the firm's representatives, brought to the company under the auspices of the marine research league and the Seattle Whaling Company; F.W. Owens, company representative; Macon E. Willis, general agent of the company (1934). Names in parenthesis represent men who may have only worked in that year; other years, men worked multiple years.

Advance agents provided prewritten articles and photographs for local newspapers. Usually, articles would state that the newspaper or mayor, in conjunction with the newspaper, was providing free tickets to kids in homeless shelters, or to the Boy Scouts and to girls' groups. In addition to the newspaper articles, tickets could be cut out of the newspaper for a free entrance or reduced fee for kids. The admission price was 10¢ in the 1930s and was increased to 25¢ in the 1940s.

The company assumed various names, including the Catalina Whaling Company (1933), the Eureka Whaling Company (1934), the Seattle Whaling Company (1935), the Mammoth Marine Hippodrome Show Train (1939), the Great Hutton Train Show (1941), the Great London Trainway Exhibition (1941), the Pan-American Train Show (1942–1943), and the Great London Trainway Exposition (1945). All of the above names were fake names for advertising and marketing. These names were used only in the years listed.

Among the captains who provided lectures were the following: Capt. Augustus E. "Oil Can Gus" Folger; Capt. C.F. Peterson (1930); Capt. Barnett, head gunner of the *Hawk*; Capt. David "Jonathan" Barnett (1935); Capt. Harry S. White (1936); Capt. Lew D. "Whalebone Lew" Nichols (1934); "Barnacle Bill" George C. Clark (1932); "Barnacle Bill" Lambert; and Capt. Mike Dolan, an ex–Major League Baseball player. Dates in parenthesis represent when these men were in use, if known. Those without parenthesis represent men who operated in multiple years.

Some of the captains had actually been whaling captains. C.F. Peterson was a well-known whaler captain; Capt. Harry Lee and Capt. Lew Nichols also were whalers. The captains would tell the story of the whalers SS *Hawk*, SS *Hercules*, or SS *Clemente* (1935), which worked with the mother ship SS *Lancing* to tow the carcass to San Pedro and, with the use of a 90-ton crane, place it on the railroad car, where the whale would be embalmed. These ships were the fleet of the California Sea Products Company, which whaled in southern California. The exhibited whales were purchased by the PWC from the whaling company. The SS *Clemente* was rented from another whaling company and was only used in 1935.

Some of the postcards had information stamped on the back about the whale in the exhibit, not the whale on the front of the card. There were only two cards done like this. The first read, "Female Sea Whale, length 55 ft. Weight, 65 tons. Killed by Capt White, December 18, 1929, near San Clements Islands. This whale feeds on anchovies, sardines and shrimps. #00 gallons of embalming fluid used to embalm. Exhibited by Pacific Whaling Co., Inc., Long Beach. Calif." The second card read, "Finback Whale captured July 16th, 1930, off San Clemente Island 70 miles South of Long Beach, California. Weight 72 tons, Length 65 feet. Tail spread 15 feet, Heart weight 750 lbs., Throat measurement 3½ inches in diameter." Information about other whales was sometimes written on the back of the cards by visitors. One of these cards listed September 6, 1929—the earliest for an exhibited date.

The company also sold a 15-page program. The first issue included eight pages of information and was titled "The Story of the Whale." The second issue, "Thar She Blows, & The Story of the Whale," had pictures of the speakers. The third issue was almost identical to the second one except that the pictures of the speakers were taken out and replaced by a picture of a whale.

Business was heaviest from 1930 to 1932, with multiple train cars traveling around from siding to siding. After about 1932, there may have only been one whale traveling around.

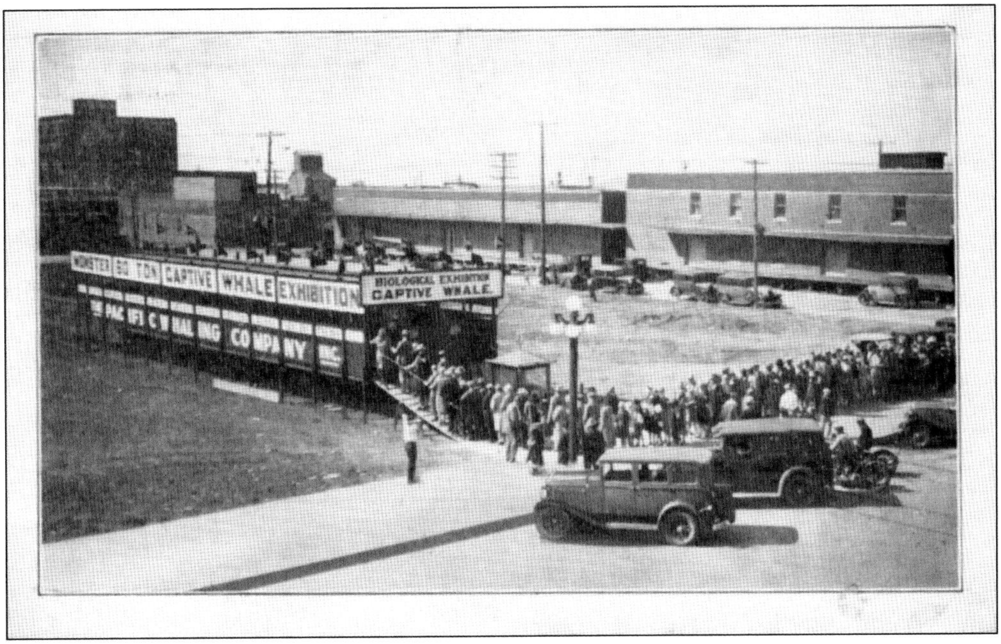

Between 1929 and 1945, the Pacific Whaling Company sent train cars around the country with embalmed whales for exhibition. Shown here are two postcards of the same exhibition.

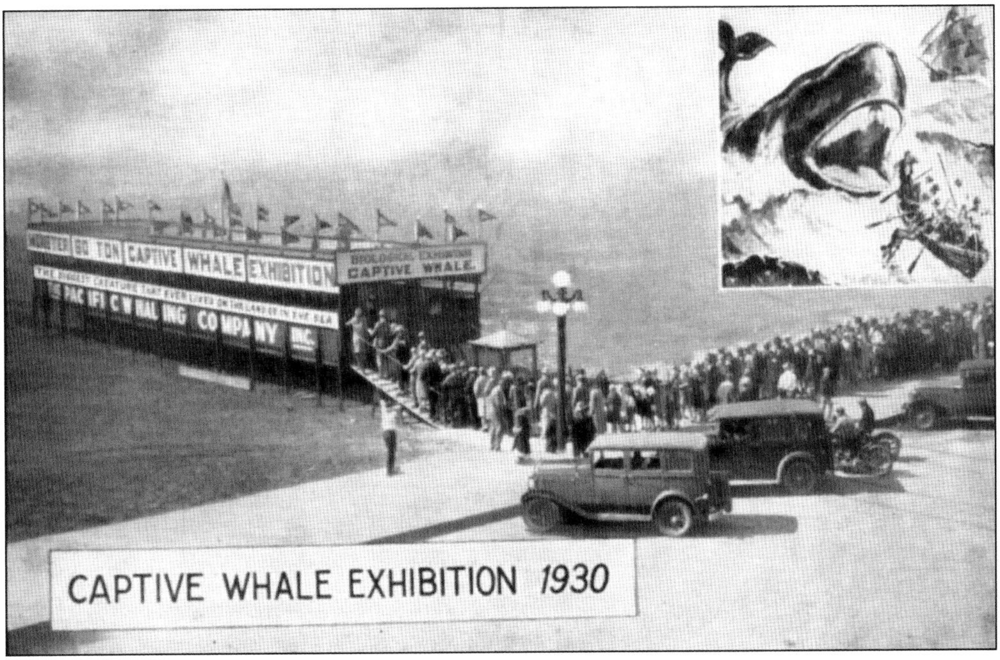

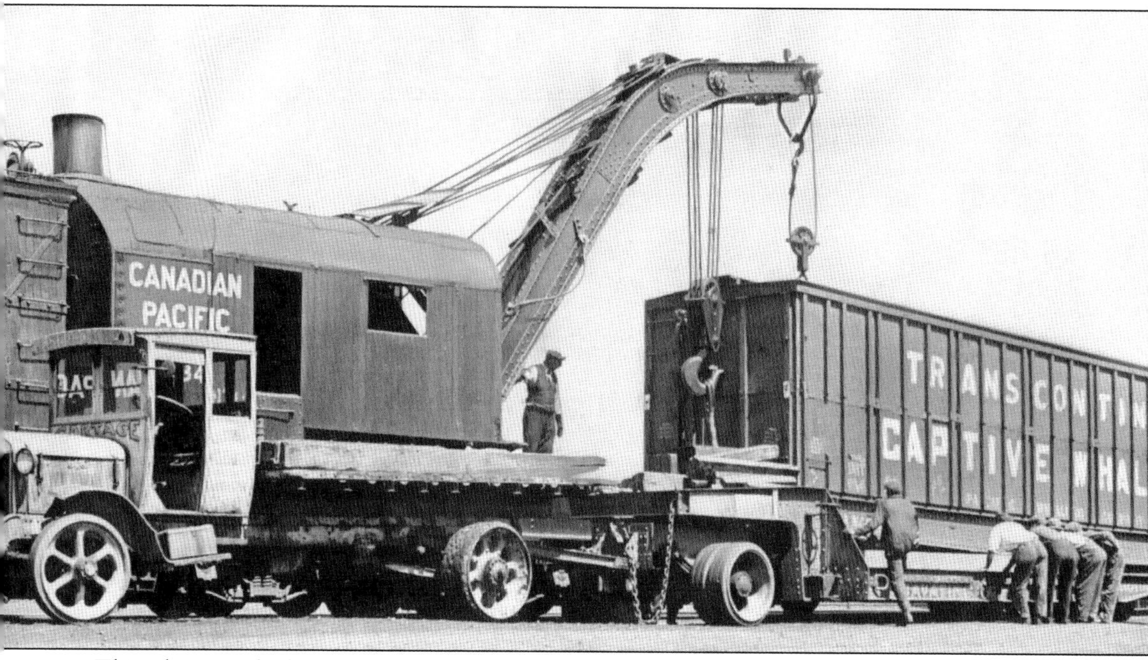

This photograph shows an exhibition tank being loaded to or from a truck trailer in Canada. Whales were known to have been purchased from the California Whaling Company in San Pedro. It is also possible that whales were purchased from a company operating out of Vancouver Island, Canada.

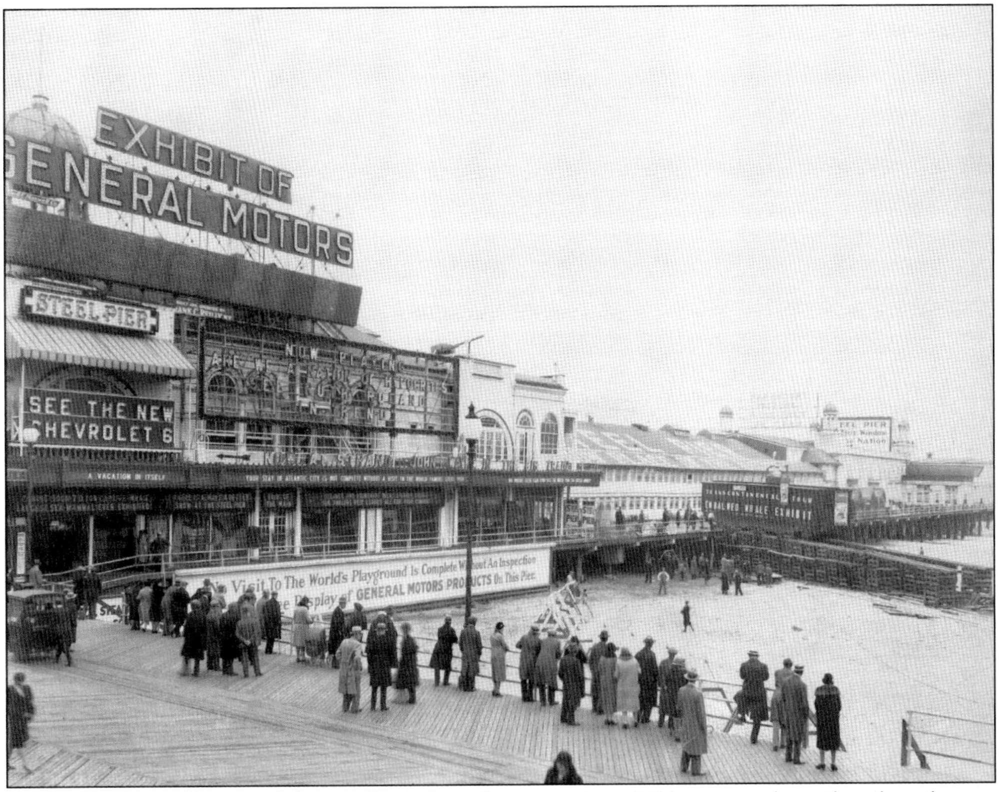

This is the Heinz Pier in Atlantic City. At right is a train exhibit car on the railroad track.

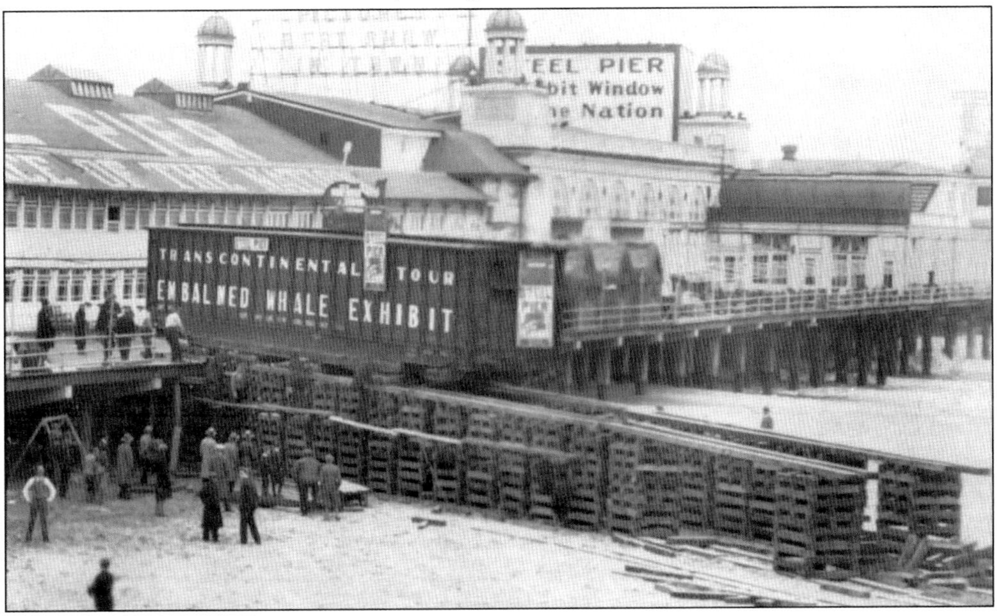

This is an enlargement of the above photograph, showing the whale exhibit train car on the Heinz Pier in Atlantic City. Exhibit trains would usually be set up on a siding in medium and large towns. Most of the exhibitions were in cities in the middle of the country, where few people would have seen a whale.

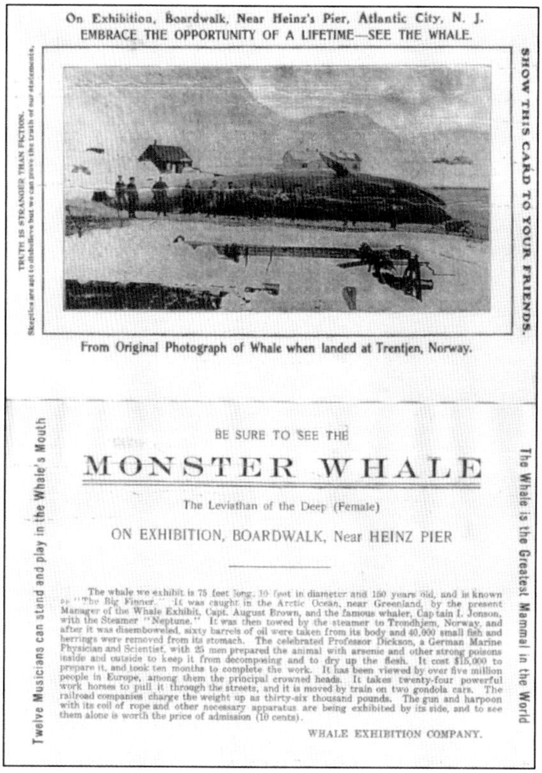
On Exhibition, Boardwalk, Near Heinz's Pier, Atlantic City, N. J.
EMBRACE THE OPPORTUNITY OF A LIFETIME—SEE THE WHALE.

TRUTH IS STRANGER THAN FICTION.
Skeptics are apt to disbelieve but we can prove the truth of our statements.

SHOW THIS CARD TO YOUR FRIENDS.

From Original Photograph of Whale when landed at Trentjen, Norway.

Twelve Musicians can stand and play in the Whale's Mouth

BE SURE TO SEE THE

MONSTER WHALE

The Leviathan of the Deep (Female)

ON EXHIBITION, BOARDWALK, Near HEINZ PIER

The whale we exhibit is 75 feet long, 10 feet in diameter and 150 years old, and is known as "The Big Finner." It was caught in the Arctic Ocean, near Greenland, by the present Manager of the Whale Exhibit, Capt. August Brown, and the famous whaler, Cap tain I. Jonson, with the Steamer "Neptune." It was then towed by the steamer to Trondhjem, Norway, and after it was disemboweled, sixty barrels of oil were taken from its body and 40,000 small fish and herrings were removed from its stomach. The celebrated Professor Dickson, a German Marine Physician and Scientist, with 25 men prepared the animal with arsenic and other strong poisons inside and outside to keep it from decomposing and to dry up the flesh. It cost $15,000 to prepare it, and took ten months to complete the work. It has been viewed by over five million people in Europe, among them the principal crowned heads. It takes twenty-four powerful work horses to pull it through the streets, and it is moved by train on two gondola cars. The railroad companies charge the weight up as thirty-six thousand pounds. The gun and harpoon with its coil of rope and other necessary apparatus are being exhibited by its side, and to see them alone is worth the price of admission (10 cents).

WHALE EXHIBITION COMPANY.

The Whale is the Greatest Mammal in the World

Shown here are both sides of an advertising card for the Atlantic City exhibit on the Heinz Pier, seen in the previous photographs.

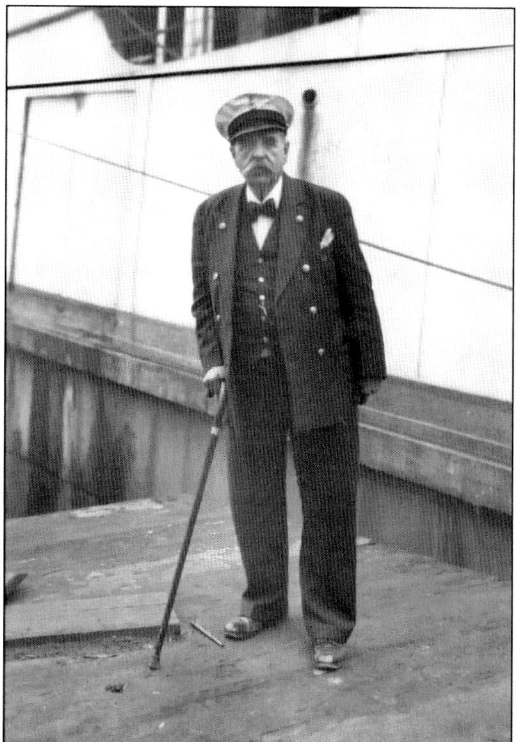

Shown here is the first captain of the exhibition, Gus "Oil Can Gus" Folger. He was also the emcee and main lecturer of the Pacific Whaling Company. Folger was perfect for the exhibition, as he had been traveling the country for 15–20 years before the PWC exhibits, lecturing in the same role. The lecturers and other men of the whaling company were said to be actual whalers, and, while some of them were, others were not.

THE PACIFIC WHALING COMPANY

OF LONG BEACH, CALIFORNIA, U. S. A.

Presents

"Colossus" the Captive Whale

AN EDUCATIONAL MARINE EXHIBITION

Under Command

CAPTAIN GEORGE CLARKE—Whale Hunter

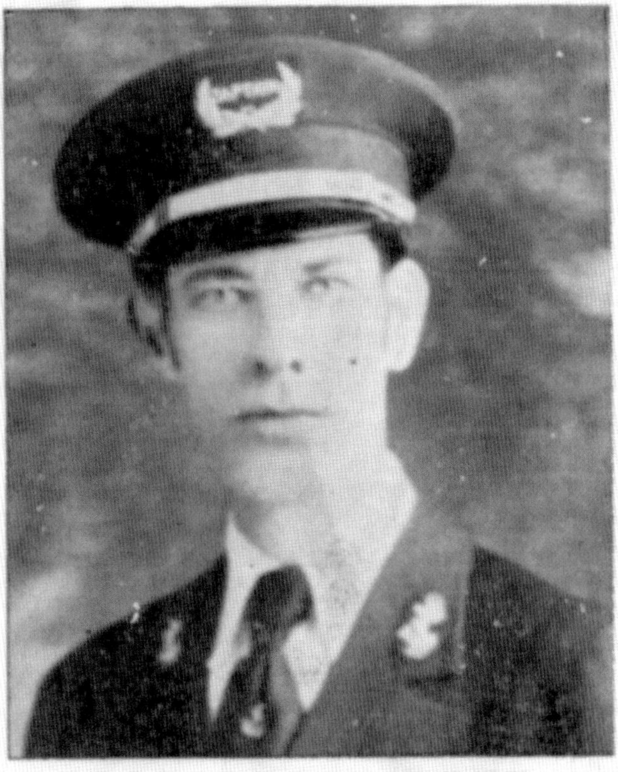

CAPTAIN GEORGE CLARKE, COMMANDER

Touring on a 100-Foot Specially Constructed Railroad Car

THE GREATEST BIOLOGICAL STUDY OF ALL TIME

This is a page from one of the show booklets. On the second page of the booklets, a photograph of the captain lecturer was provided. In this case, it is George Clarke. The official story was that these captains actually went whaling and shot the harpoon that killed the whales being exhibited. The whaleboats named by the company, the *Hercules* and *Hawk*, were actual boats from the California Whaling Company that whaled between Long Beach and Catalina, California.

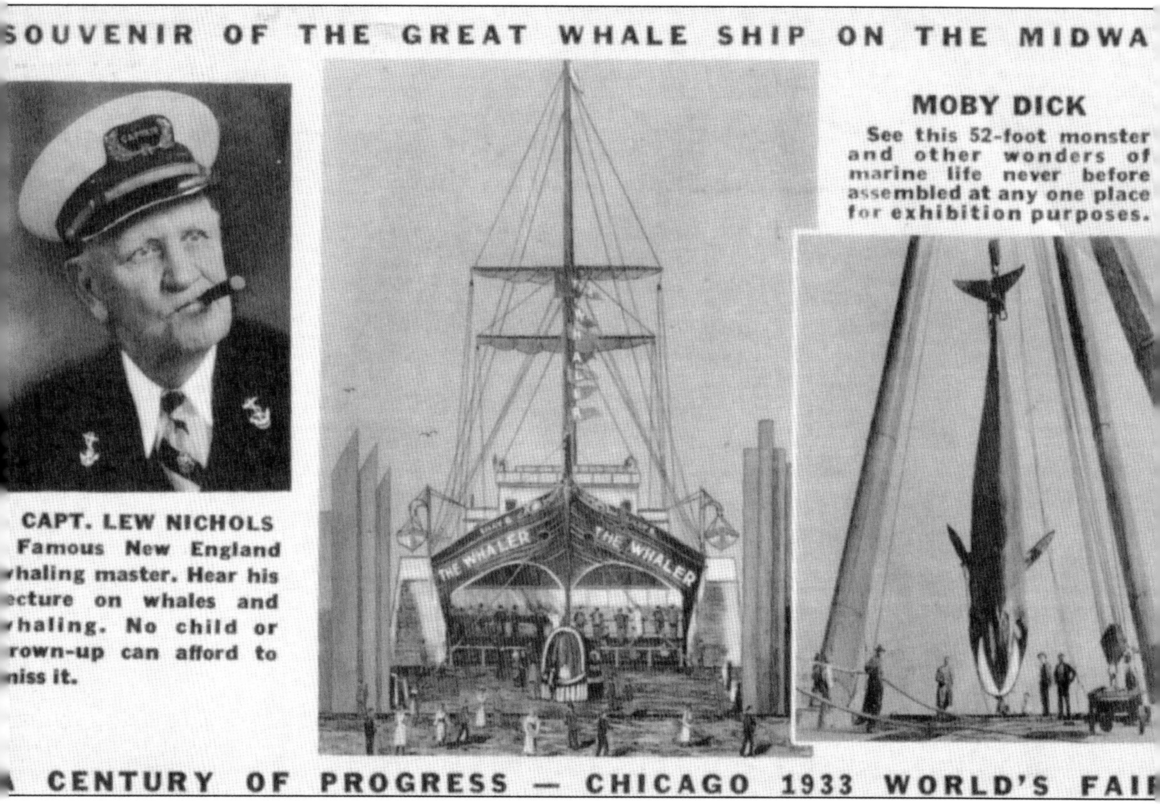

Capt. Lew Nichols, seen on this postcard, apparently did not appear in programs with his photograph inside. There were basically two programs. The first program was eight pages long and featured the first lecturer, Ben McCourt, who had the title of curator. The second program was 15 pages long and was used for most of the years of the PWC exhibits. Only the first or second page was changed, as in the Capt. Clark page seen on page 63. Records of where the PWC exhibited are found in the archives of daily newspapers all over the country. A newspaper has yet to be found with a reference to McCourt.

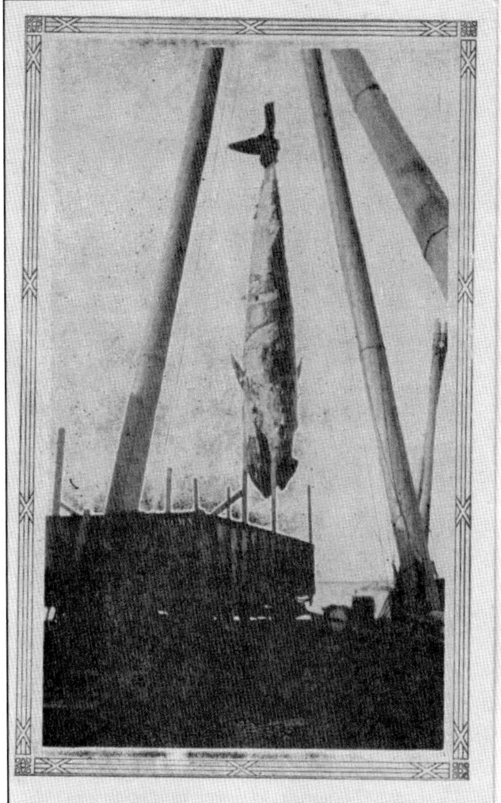

SOUVENIR CARD

First Continental Tour of a
60-TON CALIFORNIA
GRAY WHALE

City...................... Date............

Of the 27 species of WHALES, this is the smallest. This one is a male, shot 70 miles off San Clemente Island, on July 1, 1929, at 4 P. M., after an all-day chase, using regulation Whale boat, made in Norway, manned by professional killers.

Battled 17 hours after being harpooned. Harpoon weighs 150 pounds with bomb on end. Towed in from sea and lifted by a 90-ton capacity electric crane at the Los Angeles Shipbuilding Yards, where he was placed on the Special Steel Railroad Car.

Took 10 Morticians 14 days and nights to embalm him with over 5600 gallons of special fluid. His tongue weighed 1500 pounds, his heart 225 pounds, total weight 120,000 pounds; no teeth, throat size of man's fist, feeds on Sardines, Squibs, Anchovies, catches from 1 to 1½ tons at a time, eyes and ears very small but capable of hearing and seeing a distance of one-fourth mile.

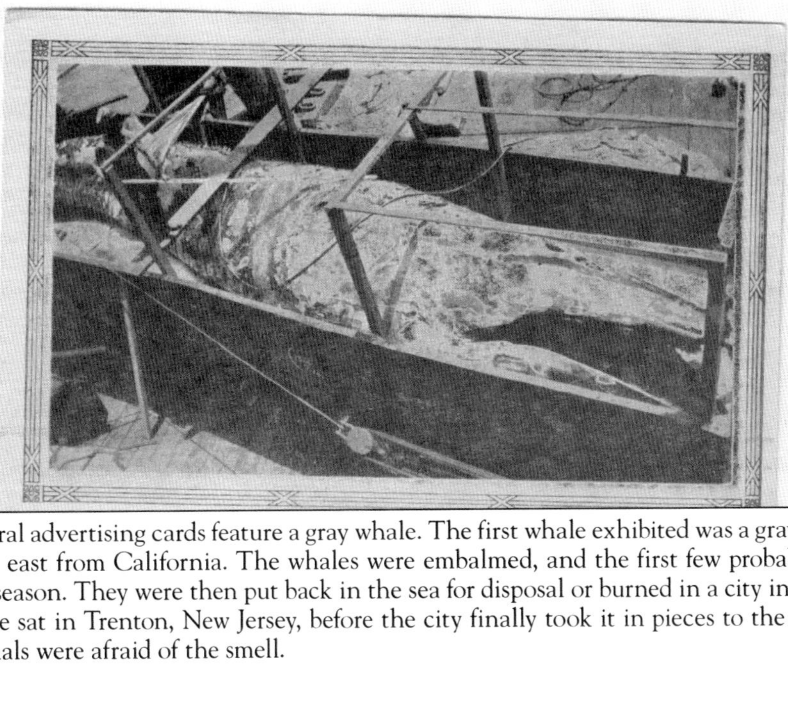

Several advertising cards feature a gray whale. The first whale exhibited was a gray whale, which went east from California. The whales were embalmed, and the first few probably lasted only one season. They were then put back in the sea for disposal or burned in a city incinerator. One whale sat in Trenton, New Jersey, before the city finally took it in pieces to the incinerator, as officials were afraid of the smell.

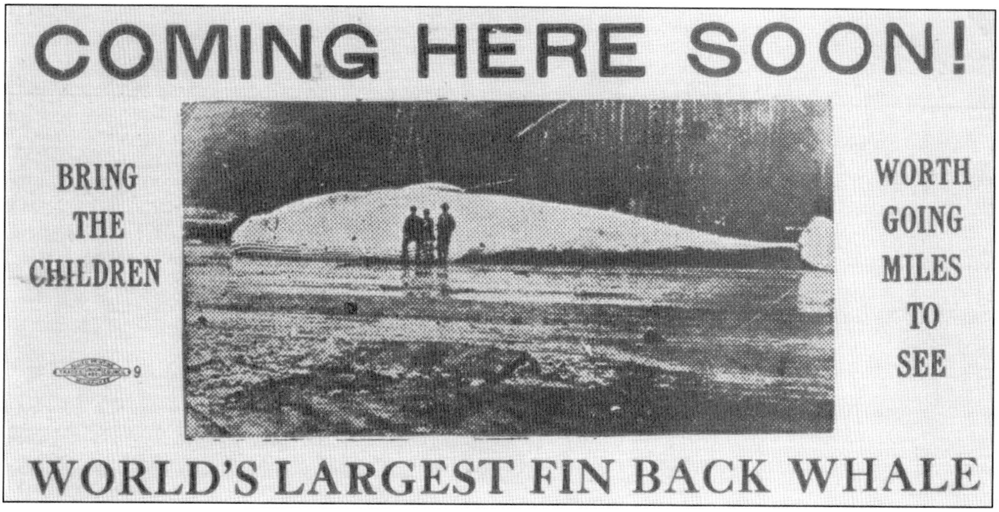

At top is an advertising card, and below it is a ticket from an exhibit. As evident by some of the photographs in this book, the exhibits were heavily attended. In addition to the whale, there were other related exhibits, with a whaler lecturer at each one to explain the items being shown. After five years, the show was revamped to add other features to draw the public, ranging from a flea circus, to the world's largest and smallest cows, and other circus-type displays.

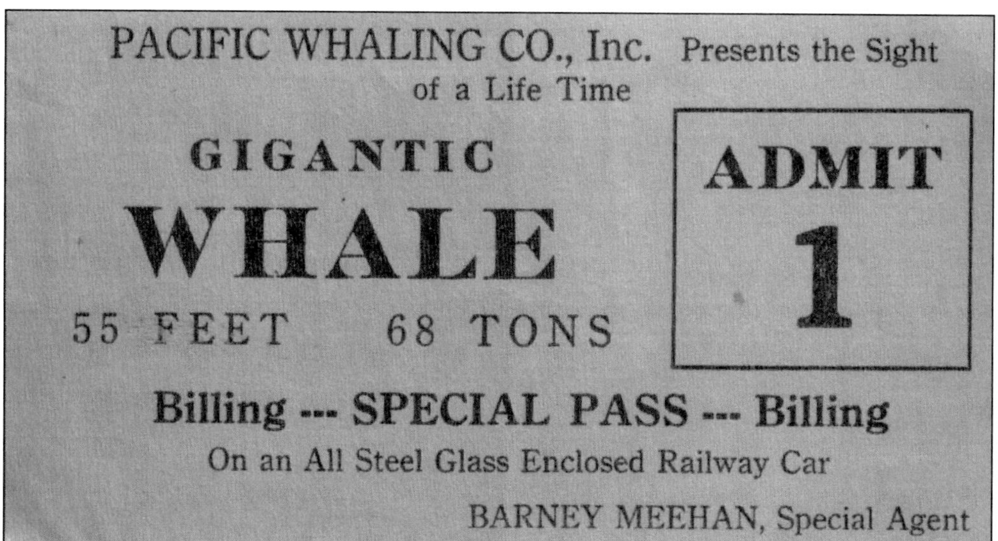
PACIFIC WHALING CO., Inc. Presents the Sight of a Life Time

GIGANTIC WHALE

55 FEET 68 TONS

ADMIT 1

Billing --- SPECIAL PASS --- Billing

On an All Steel Glass Enclosed Railway Car

BARNEY MEEHAN, Special Agent

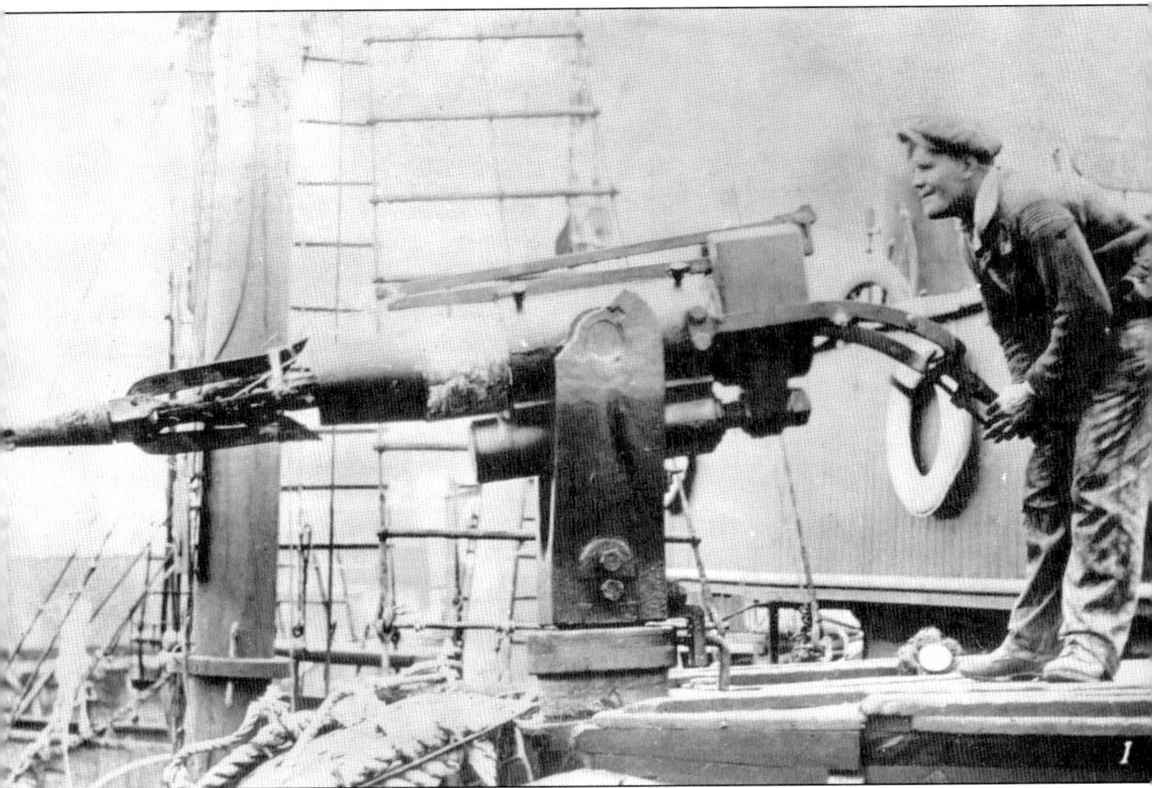

The company also sold a set of six postcards, numbered one through six. The cards were also available individually, without numbering. Handwriting on this, the first card, indicates that this is Mad Harry Andersen of the Consolidated Whaling Company, Victoria, Canada. The information, correct or not, must have come from a lecturer.

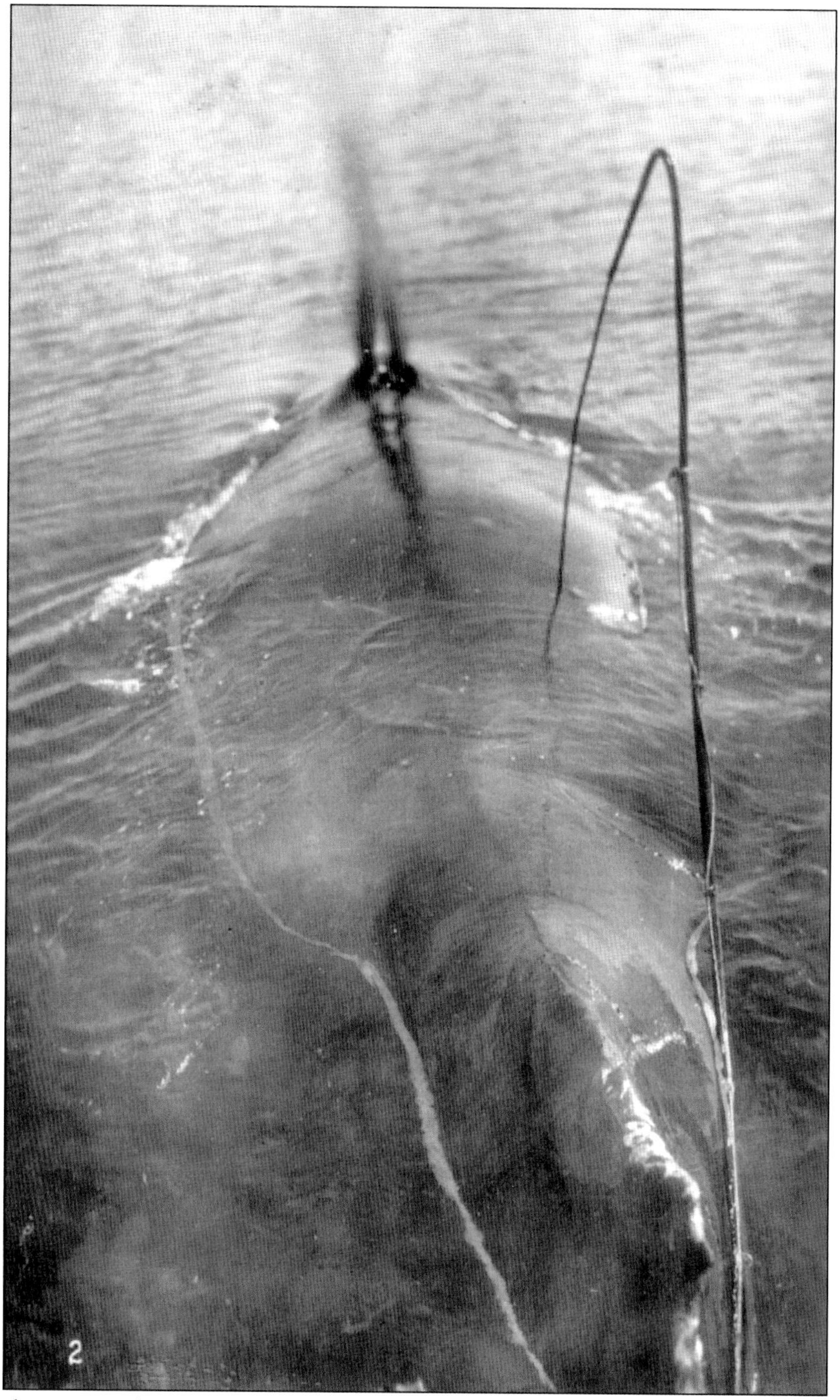

Shown here on card no. 2 is a large whale, probably a fin whale. A harpoon is visible on the right side of the whale, and the animal is spouting blood instead of water. This indicates that the whale has been mortally wounded. At this time, the boats back off, as the whale is very dangerous to be around.

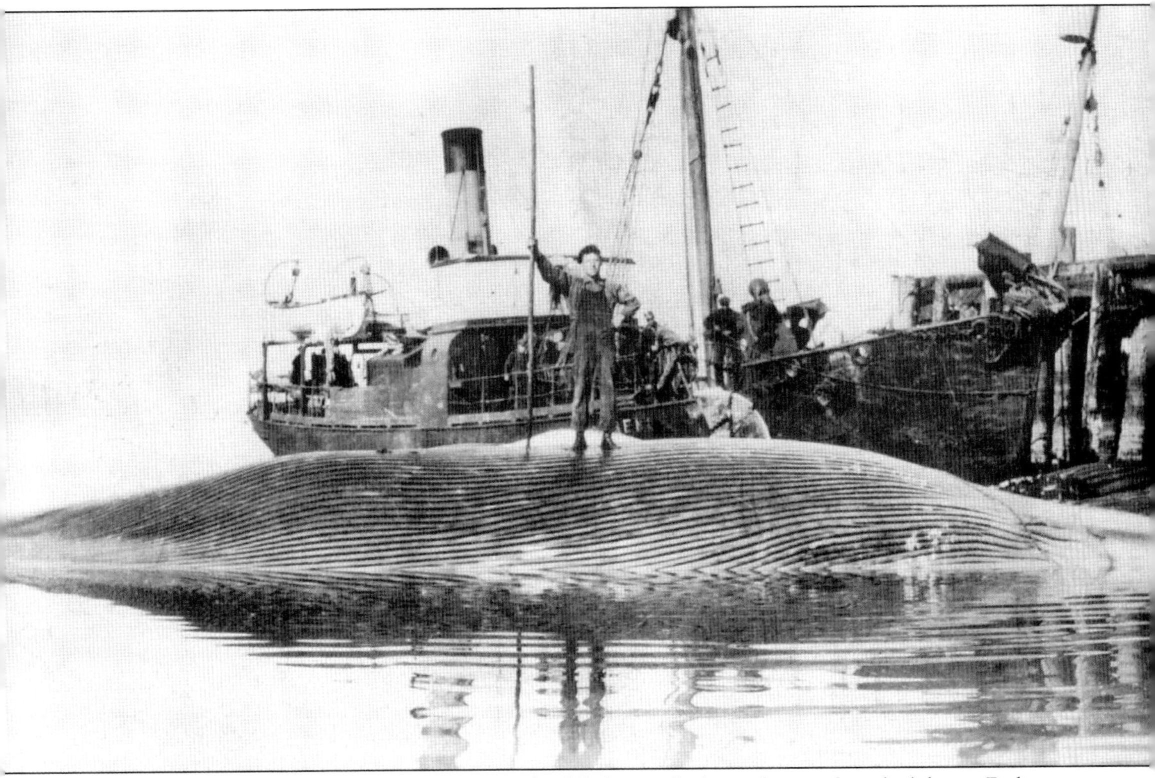

Card no. 3 depicts a worker standing on a dead baleen whale in front of a whaleboat. Robert Webb helped the author, around 1986, to identify this boat as an Akers-built whaler named the *St. Lawrence*, belonging to a Canadian whaling company. Akers is short for Akers Mekaniske Verksted, in Akers, Norway.

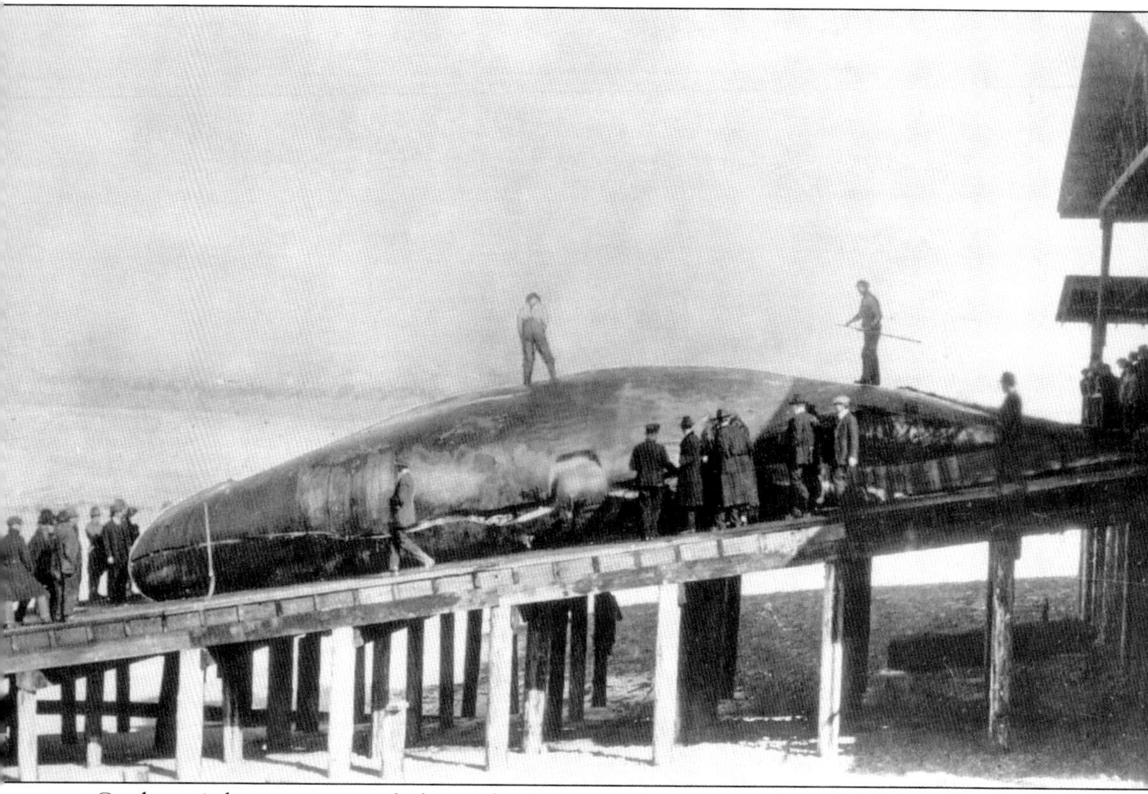

Card no. 4 shows a sperm whale on the Moss Landing Ramp of the California Sea Products Company. The photograph was taken at 10:00 a.m. on January 22, 1919. The head flenser would have the position on top of the whale to begin the first cuts. The public was allowed to walk around the whale, but soon they would have to be moved back so the whale could be cut up.

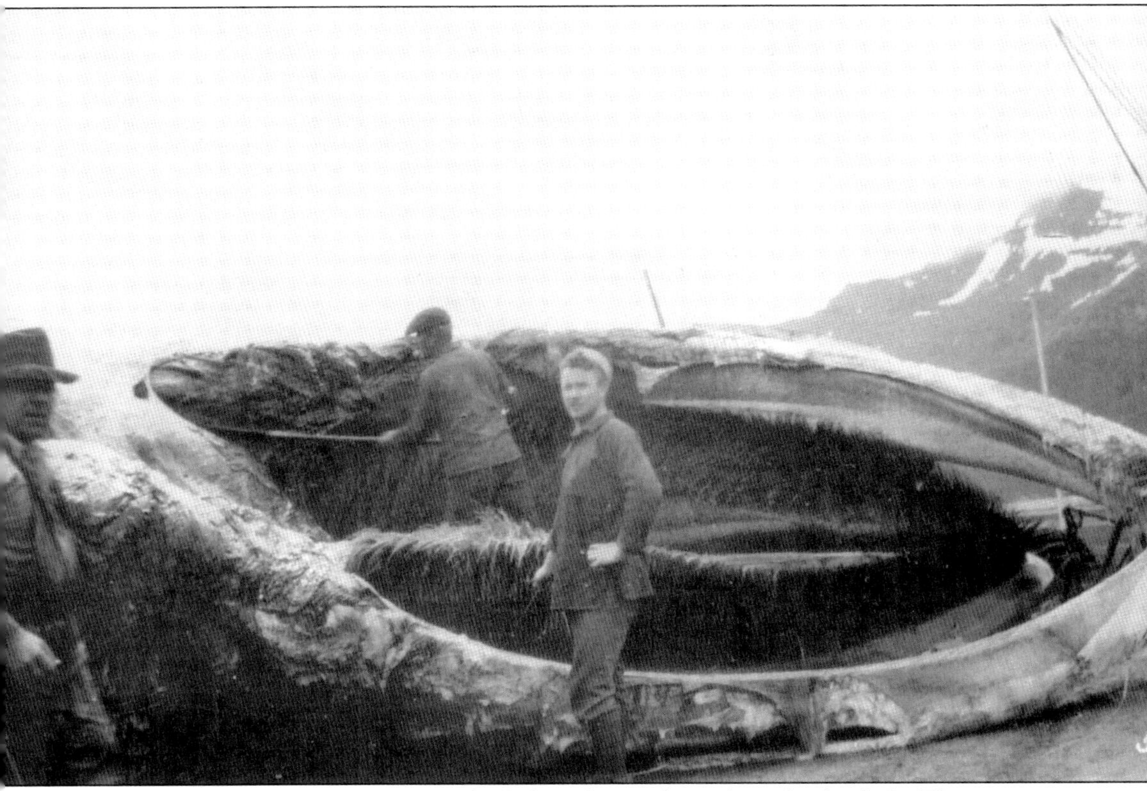

Card No. 5 shows workers removing the baleen from a fin or humpback whale. The snow on barren mountains in the distance indicates that the station here is in Akutan, Alaska. All of the stations mentioned were operating at roughly the same time as the exhibitions, in the late 1920s and early 1930s. Thus, these photographs could be used in exhibitions.

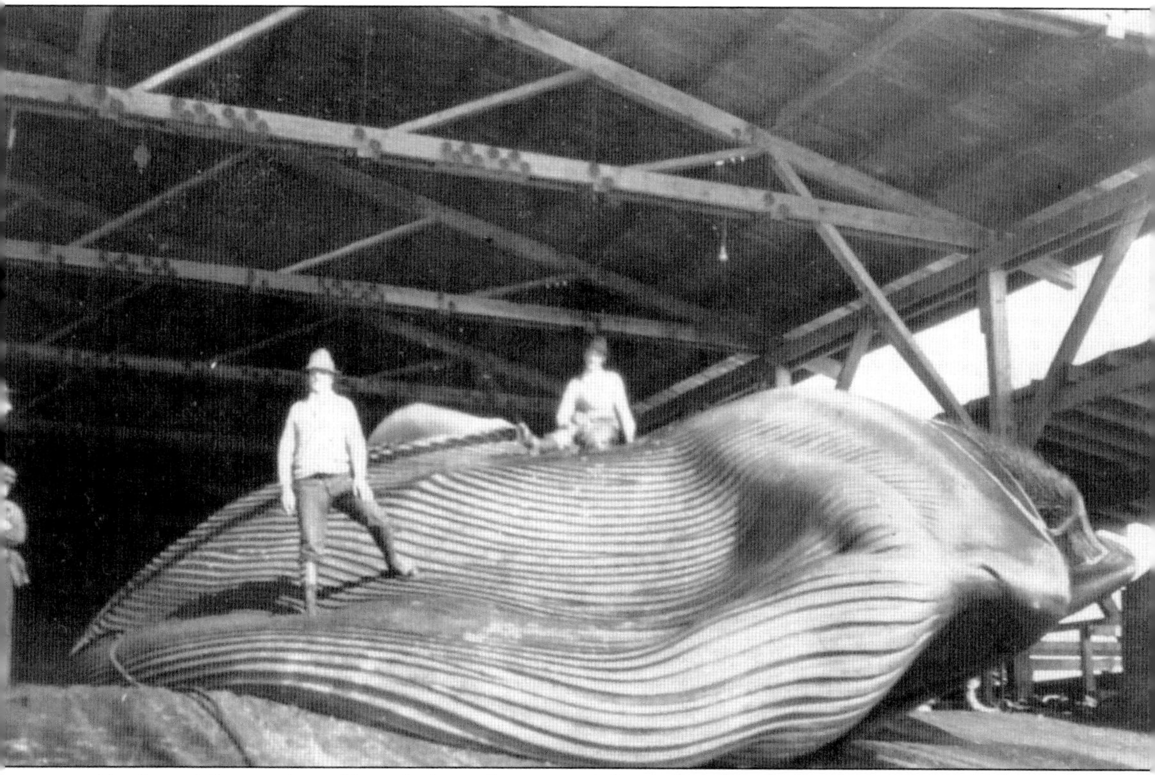

Card no. 6 shows a large blue whale sticking out of the end of the whaling station at Moss Landing. An original photograph was recently found that identified the photographer as L.S. Slevin of Carmel, California. The photograph is part of his collection. It was then in an album of whaling photographs in the collection of E. Lee Dorsett, and it had a sticker to indicate it ended up in the collection of whaling material belonging to Barbara Johnson. It is now in the collection of the author. The lower part of the original is cut off. It reads "Moss Ldg Cal 1919, Slevin catalog number 3030." On the back is Slevin's stamp.

Local female dance troupes were used from time to time in the newspapers to promote the exhibitions. Here, two women stand in the mouth and on top of this baleen whale. Other newspaper photographs show six or seven women, arm in arm with one leg in the air.

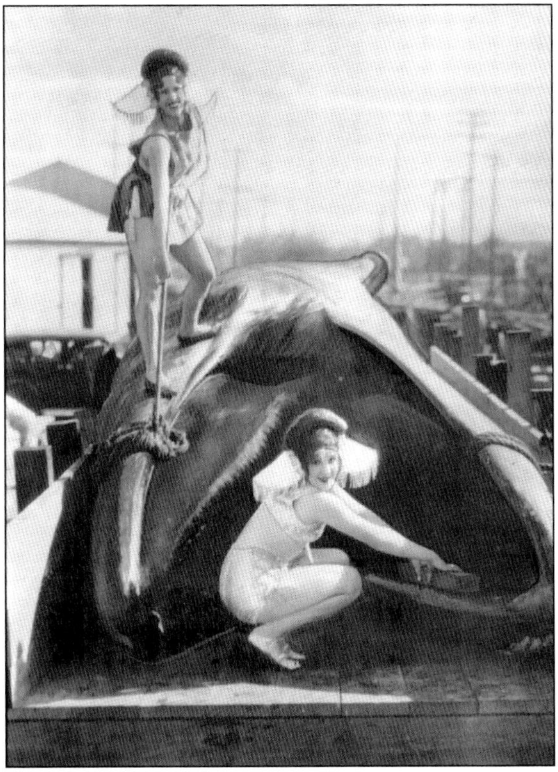

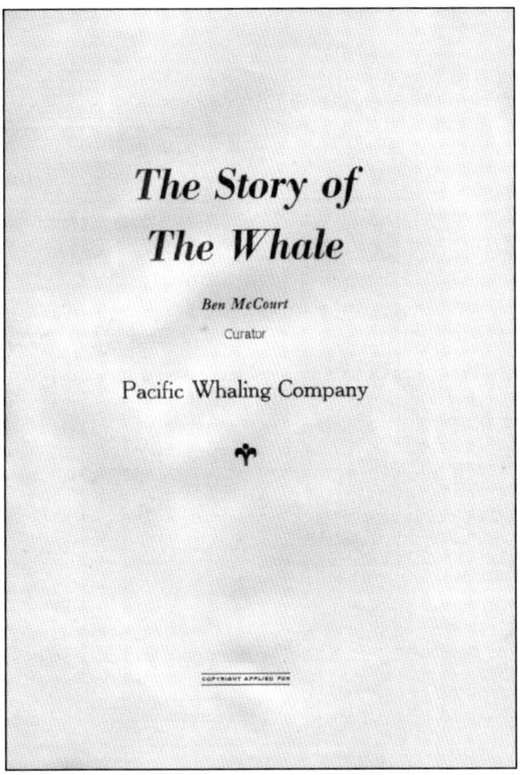

The Story of The Whale

Ben McCourt

Curator

Pacific Whaling Company

COPYRIGHT APPLIED FOR

This is the first page of the 15-page booklet. There is no indication of who the lead lecturer was. The booklets discuss whales, their different types, and explain that the animals are warm-blooded mammals. The booklets also detail the whaling industry and the products that are made from the whale.

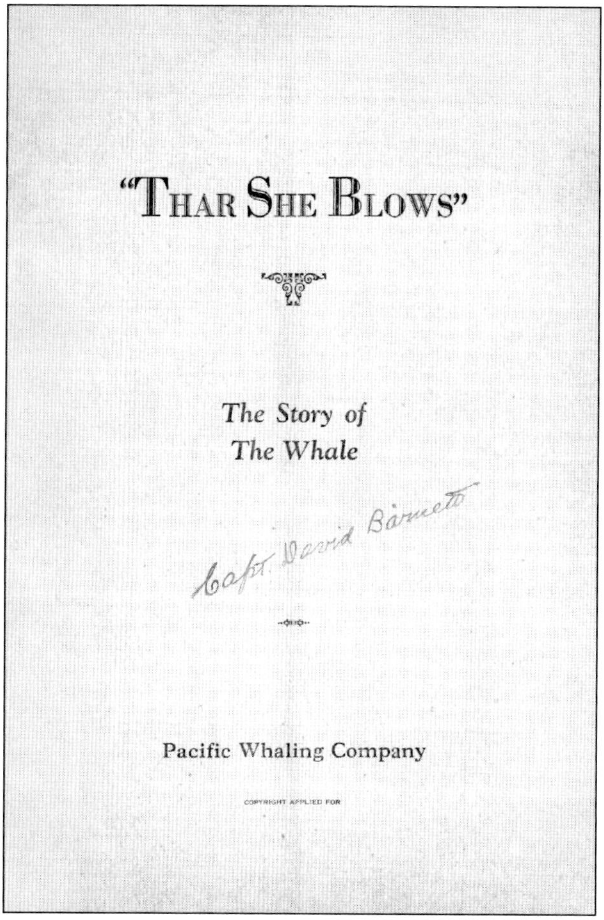

"THAR SHE BLOWS"

The Story of
The Whale

Capt. David Barnett

Pacific Whaling Company

COPYRIGHT APPLIED FOR

This booklet has been stamped on the inside with the name of Capt. David Barnett. He was one of the main lecturers, but there is apparently no booklet with his picture in it.

This photograph is from an antique black-and-white postcard of Hammerfest, Finnmark, Norway. Here, people stand next to a blue whale. This postcard was published by Anth. Kallands Forlag, Hammerfest, about 1899. The PWC used this card in some of its 15-page booklets.

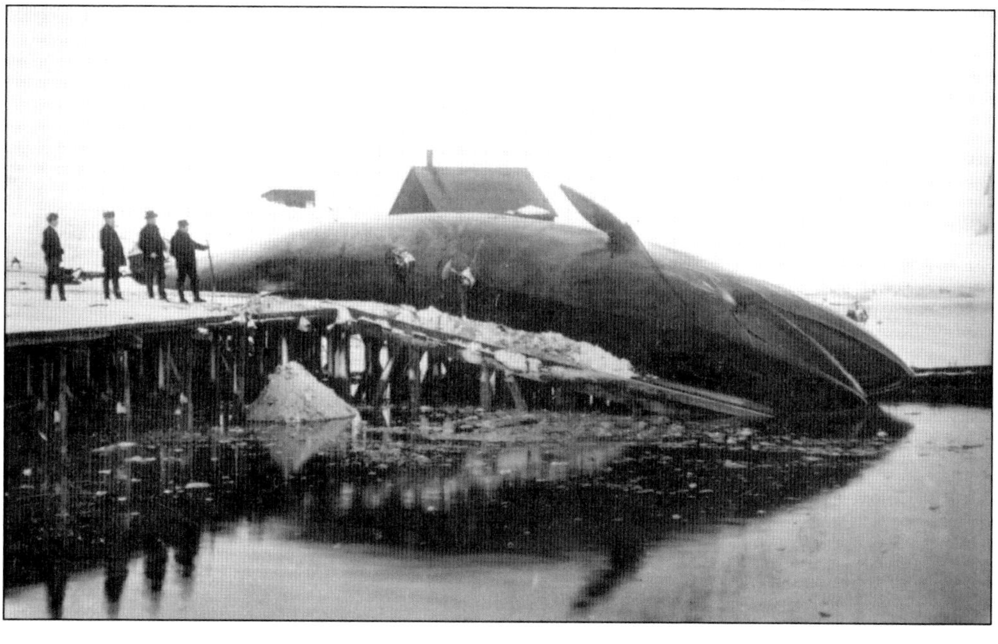

Five

California Whaling in the 1920s and 1930s

Captain F.K. Dedrick was born Frederick Kristian Dietrichson on September 6, 1867, or 1868, in Stodoen, near Bergen, Norway. While the timing of his exact arrival in California is not known, he is placed on the West Coast in 1885 as a mate on coasting schooners. He served on various vessels for the next several years. He was naturalized in San Francisco Superior Court on September 7, 1892, the day after his 25th birthday. He received his captain's license No. 55 by the Steamboat Inspection Service in Seattle on August 11, 1899. He married Lena Hemberger of San Francisco in 1898. Their son Frederick David Dedrick was born in San Francisco on May 28, 1900.

Captain Dedrick was master of the schooners *Gotama*, *Defender*, and *Jame Rolph* under the employ of Hind & Rolph Company, San Francisco. James Rolph, later mayor of San Francisco and governor of California, knew and admired Captain Dedrick, who went north in the *Gotama* with the Salmon Fleet.

He retired from sea service in 1908 and ventured into his own business, which either dissolved or was sold in 1911. The next business he developed was incorporated as the West Coast Whaling Company, and he secured a franchise from the town of Trinidad, Humboldt County. Under the terms of the contract, work on the plant had to start within 90 days. The California Sea Products Company did not incorporate until 1914 and did not start construction until after the war in 1919 (Moss Landing) and 1920 (Trinidad). The Moss Landing plant was 350 feet by 105 feet, with an inclined ramp to the water's edge.

The first catch, a sperm whale, was taken at 10:00 a.m. on January 22, 1919, from the Moss Landing station. The tugs *Traveler* and *Hercules* were the first vessels used by the company. After many delays, the harpoon guns arrived in San Francisco, and the *Hercules* left on January 21st for Moss Landing. The next morning, in sight of shore, a 60-foot sperm whale was taken.

The whaling vessels *Hawk* and *Port Saunders* were purchased in Newfoundland. Built at the Akers Mekanisk Verksted plant in Norway, the two vessels were purchased in May and paid for, but they were not delivered. So, in September 1919, the company brought suit in US District Court against the Newfoundland Shipbuilding Company for $133,390 or consummation of the sale of the two steam ships. The company was further delayed in using the two Norwegian whalers while the registry was transferred from British to American registry.

Captain Dedrick used the same equipment and methods that had been employed in British Columbia and Alaska stations in the years prior to the California Sea Products Company. Sven Foyn developed the modern whaling steel catcher boat, harpoon cannon, and whaling shore stations.

From Moss Landing in Monterey County, the whalers worked the coastline and the sea in a 50-mile radius. The locations mentioned in the catch records were off Monterey Bay, Pigeon Point, Santa Cruz, the Cement Works (Davenport), Half Moon Bay, and the Farrallon Islands. The majority of the catch was made up of humpback and finback whales, with some other species also being taken (sperm, sei, bottlenose, and California gray and blue whales). The combined Moss Landing and Trinidad operations took approximately 200 whales per year.

The company operated four whalers from the two stations until 1925, when the catches were diminishing and the decision was made to begin using a floating factory ship. The stations produced whale oil, sperm oil, fertilizer, and bone meal. The Moss Landing station operated until 1926, and the Trinidad station ceased operations in 1925.

In 1926, the company acquired the Union Oil tanker *Lansing* and the monitor *Monterey*. These were retrofitted for ship-based whaling operations. The *Lansing* was retrofitted for whaling in Alameda as a floating reduction plant, similar to the Norwegian whaling mother ships, while the *Monterey* would be used for storage. It was desired to send the fleet north in 1926, but unavoidable delays prevented this from happening. Instead, the company decided to operate the fleet off of South Bay, San Clemente Island. This marked the first time in 50 years that commercial whaling had been conducted off San Pedro Harbor. Capt. F.K. Dedrick was in charge of the *Lansing*. The fleet was expected to relocate to the Lower California (Mexico) district as the season progressed.

The fleet of the *Lansing* and four catcher boats left San Francisco Bay in the summer of 1927, headed for Alaskan waters, when an accident took place between the *Port Saunders* and the lighthouse tender *Madrone*. It seems the *Madrone* cut the line of whaling ships steaming past and ran directly into the side of the *Port Saunders*, which settled to the bottom, having had its side stove in. The *Port Saunders* was raised and taken to the Bethlehem Shipbuilding yards and repaired for the 1928 season.

The rest of the fleet continued to Alitak Bay on Kodiak Island, returning to San Francisco at the end of the season. The catch in Alaska started out good, averaging three whales per day, but it ended up being a rather disappointing season, averaging one per day. Gales off of Alitak, Alaska, in September caused the fleet to move to Kamechak Bay. This was the one and only time the fleet would go to Alaska. The fleet returned to San Clemente for the start of the winter season. A total of 1,237 whales were taken in the season. The California Sea Products fleet was not the only fleet in Mexican waters in 1927. The Mexico Whaling Corporation of Norway operated a floater in the Gulf of California and took 390 whales, netting 12,000 barrels of oil up to March 15. A third fleet, of the Los Angeles Whaling Company, was making preparations to go whaling in Lower California. The *Port Saunders* resumed operations with the fleet in the fall of 1928.

Company officers in 1928 were the following: chairman of the board Robert Oxnard; president and manager F.K. Dedrick; vice presidents E.J. Pringle and Kirkham Wright; treasurer Kirkham Wright; secretary R.G. Fontaine; assistant secretaries E.J. Pringle and Ralph H. Handy; assistant manager R.G. Fontaine; E.J. Pringle, counsel; acting treasurer R.G. Fontaine; and assistant secretary C.S. Curtis.

The Los Angeles Whaling Company was to buy the *Washtenaw* from the California Petroleum Corporation in June, with the intention to convert it into a factory tanker. With her two killers, the fleet was expected to leave Los Angeles Harbor for the 1928 season. In January 1928, however, it was reported that the company was looking for a replacement for the *Washtenaw*, which sank before it could be put in service. The vessel sank in San Pedro in September 1927 and was forfeited by the Los Angeles Fisheries Company, whose officers were looking for a factory ship to work with its two killers and to resume operations.

The California Sea Products fleet returned to Catalina for the start of the 1928 season, while the Mexico Whaling Company, which was outfitted in San Pedro, went to Magdalena Bay on the southwest coast of Baja California. The Mexico Whaling Company's fleet was called home to Norway before the start of the fall whaling operations. It was expected not to return to the waters off Lower California. Its factory ship, *Esperanza*, and three killers sailed early in June, leaving only the killer *Columbus* at Long Beach, to be sold or disposed of.

At the end of the decade, the California Sea Products fleet was alone in Southern California waters, the Norwegian Mexico Whaling fleet having been called home, and the Los Angeles Whaling Company tied up without a factory ship.

Here, a baleen whale is being drawn up the slipway in the rear of the *Sven Foyn*. Capt. Sven Foyn invented the rear slip factory ship, steel whale catchers, and the harpoon cannon used to catch whales in the 1890s and after.

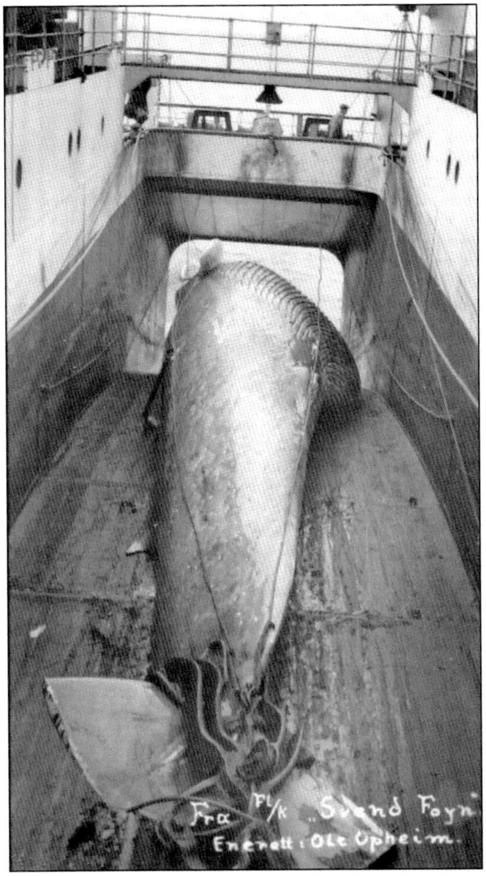

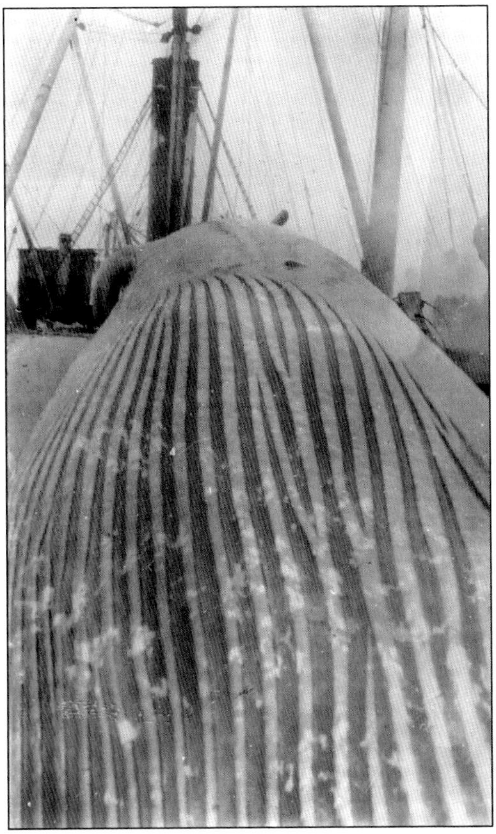

This is a closer view of the throat grooves in a baleen whale being pulled onto the *Sven Foyn*. When eating, the baleen whales take in large amounts of water, and the folds extend greatly to hold the water. The whale then expels the water through the baleen filter and is left with the krill or fish that it is eating.

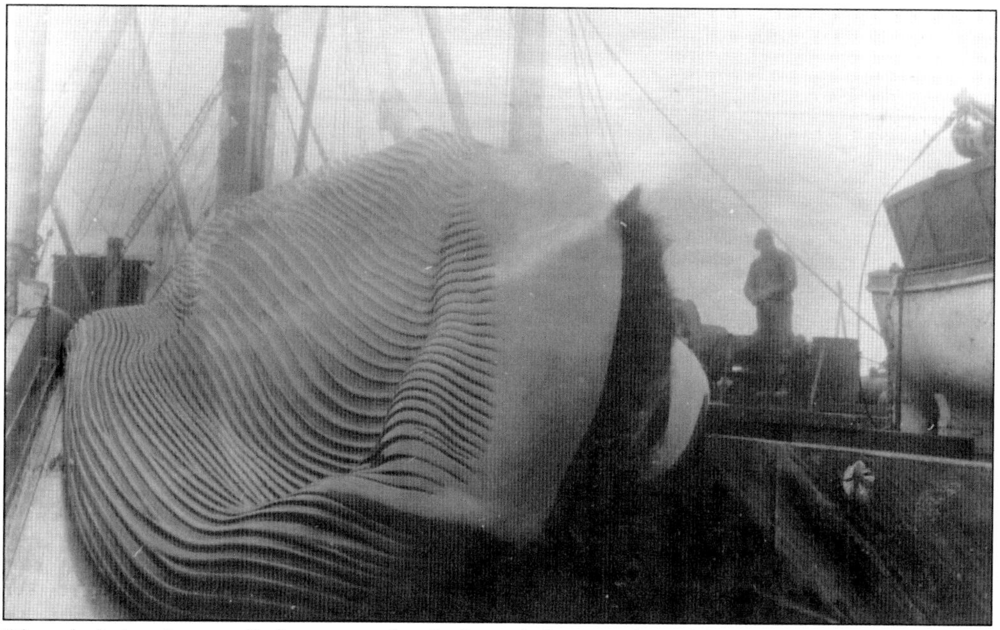

The whale has been pulled up onto the deck, and the mouth and lower jaw can be seen. The throat grooves are clearly seen here.

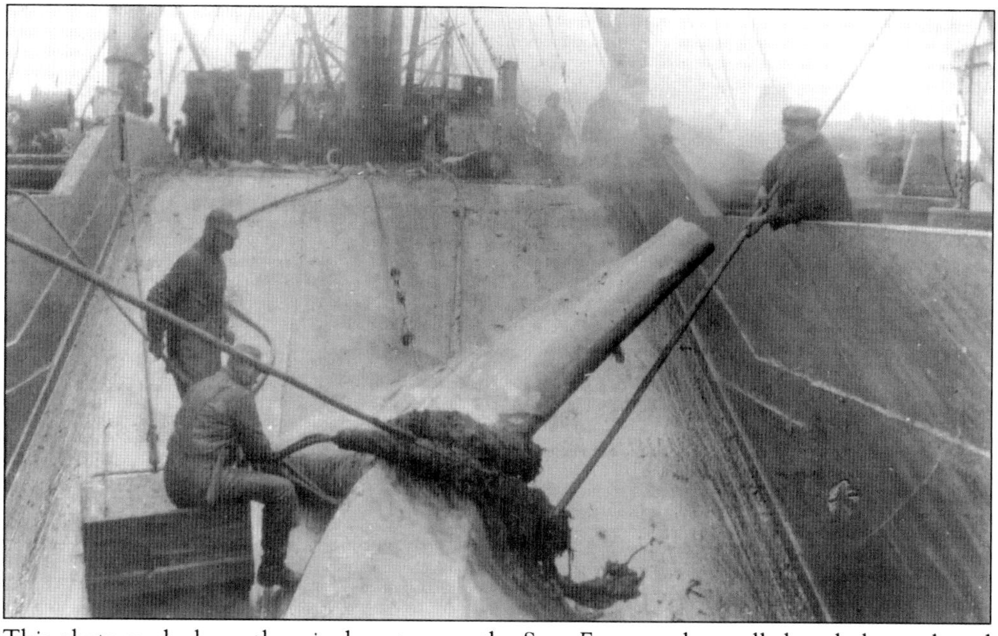

This photograph shows the winch system on the *Sven Foyn*, used to pull the whales on board for flensing.

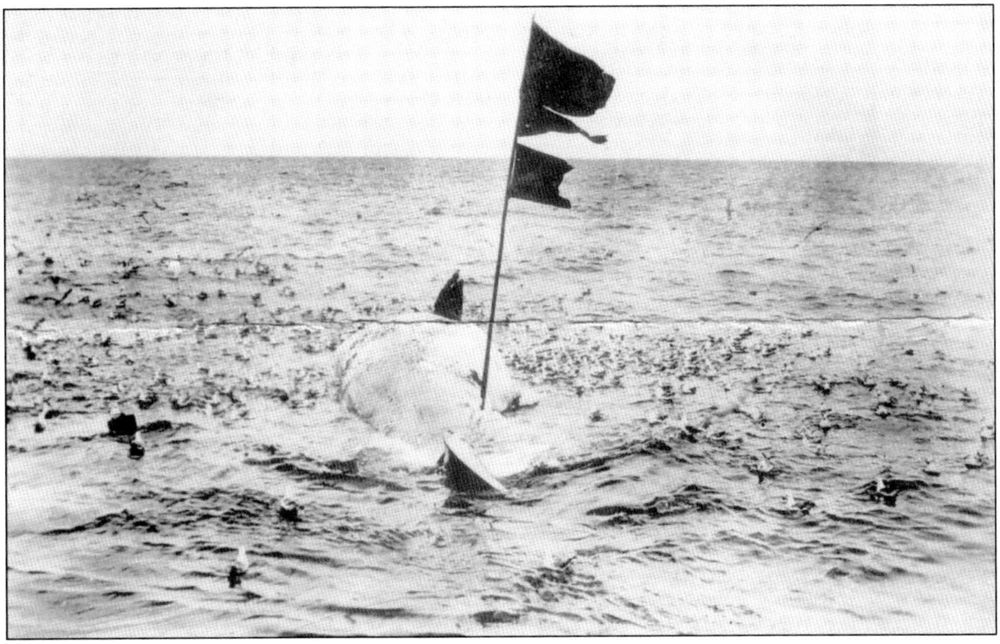

Whales are filled with air in order to float. After the whale is inflated with air, the holes are plugged to prevent air escaping. The flag marks the company to whom the whale belongs. The catcher will pick up the whales on the way back to the mother ship and deliver them for processing.

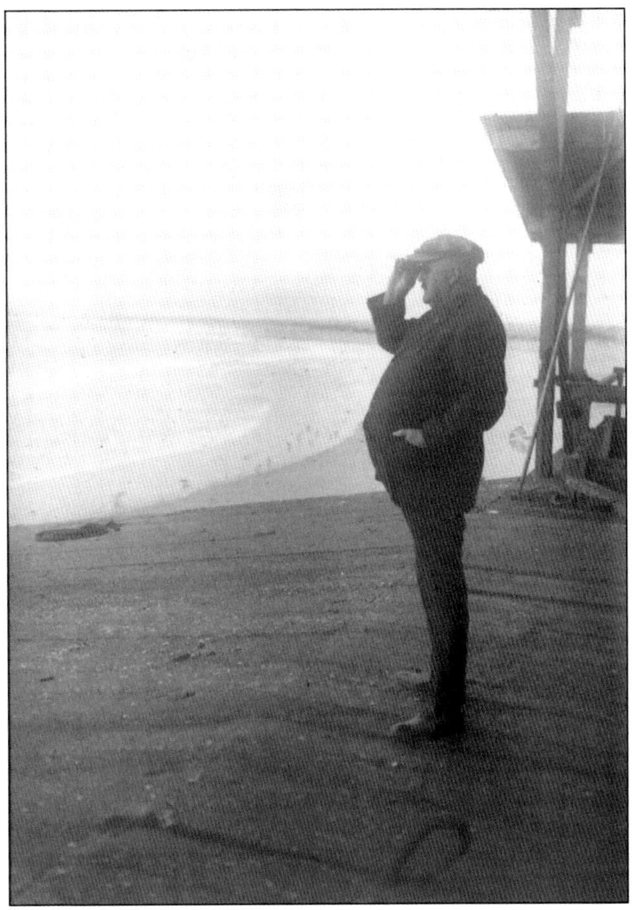

This is a photograph of Capt. Frederick Kristian Dedrick, the owner of the California Sea Products Company. He is standing on the Moss Landing plant deck in Monterey Bay. This photograph was taken by L.S. Slevin of Carmel.

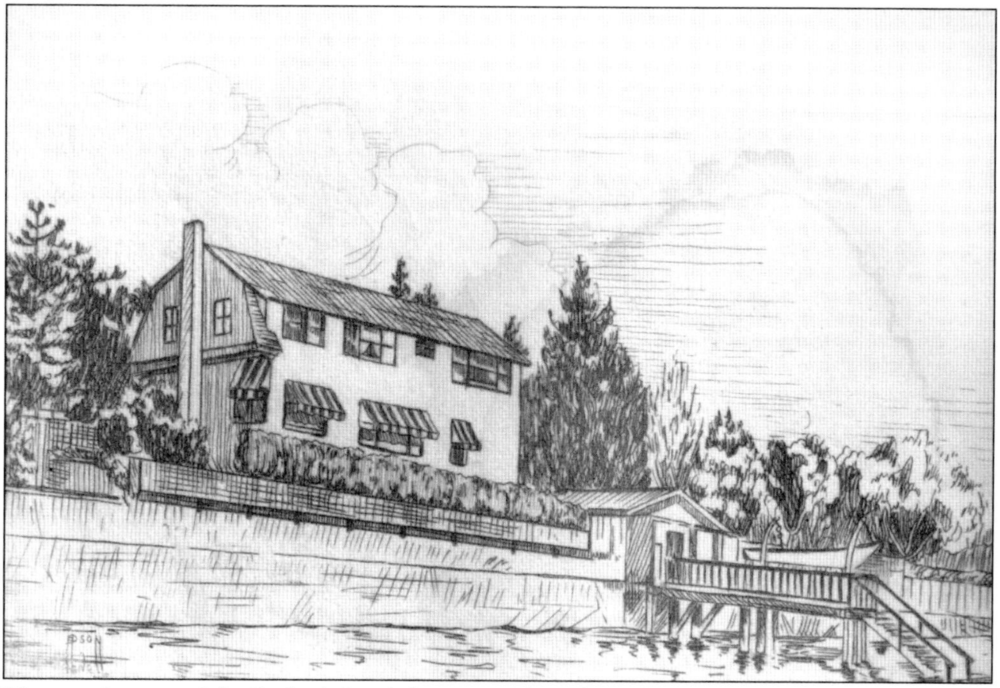

This is a drawing of the Dedrick family home in Alameda, California. The house was originally built on the water, but the area was filled in and so was no longer on waterfront property.

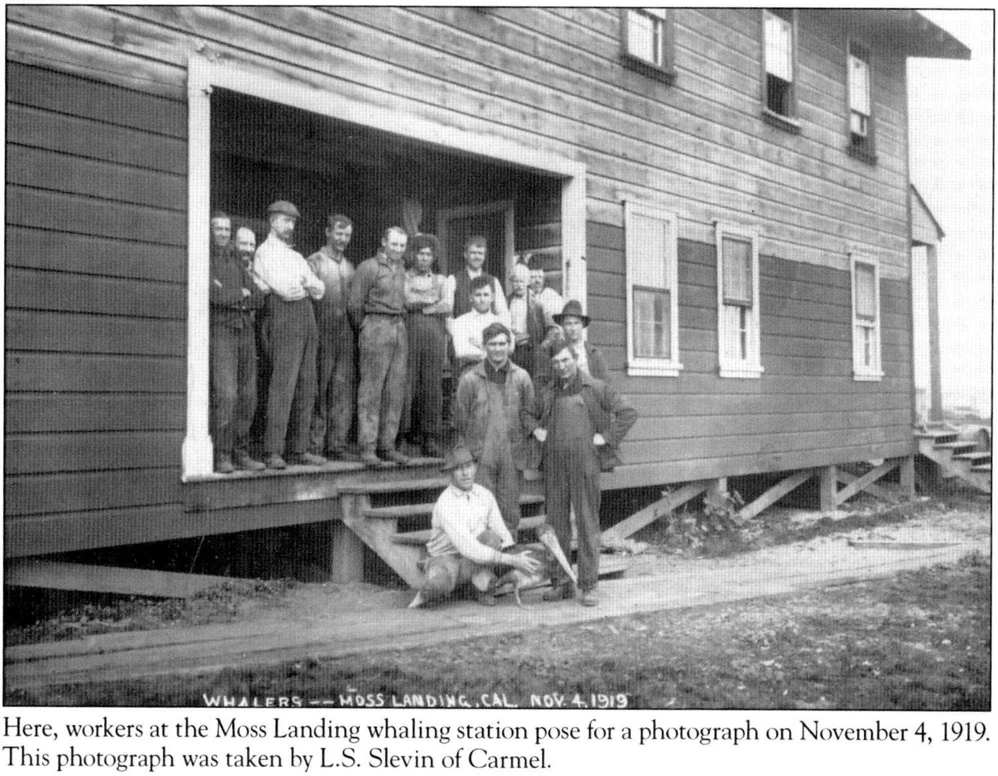

Here, workers at the Moss Landing whaling station pose for a photograph on November 4, 1919. This photograph was taken by L.S. Slevin of Carmel.

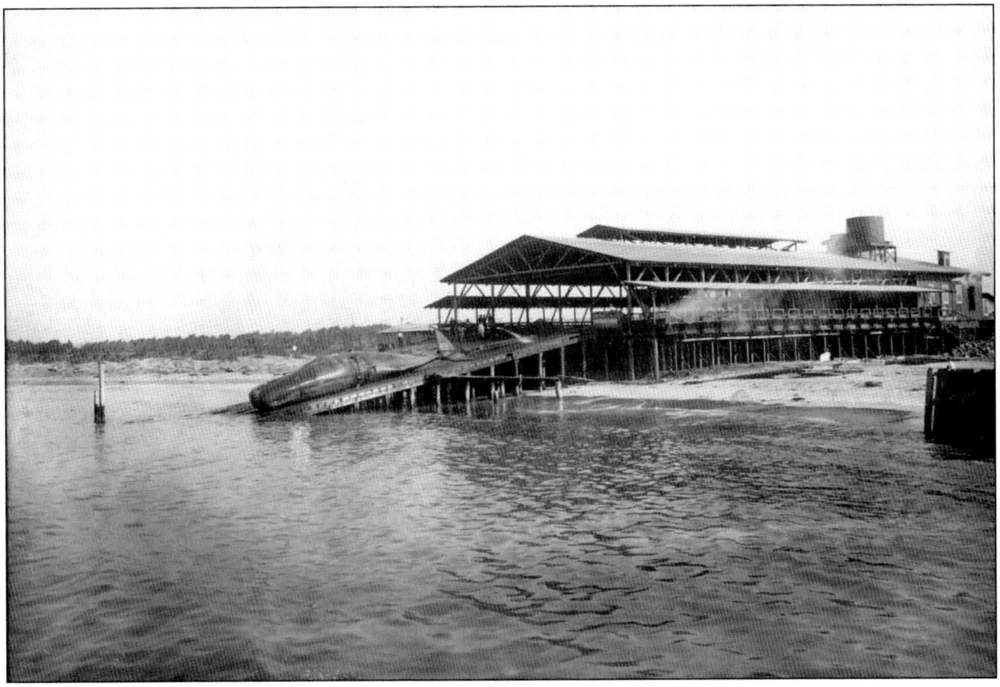

This image shows the first whale taken at Moss Landing on November 11, 1919. Captain Dedrick ran the Moss Landing Whaling Station of the California Sea Products Co.

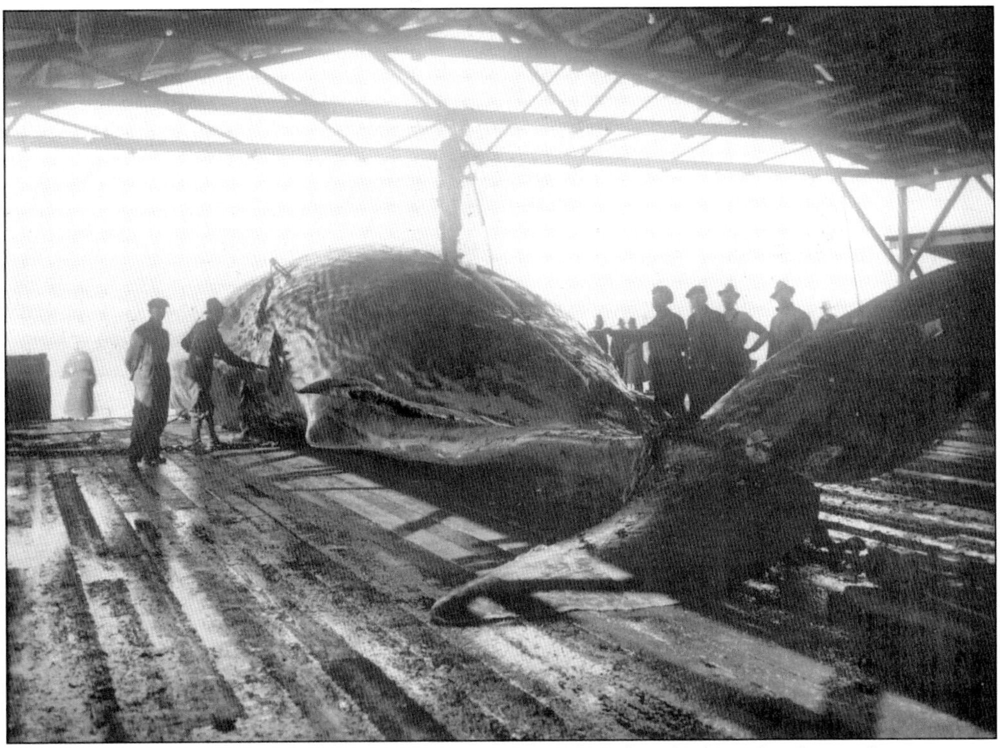

The sperm whale has been hauled into the station. The rippling look to the skin is characteristic of the sperm whale. The flensing will start soon.

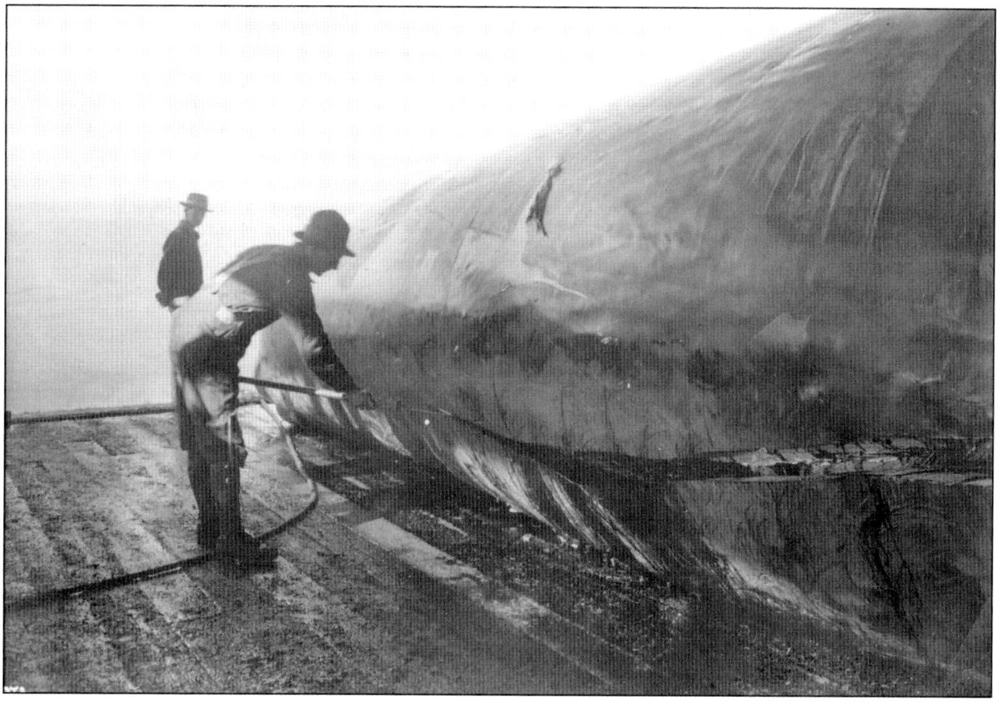

Shown here is the first cut of the whale by the head flenser. The first cut is a horizontal cut along the length of the whale. The rest of the cuts will be vertical, so that the blubber can be cut off in large "blanket-pieces."

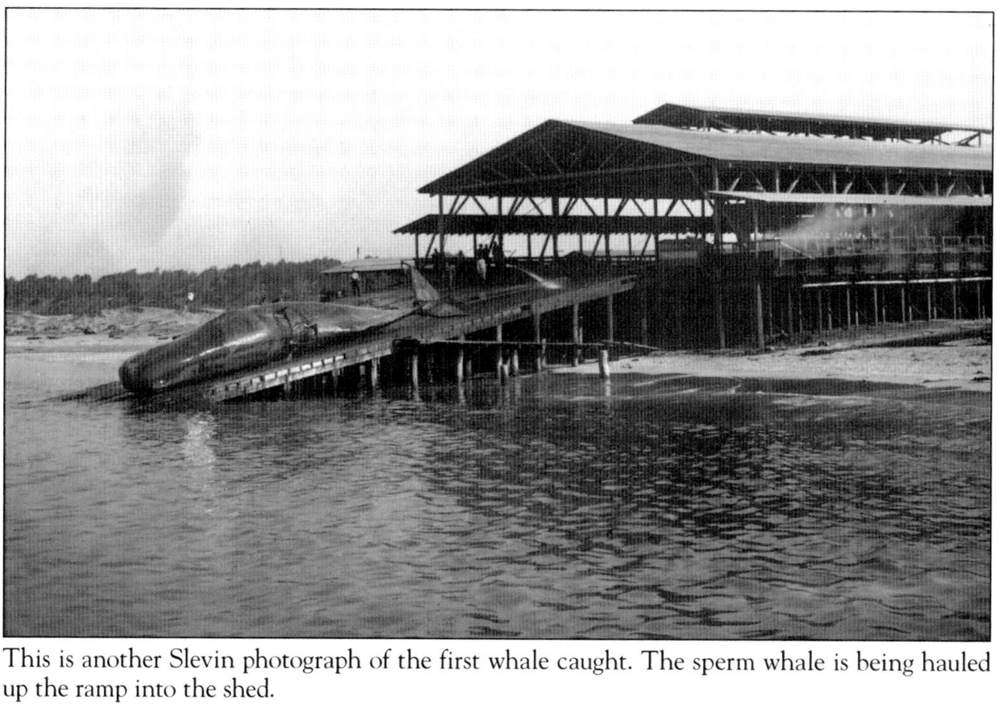

This is another Slevin photograph of the first whale caught. The sperm whale is being hauled up the ramp into the shed.

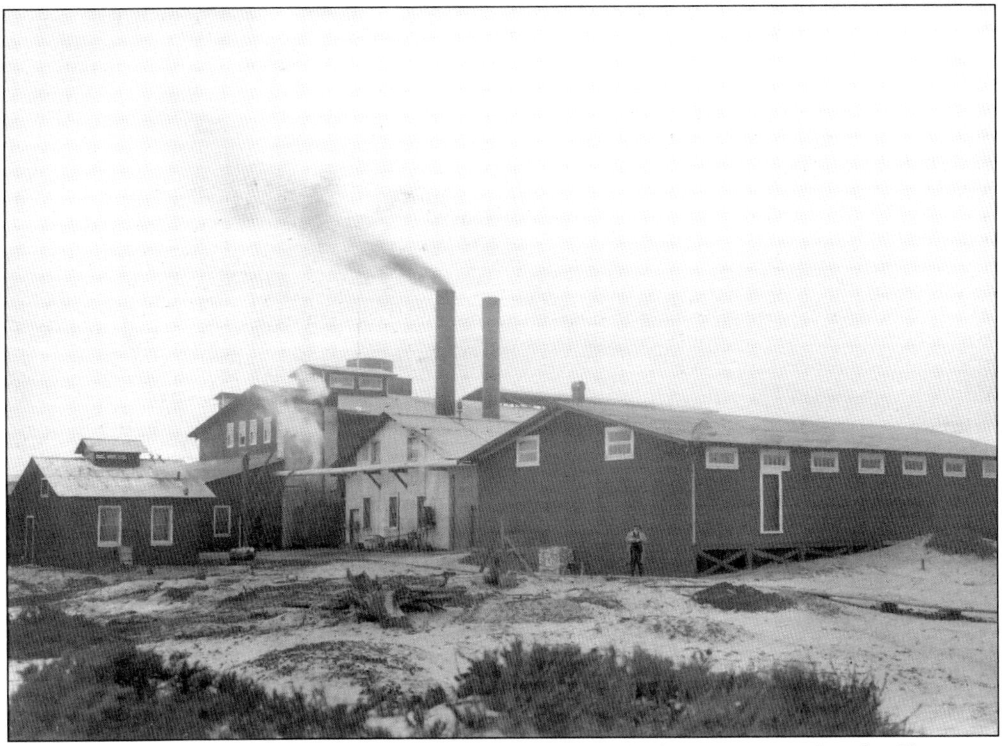

This is a photograph of the front of the Moss Landing whaling station, taken by Slevin on November 4, 1919. The ramp is to the right in this photograph.

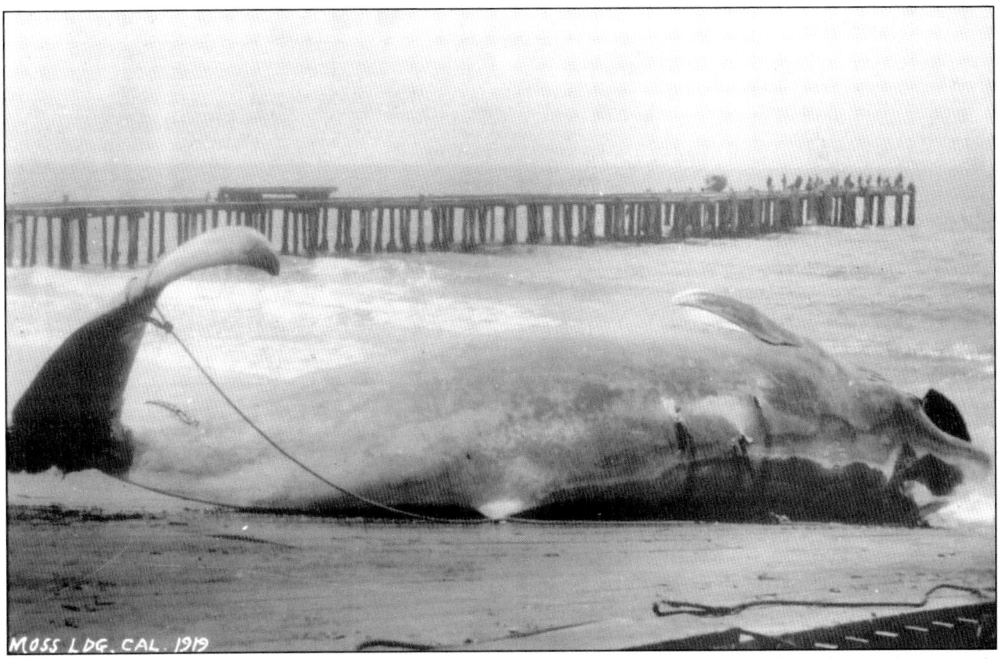

This whale, probably a fin whale, was caught later in 1919. The exact date of this Slevin photograph is unknown.

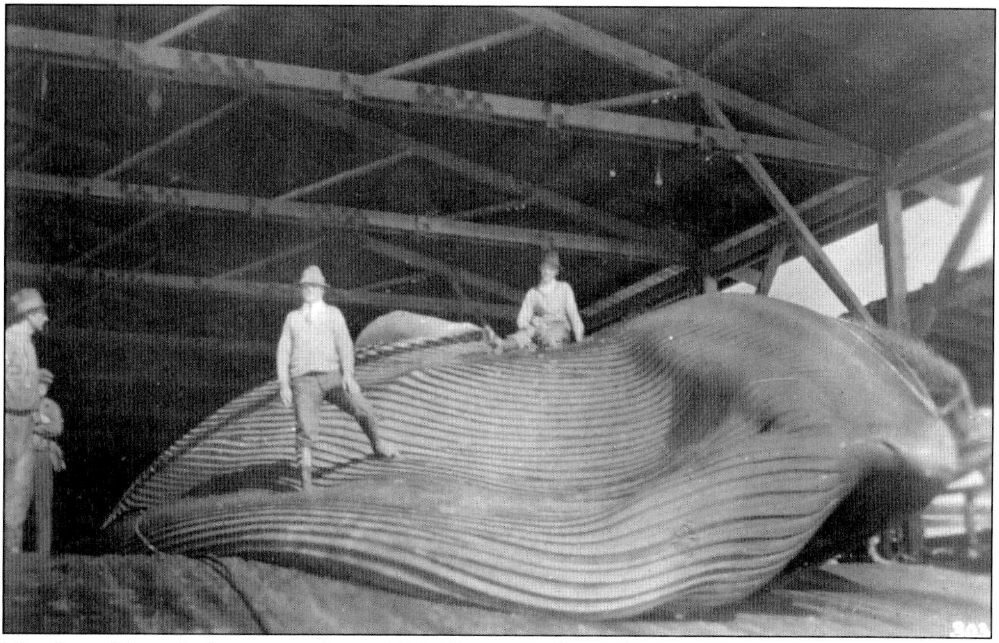

This large blue whale was caught in 1919. The animal is so long that it does not go all the way up the ramp. This photograph was taken by L.S. Slevin.

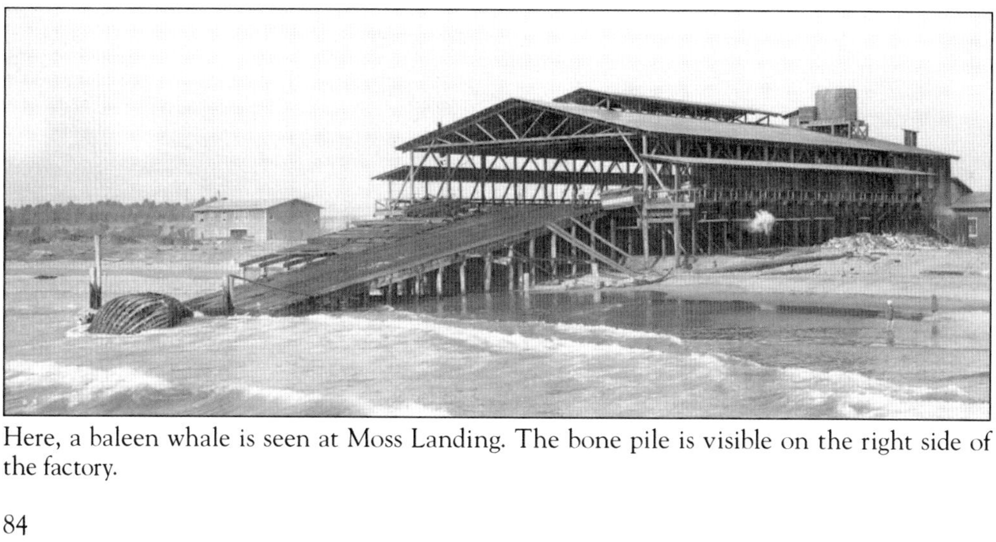

Here, a baleen whale is seen at Moss Landing. The bone pile is visible on the right side of the factory.

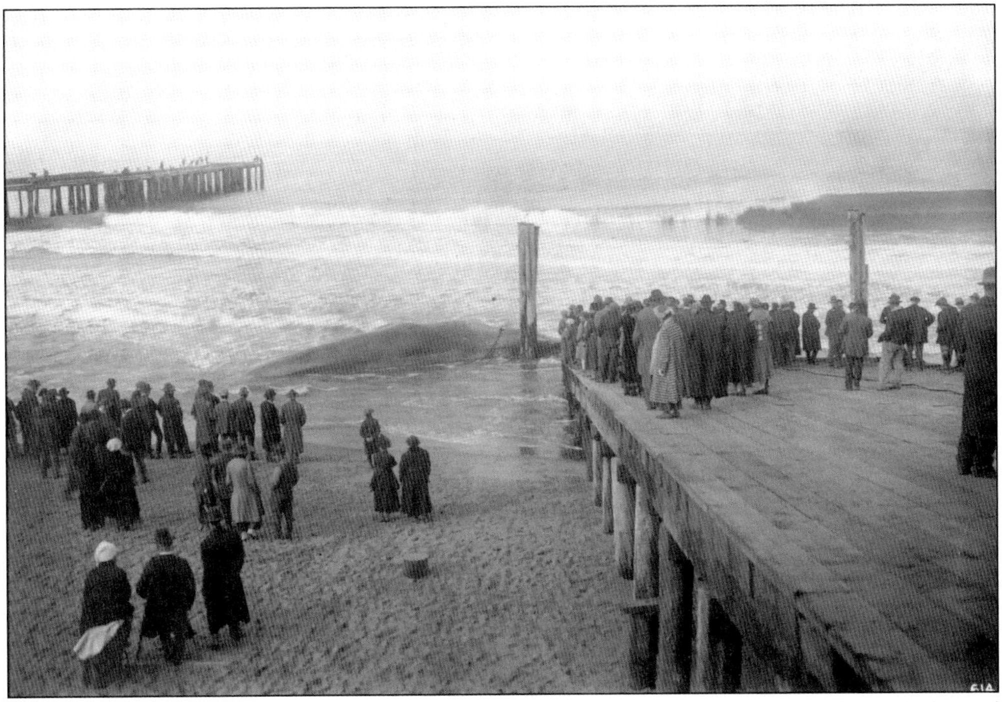

This photograph, taken from the top of the platform, shows curious onlookers and the whale, tied up at the station. Dated January 23, 1919, this photograph must have been taken in 1920.

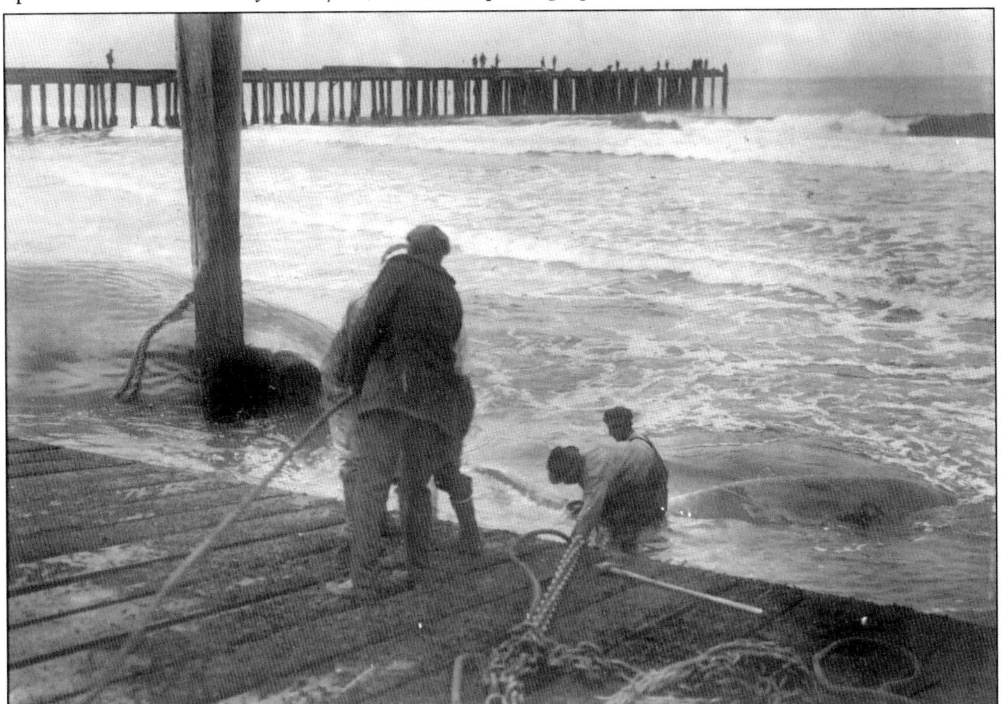

This Slevin photograph shows the end of the Moss Landing ramp. The cables have been pulled to the end of the ramp, to be put around the tail of the whale. There are two whales in the water.

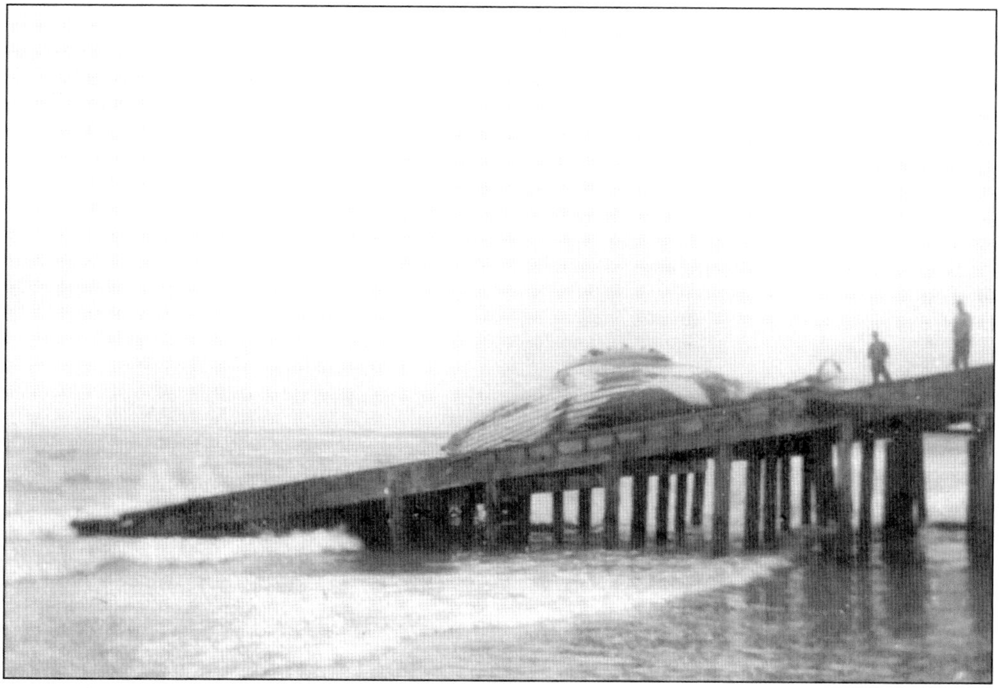

Here, a humpback whale is on the Moss Landing ramp. It has been pulled up about halfway.

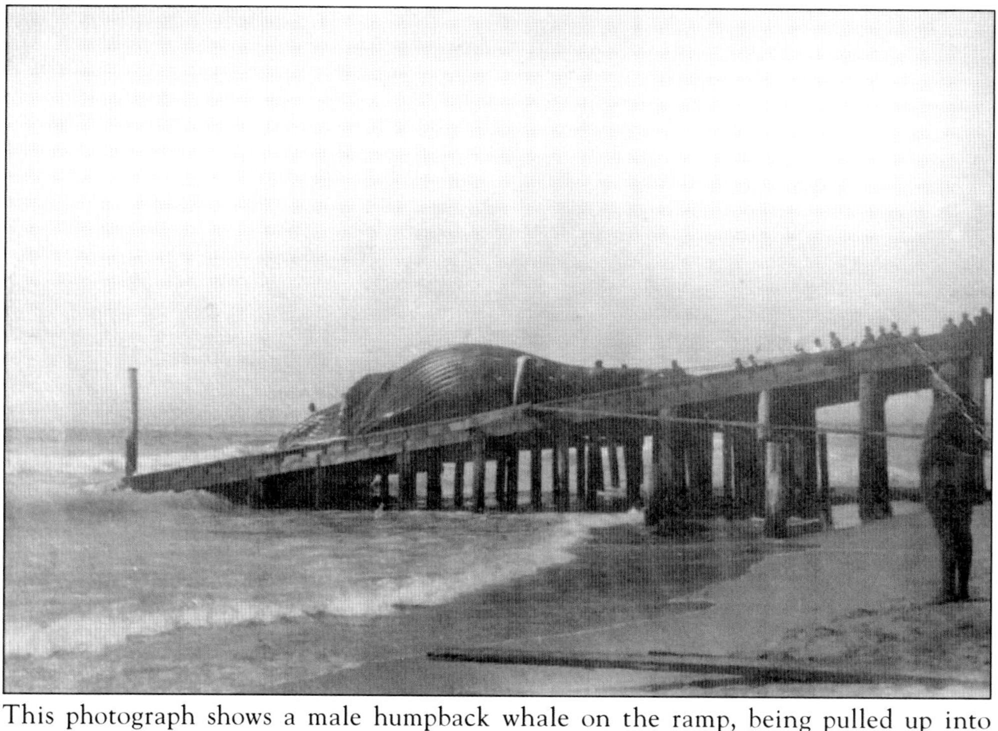

This photograph shows a male humpback whale on the ramp, being pulled up into the cannery.

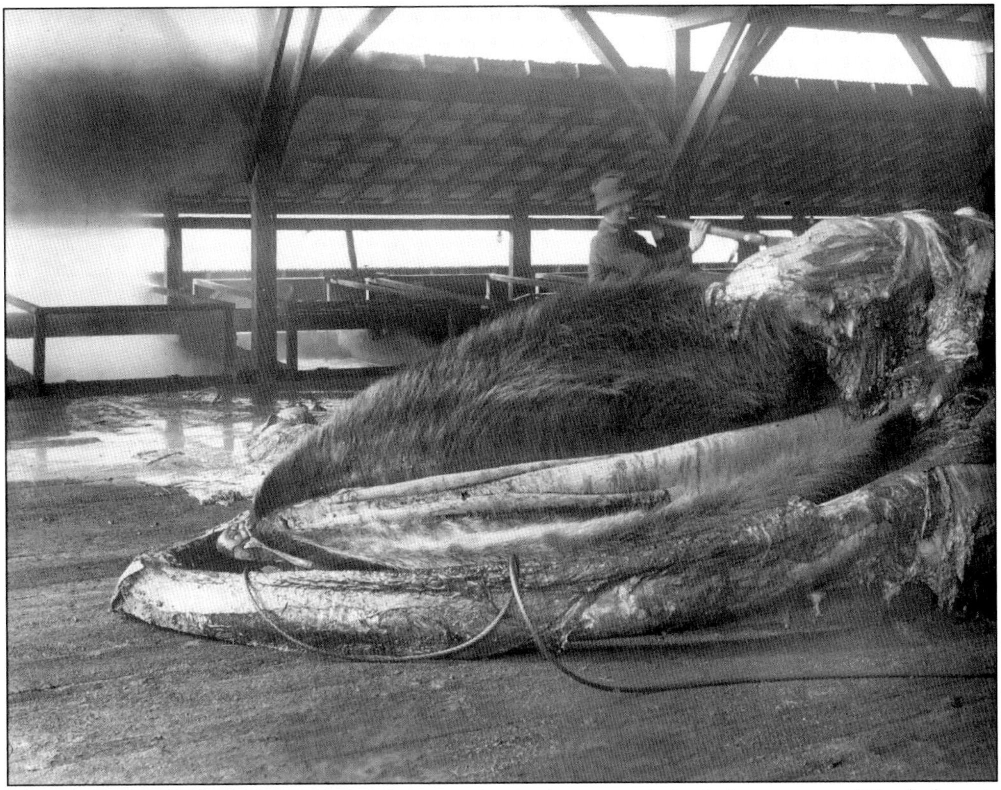

This is the head of a baleen whale, showing the jawbones and the baleen on top. The baleen is used to separate the food from water.

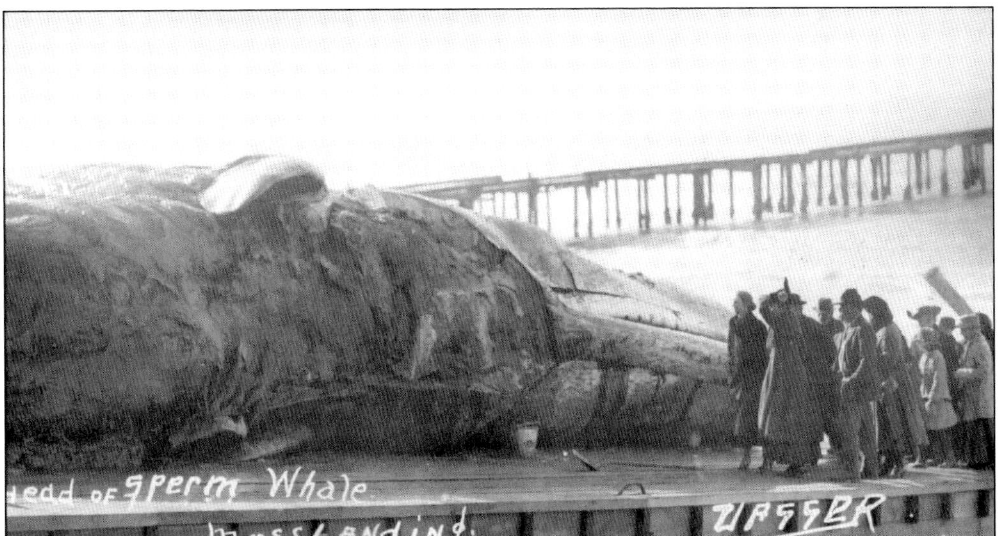

Here, the head of a sperm whale at Moss Landing is being inspected by tourists.

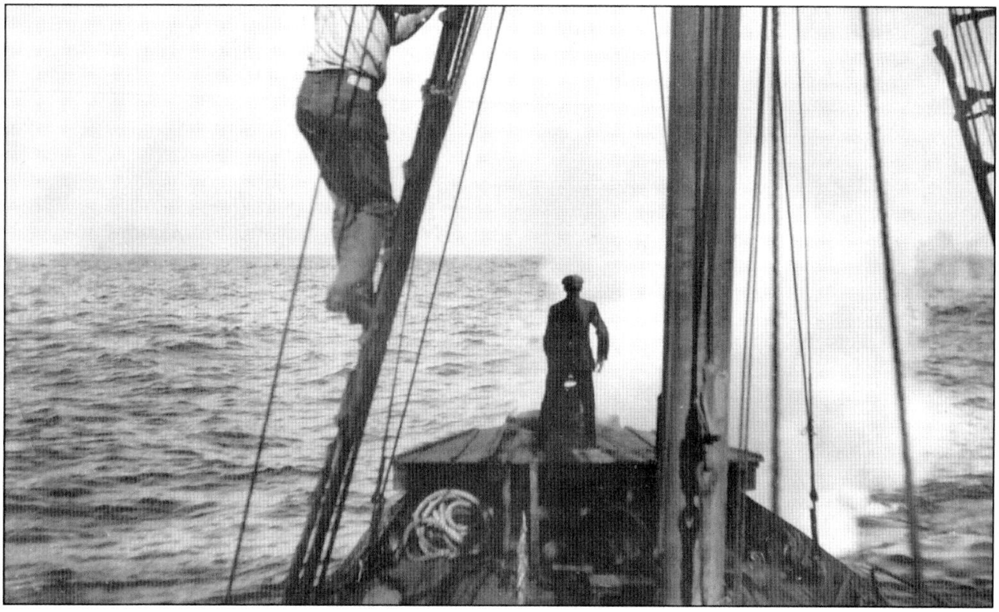

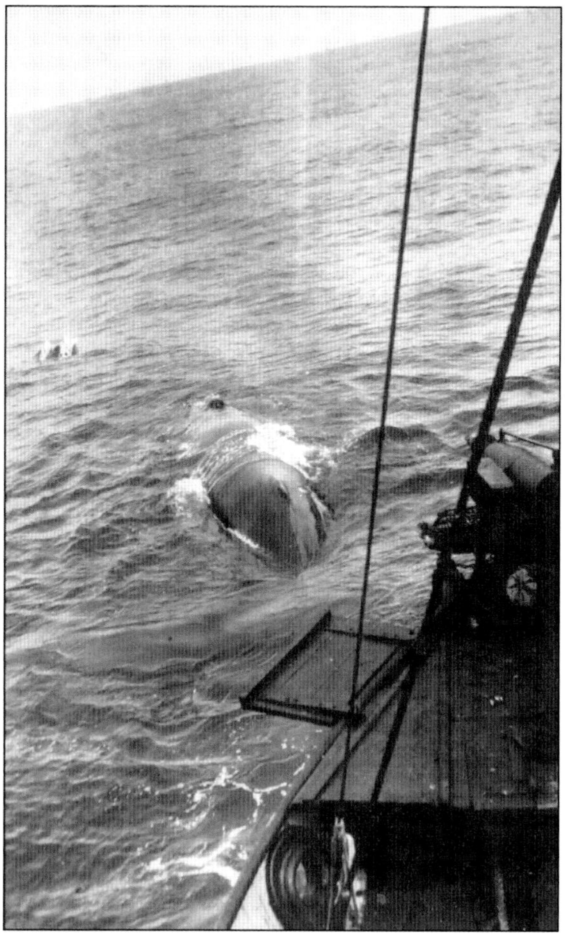

A harpoon is being fired from the bow of one of the whaleships.

In this photograph, a whale is lying in the water by the side of the killer ship after being shot. A line will be thrown around the tail, and the whale will be tied to the side of the whaler for towing. If it is to be inflated, the whale will be left with a flag in it to mark ownership and location.

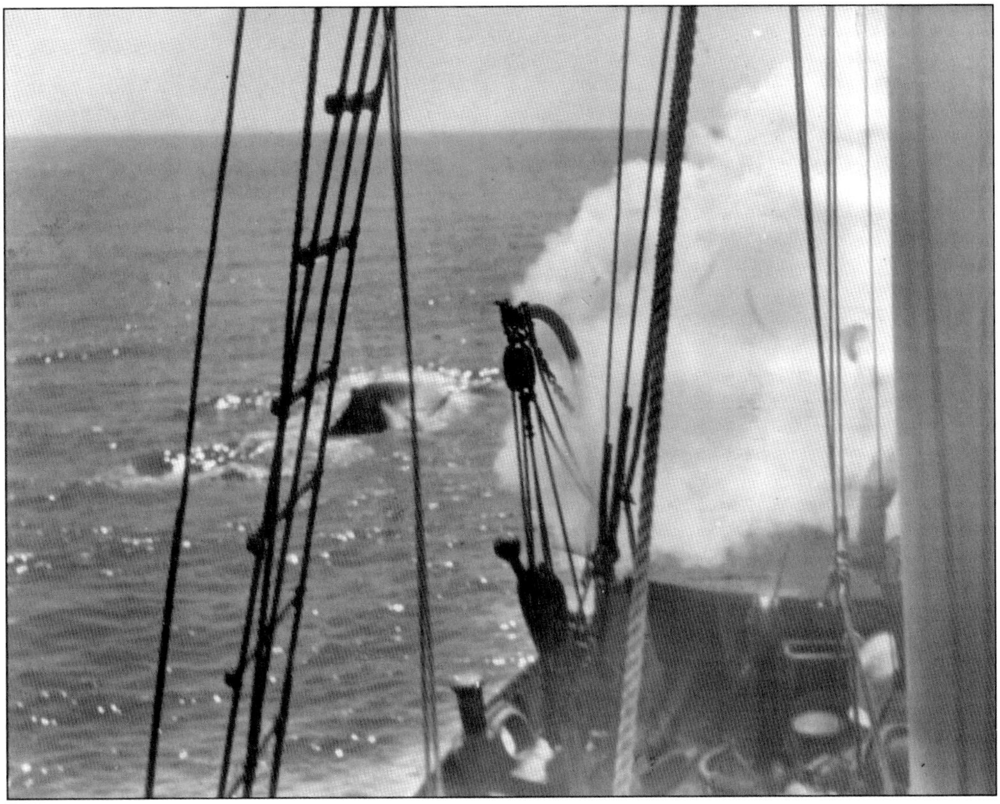

This blue whale was harpooned off Catalina Island in 1927. The whalers ranged from the Mexican border to Long Beach and the channel between Long Beach and Catalina.

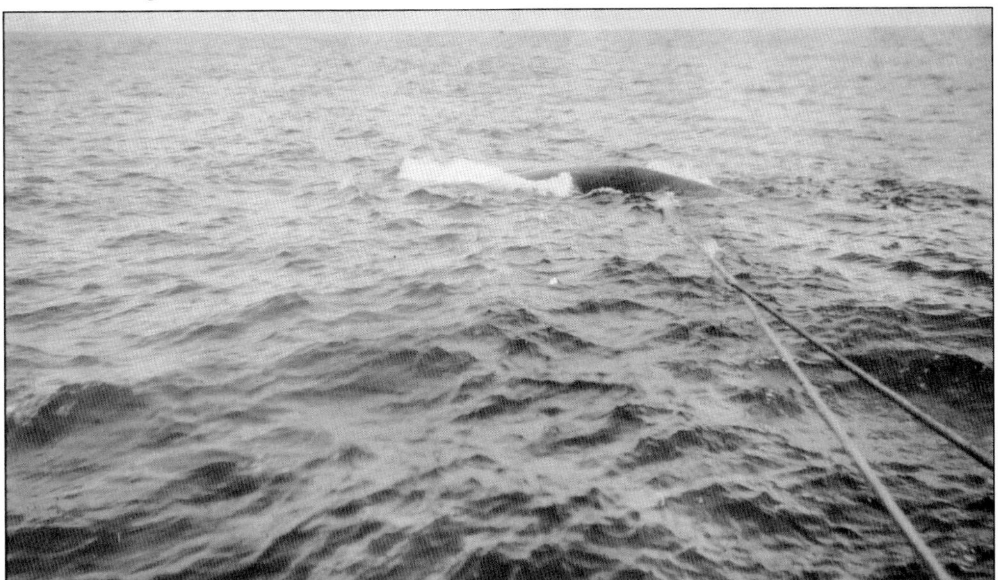

This whale has been harpooned but is still alive. It is towing the whaleboat. When the whale tires out, it will be harpooned again with an explosive harpoon. After a vital spot is hit, the whale will usually spout blood and then die.

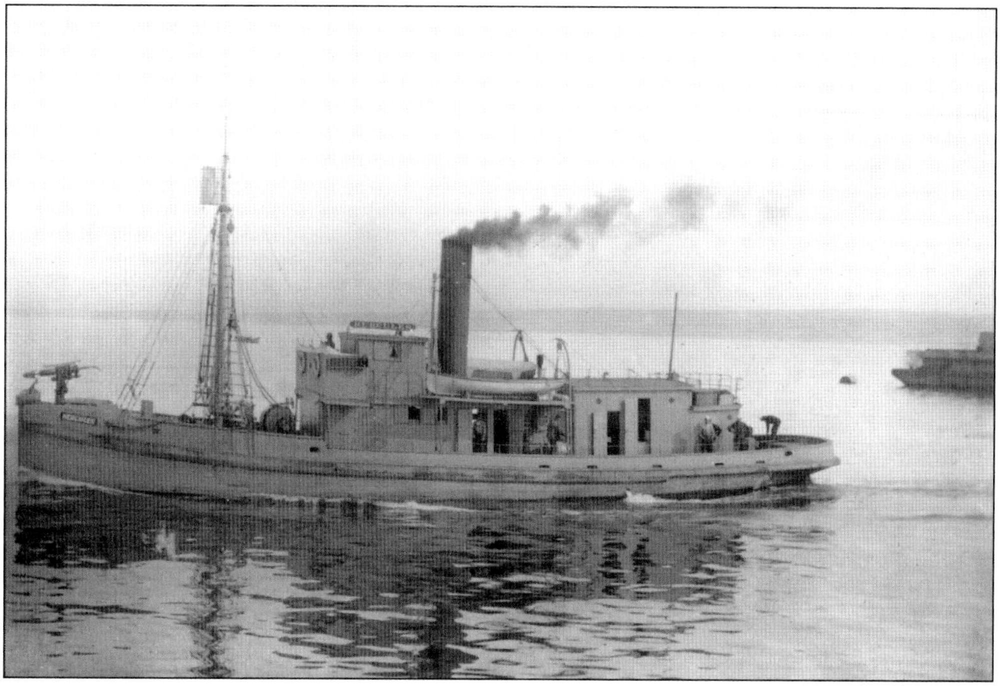

This ship is the whale killer *Hercules* of the Moss Landing whaling station. Note the harpoon gun on the bow and the crow's nest barrel atop the mast for spotting whales. The *Hercules* also has an open deck on top, from which the ship was operated. This photograph was taken by L.S. Slevin.

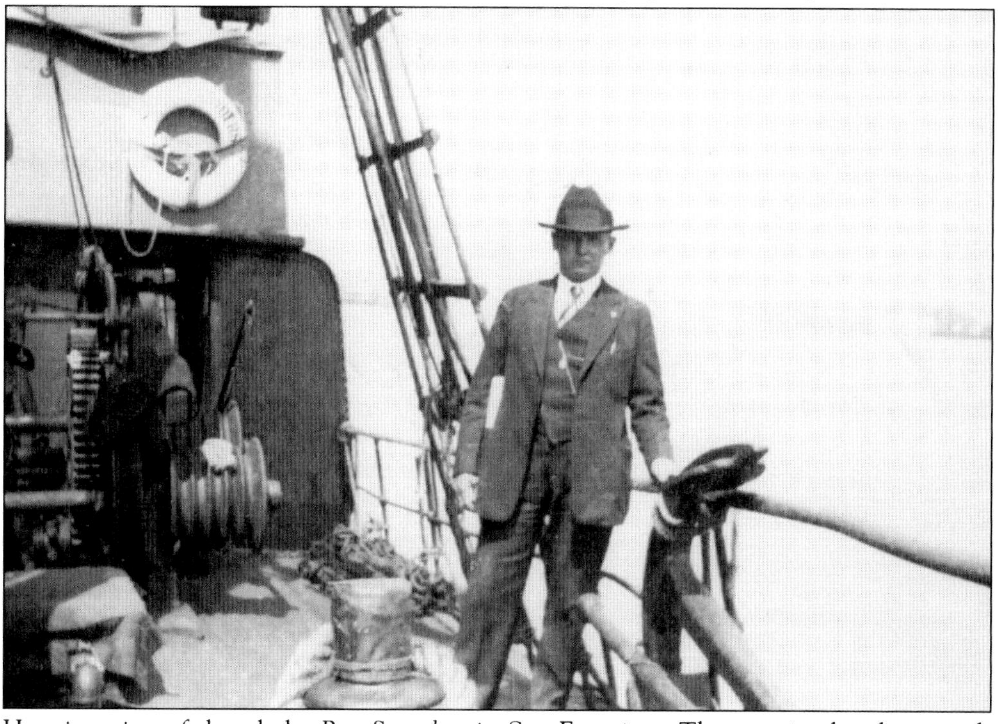

Here is a view of the whaler *Port Saunders* in San Francisco. The man in the photograph is unidentified.

The *Port Saunders* was sunk after it was hit by the lighthouse tender *Madrona* in San Francisco Bay. The accident occurred as the fleet left for Alaska in 1927. The ship was relocated in a few days and taken in for repairs. This photograph was taken at Bethlehem Steel, where the boat was taken for repairs. The extent of the damage is evident.

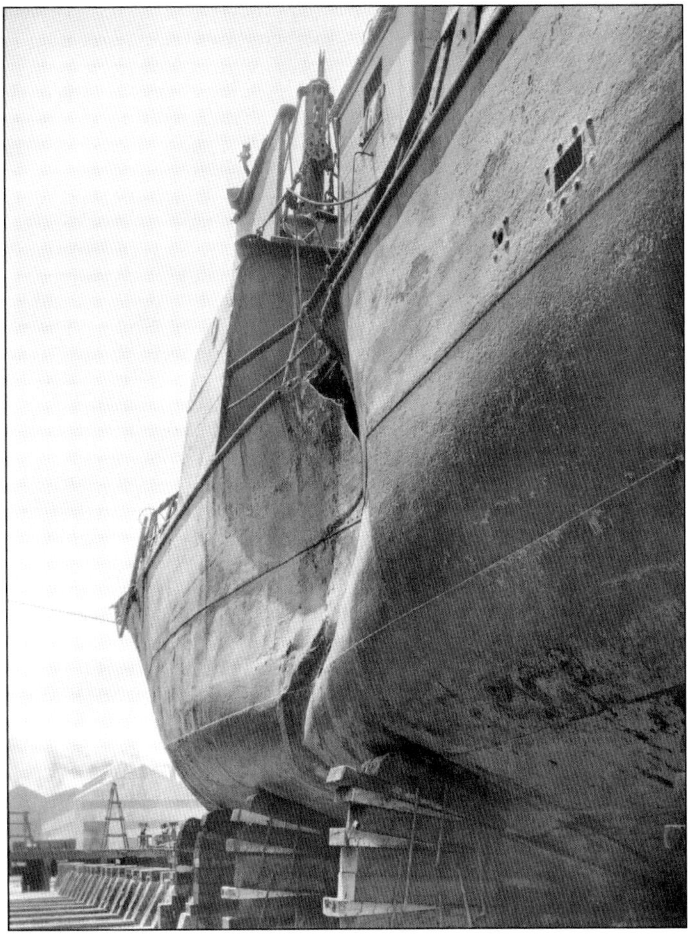

This is a photograph of the *Port Saunders* at Moss Landing station, tying off whales for the station.

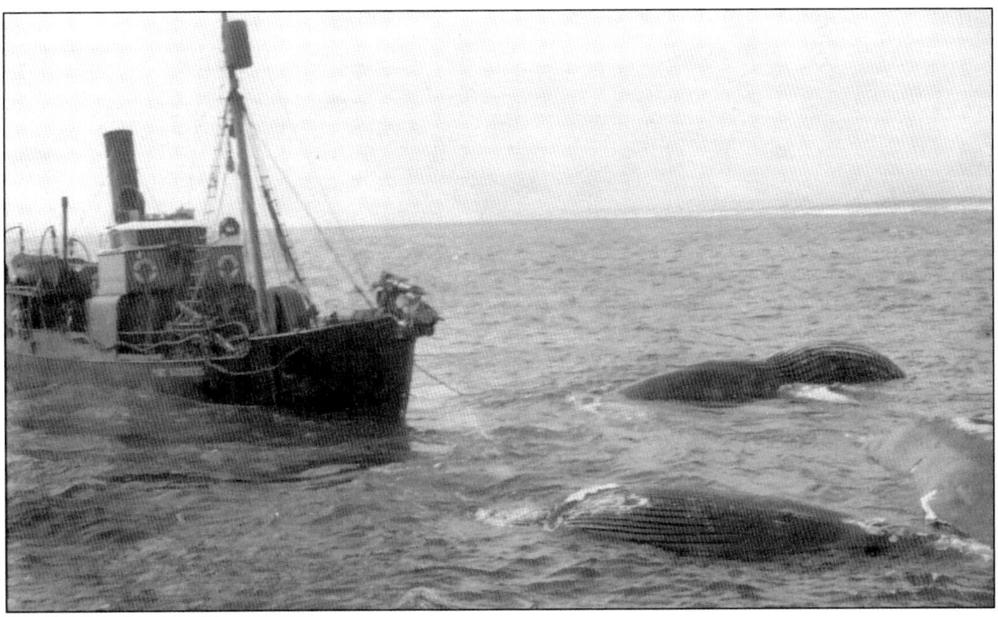

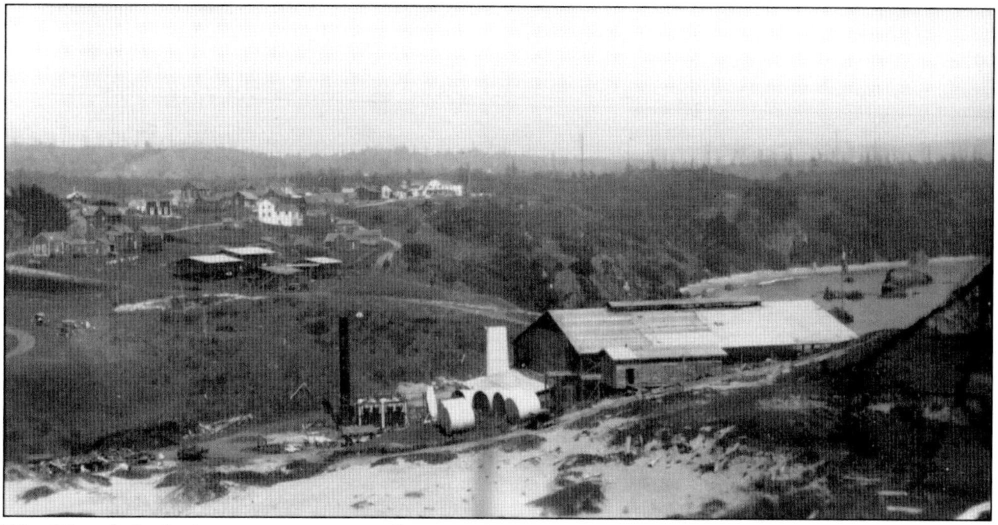

The Trinidad whaling station is seen here under construction in 1920. The station opened for processing that year. Trinidad is north of Humboldt Bay in Northern California.

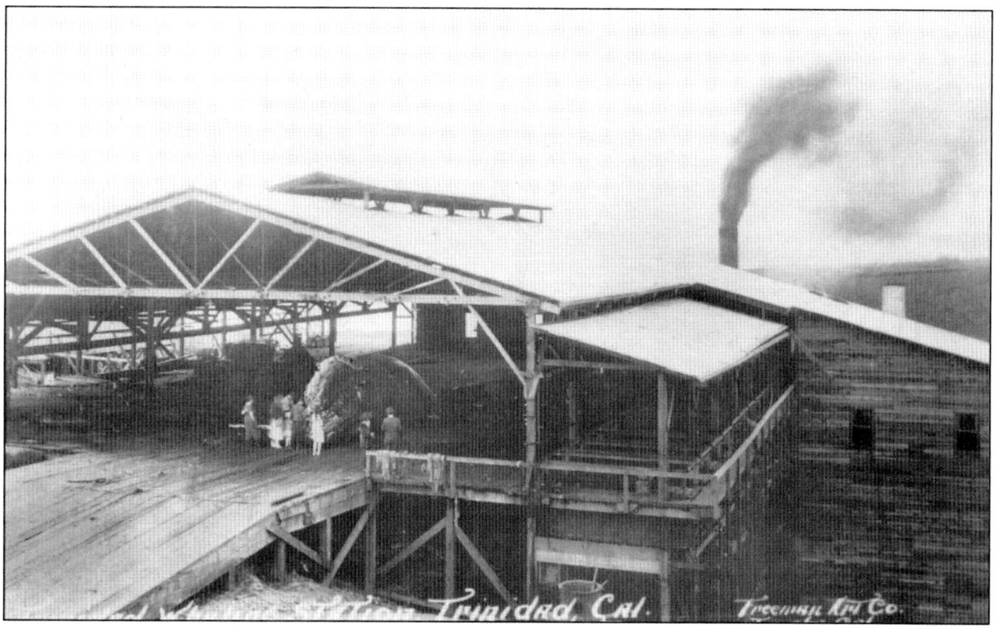

Shown here is the whaling station at Trinidad after it was opened in 1920.

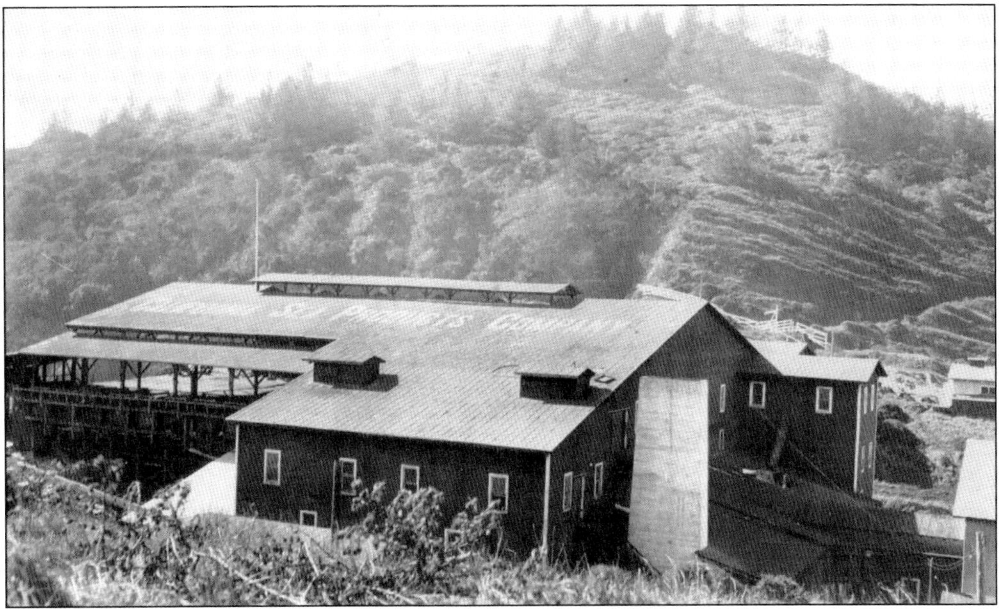

This is a photograph of the rear of the completed Trinidad station in 1920. The station has a very long ramp, as the facility was built on a hill some distance from the water.

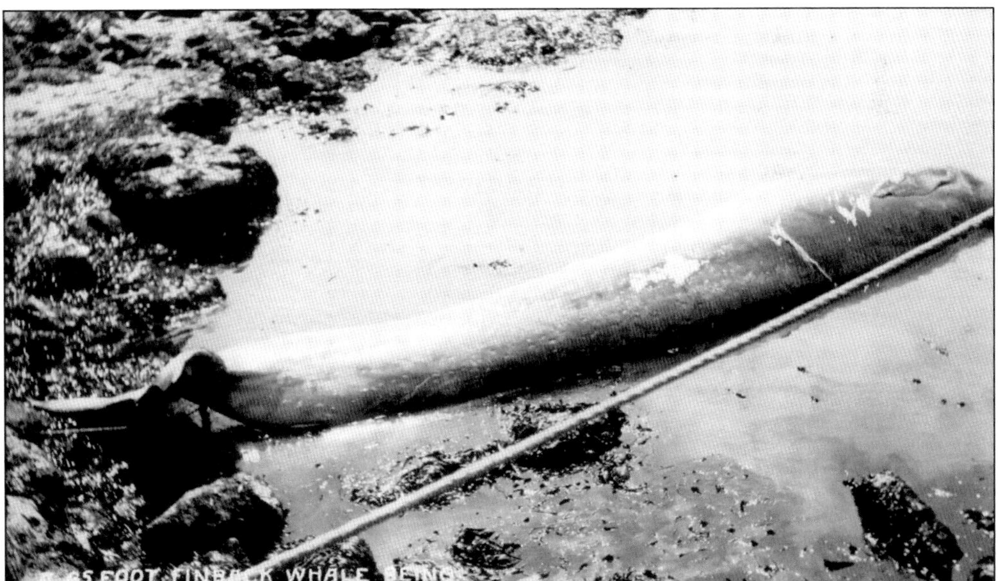

A 65-foot finback whale has been towed in to the foot of the ramp. It will be winched up from here to the station.

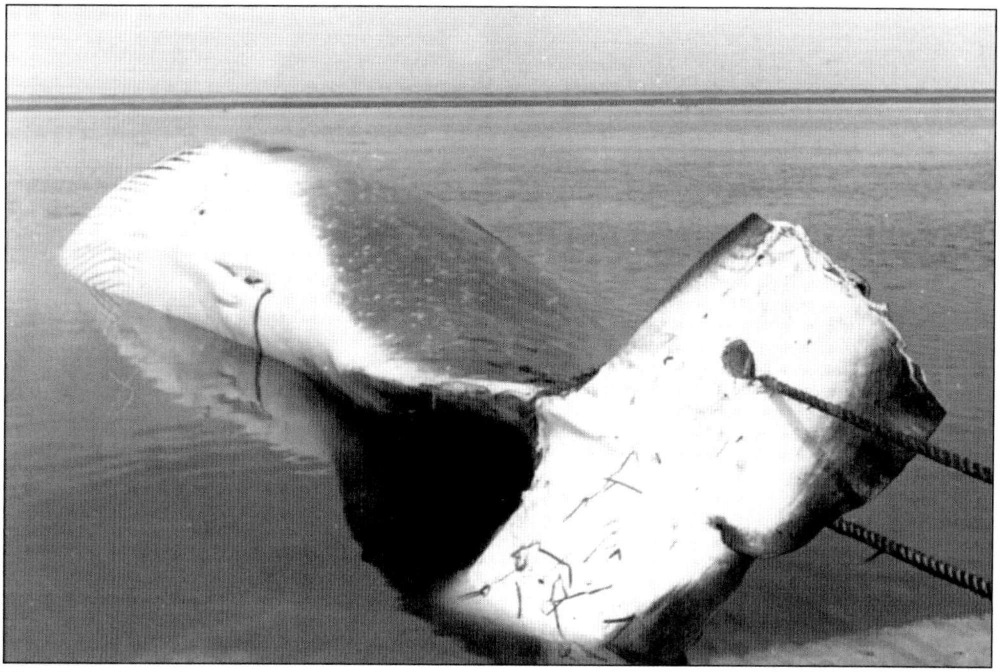

This finback whale has a hole through the tail. The end of the cable is attached so that the whale can be pulled up. Note that the ends of the whale's tail have been cut off. This was done by the whalers in the boat so that the fins would not create resistance as the whale was being towed.

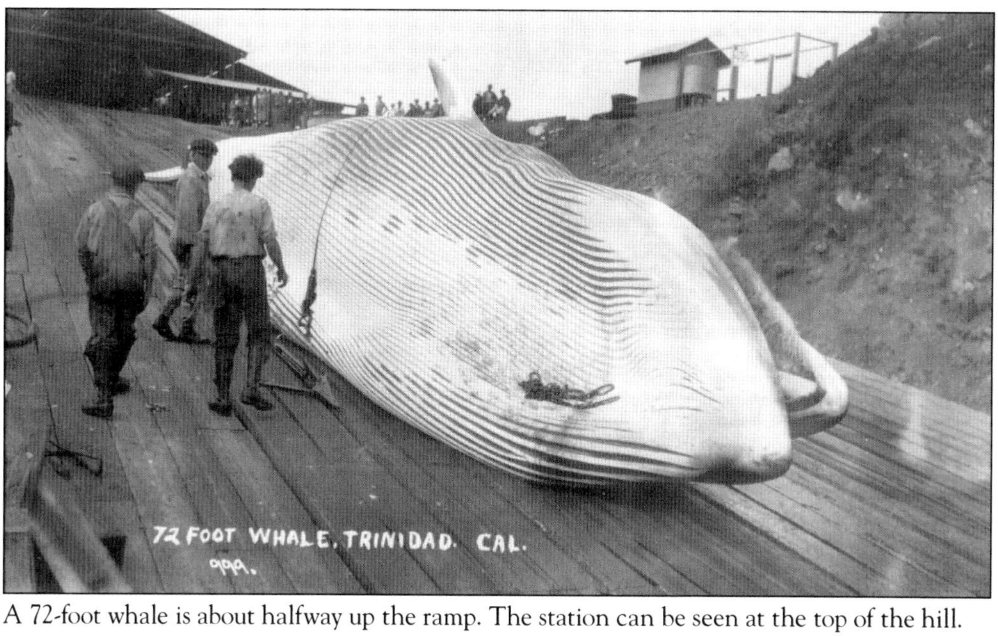

A 72-foot whale is about halfway up the ramp. The station can be seen at the top of the hill.

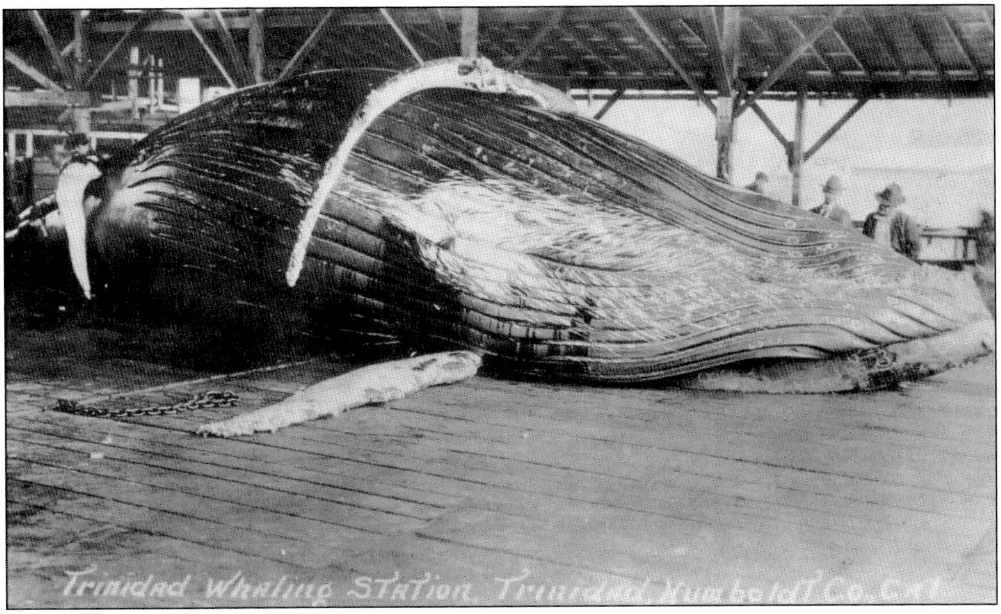

This is a good view of a humpback whale in the Trinidad station. The long, winglike front flippers are the best way to identify the humpback whale.

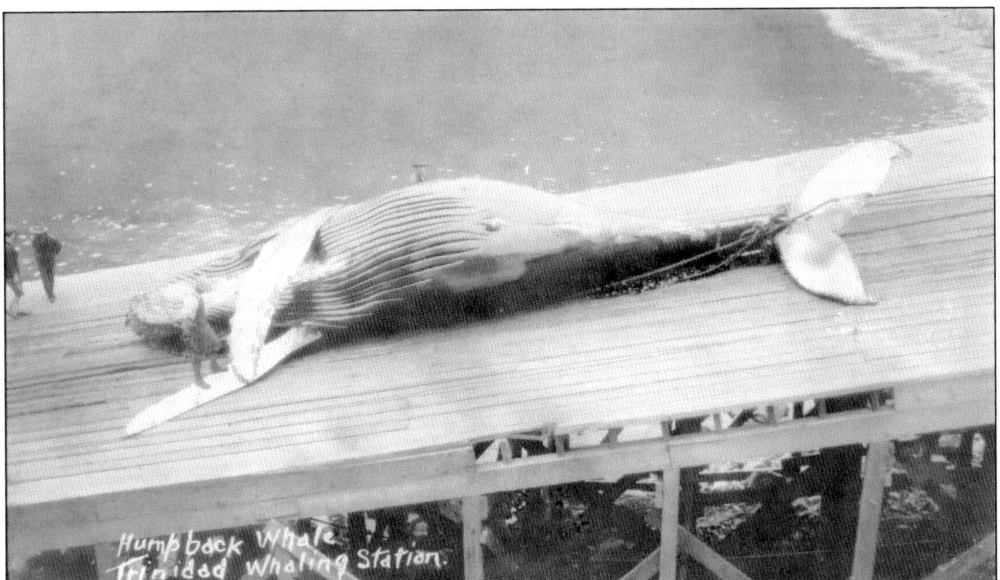

This humpback whale is about halfway up the ramp to the Trinidad station. Again, the front flippers are quite visible here.

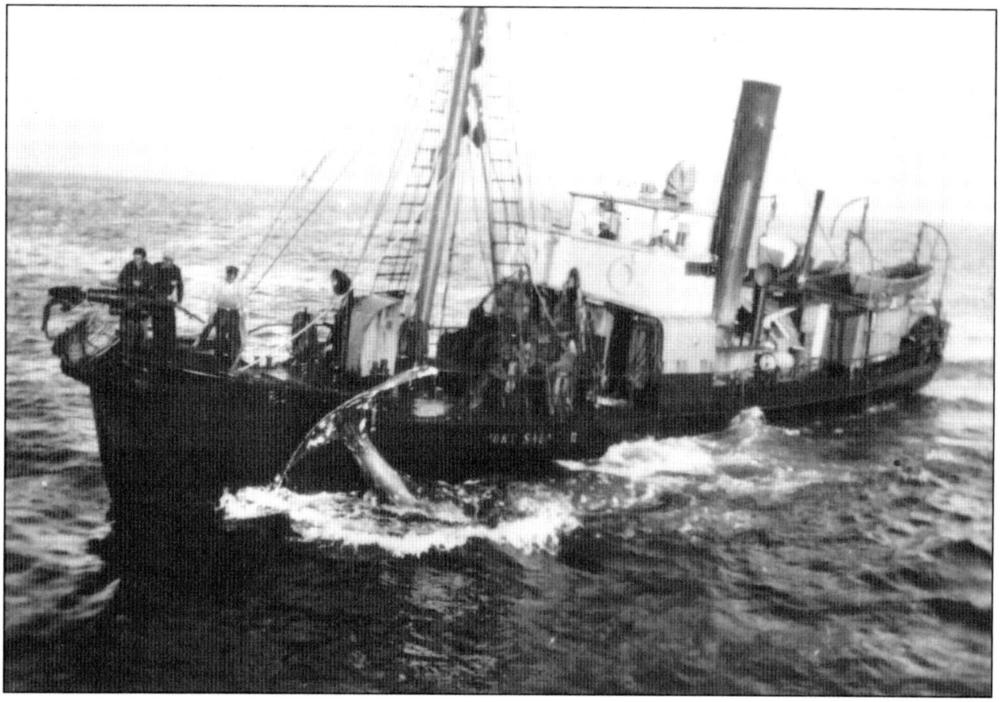

The SS *Port Saunders* is pictured returning to the mother ship, SS *California*, with whales to be processed on the SS *California*. The *Port Saunders*, made in Norway, was purchased from a British whaling company. She whaled for the California Sea Products Company from 1912 to 1932, then for California Sea Products from 1932 to 1936, then for the San Francisco Sea Products Company from 1939 to 1942, and for Maritime Industries from 1942 to 1945. She caught fire while being used off-season at Porta Costa, California, and drifted toward the C&H Sugar plant in Richmond, California, in the Carquinez Straits.

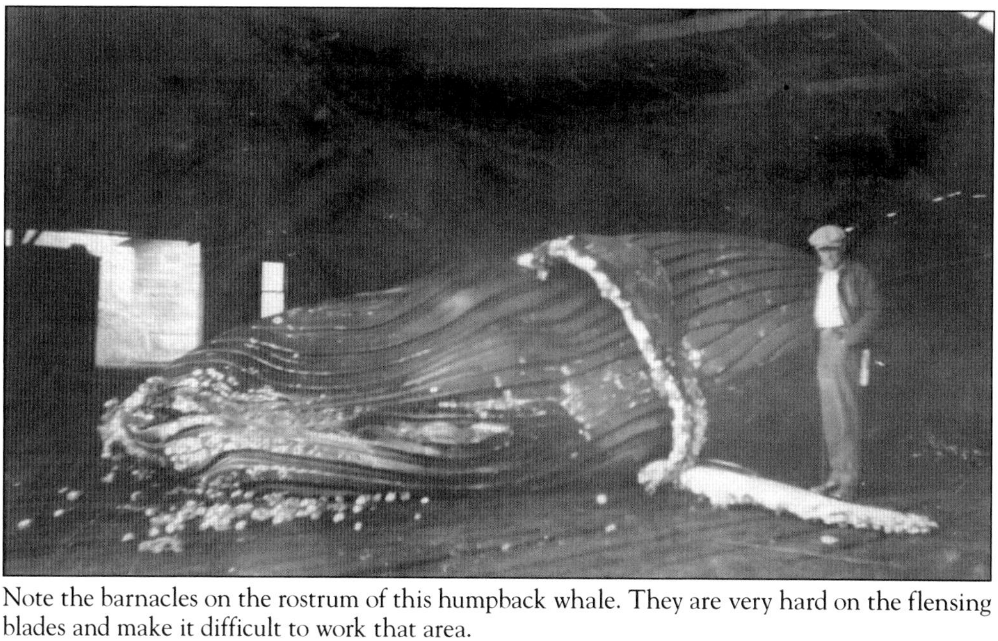

Note the barnacles on the rostrum of this humpback whale. They are very hard on the flensing blades and make it difficult to work that area.

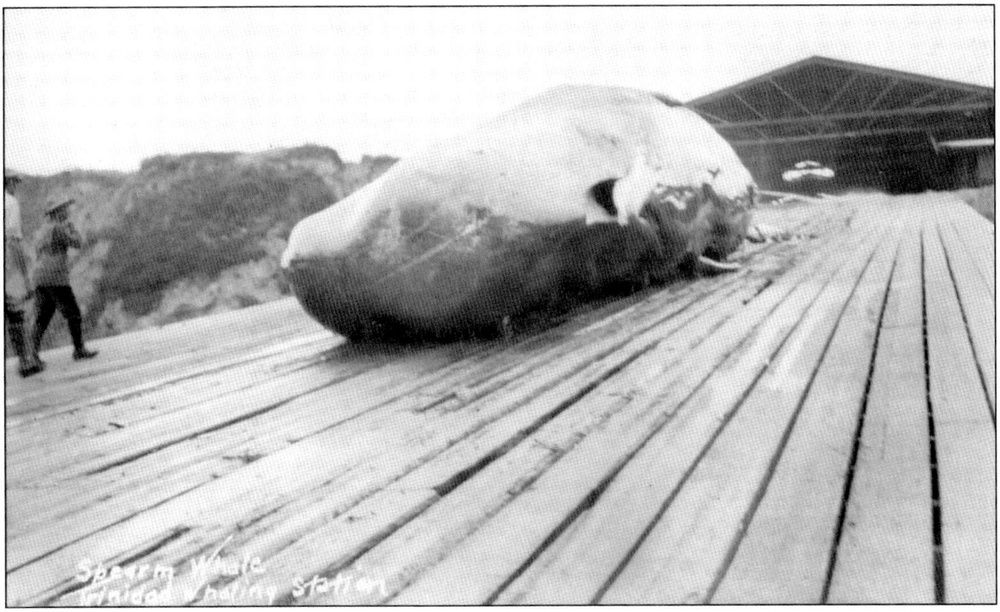

A sperm whale is pictured on the ramp at Trinidad Whaling Station. Note the large bulbous head and the smaller-looking jaw to the right. The jaw, however, is filled with large conical teeth, used to catch large squid and fish.

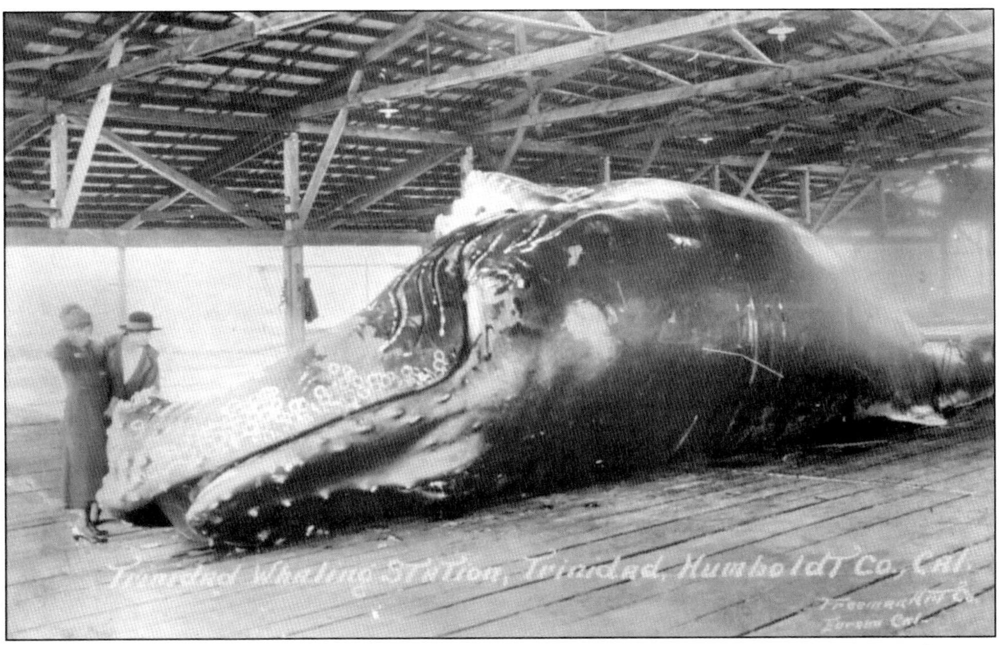

This appears to be another humpback whale, by the look of the barnacles. The front flippers cannot be easily seen from this angle.

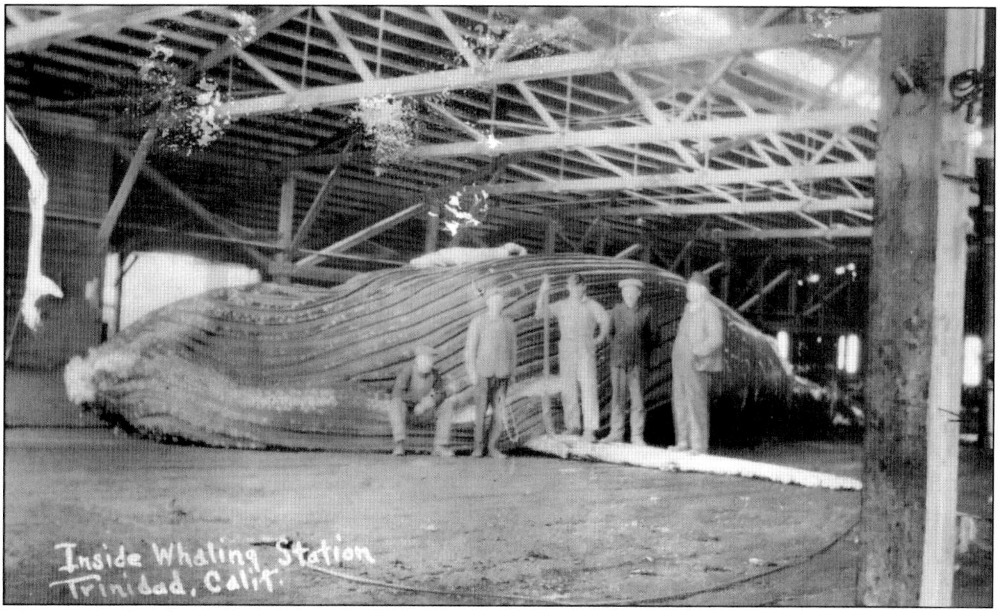

This is another humpback whale in the station. The flensing crew poses for a photograph. The head flenser is in the center, holding his cutting blade.

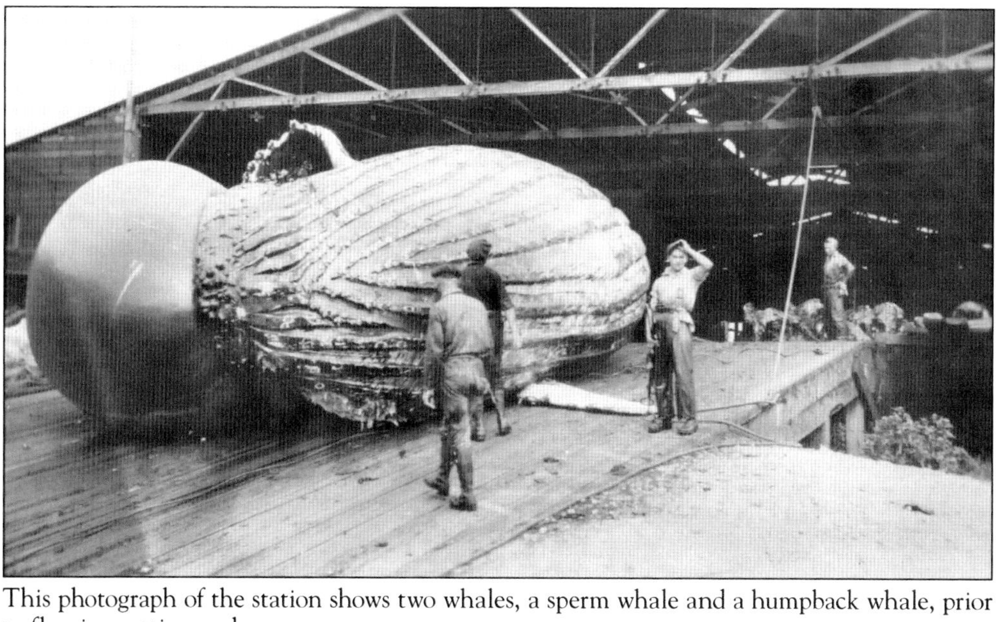

This photograph of the station shows two whales, a sperm whale and a humpback whale, prior to flensing getting under way.

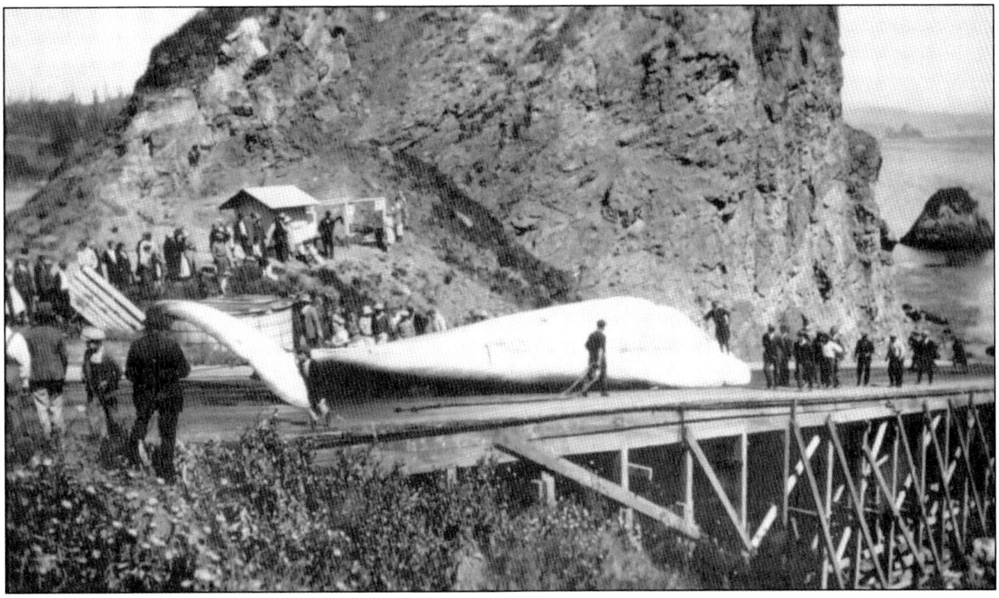

This could be a blue whale on the Trinidad platform. Several people are watching the process from the hill.

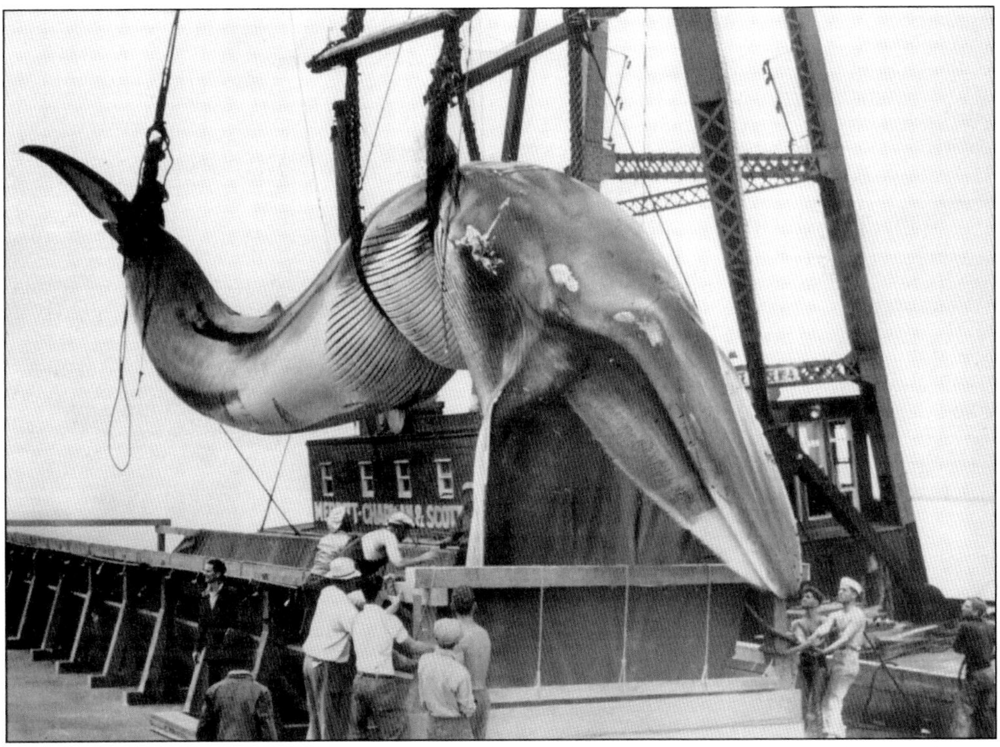

This fin whale is being hoisted by a large derrick and will be put in the constructed carrier. It may be on its way to be embalmed and used for a train exhibition. The Pacific Whaling Company had been buying whales for its exhibition needs.

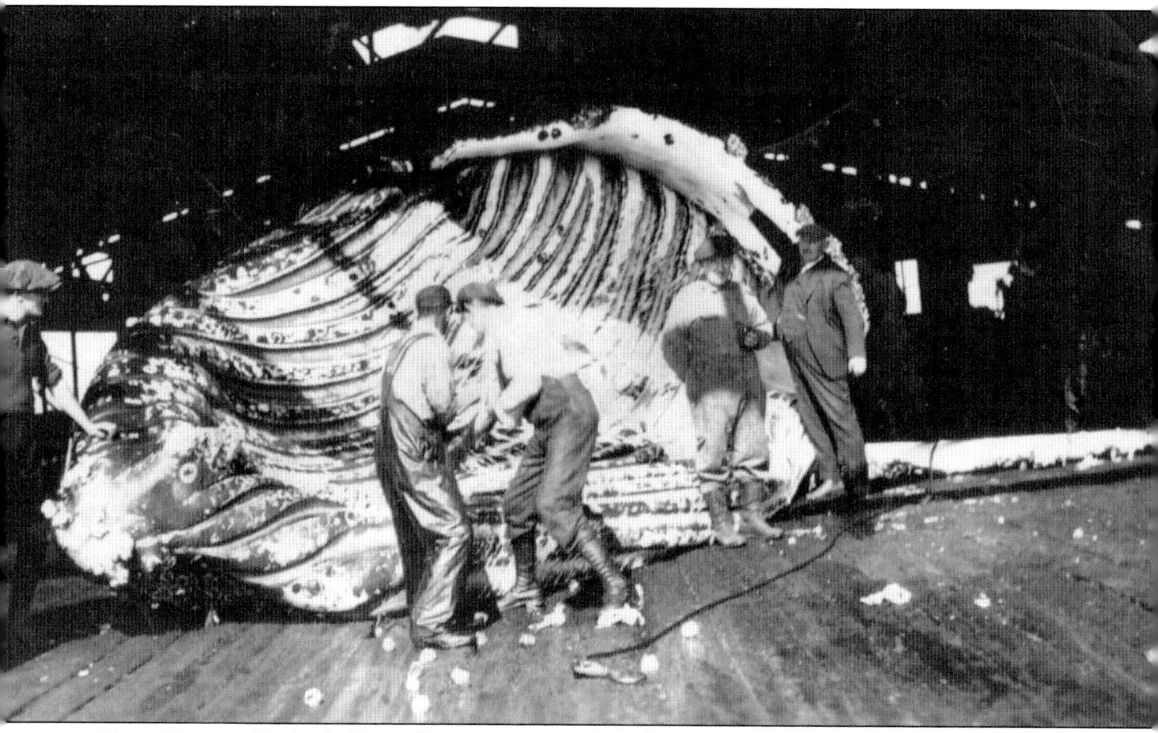

Here, Captain Dedrick (far right, wearing a suit with his right arm extended up) and his son Freddie Dedrick (far left) are pictured with three unidentified men at the Moss Landing Whaling station (operating 1919–1926). The piece of whale carcass is being moved with a hoist. Freddie was killed early in 1936 in an accident when he was struck by the recoil of the cannon, or a piece of a bomb struck him when it exploded in the whale. His father, Capt. Frederick Kristian Dedrick, also died in 1936, from complications from a throat connection.

Six

CALIFORNIA WHALING IN THE 1940S

The San Francisco Sea Products Company whaled using the factory-ship *California*, which was tied up in San Francisco Bay in 1939. Almost daily, the whalers would steam under the Golden Gate Bridge, between Angel Island and Sausalito, and up to China Basin to provide their catch to the whaling station. However, the changing laws forbade a floating factory to be used in 1940, and the company needed to find a new location for a land station for which to operate.

C.F. Hine and A.D. McBride, the new owners of the San Francisco Sea Products Company, felt that Humboldt Bay offered the best location. The Trinidad whaling station, north of Humboldt Bay, did well for several years, 20 years before that. Due to public complaints about the smells deriving from the processing at Trinidad, the owners did not try to place another plant there. They selected Fields Landing, at the point where Highway 101 meets the coast, about 10 miles south of the city of Eureka.

Hine and McBride petitioned the board of supervisors in early April for the Fields Landing location, promising that they had solved the problems regarding offensive odors emanating from the factory. In San Rafael in 1939, the factory ship *California* operated within 100 yards of a San Rafael neighborhood and in close proximity to a pleasure beach, where, in the summer, thousands of people would picnic and party, having no idea there was a whaling operation within a few hundred yards.

Humboldt County approved the whaling operation in late April 1940. The Mercer-Fraser Company of Eureka began construction of the plant around May 1, and the $60,000 factory was completed by the end of the month. The *Gleaner*, purchased along with the factory, crossed the bar on May 1 and was tied up at the Fields Landing plant. The first whale was brought in on June 14, a 54-foot-long female sperm whale that weighed 60 tons. Hundreds of people came to see it. The whales were exhibited, and admission was charged to see them. In the first month, the *Gleaner* brought five whales—two sperm, two finback, and one humpback whale. The station continued to whale until the end of the 1942 season. Only a few precautions had to be taken for the war. At this time, all employees had to be fingerprinted and the vessel cleared by the Coast Guard.

New regulations required the whales to be inspected by the nearest government entity. This requirement fell to the life-saving branch of the Coast Guard, located in Samoa, near the north side of Eureka. When whales were received at the station, a call would be placed to Samoa, and an inspector would be brought across the bay to the station. Whaleboats were hard to come by because of the war. In 1943, the whalers used were the *Hawk II*, a purse seiner leased from San Diego, and the *White*, a whaler on loan from Canada, with government permission.

Whaling continued in 1943 at the station, but the number of whales caught was below that of the previous years. There was a small amount of whaling in 1944. Due to the war, the operation was idle for the next two years. The whaler *Aberdeen*, on loan from Canada, went out in 1944, but the season was plagued with low visibility due to fog. The station had been renamed Maritime Industries beginning in 1943, and in 1944 it was announced that Max and Consuelo Hoffman were the new owners of the whaling station at Fields Landing. The whaling license expired in 1944 and was not renewed until 1947.

When the station reopened in 1947, boats were once again an issue. However, the company was able to operate by agreeing to contract Gib Hunter and Hermann Foland, who had purchased from the government surplus minesweepers and fitted them out as whalers. Hunter & Foland was to be paid an amount of money per whale brought to the station. Max Hoffman, president of Maritime Industries, would manage flensing the whales and process them into oil and fertilizer. The station continued to operate in 1948, but in midyear, the operation was bought out by Hunter & Foland, which continued to operate the station with vessels *Dennis Gayle* and *Lynnanne* throughout the decade.

The real story of the 1940s was the operation of the station in 1943. San Francisco Sea Products had concluded business in 1942 and did not plan to operate in 1943. Max and Consuelo Hoffman bought Maritime Industries in 1944 and ran the business until Hunter & Foland took over until 1952. That left a gap in the business, as the station operated in 1943 as Maritime Industries for one year before the Hoffmans took over. Someone incorporated the business as Maritime Industries and operated the plant for one season as a wartime industry. Newspapers and magazines stated that there was a change of management, however, the public was not told who actually owned the business.

The articles of incorporation filed with the California secretary of state indicate that the directors of the company were John D. Gallaher, Maude E. Woodward, and Grace Cairncross. A check of the San Francisco directory shows these people to be a lawyer and two office employees of the law firm that filed the paperwork with the secretary of state. This practice was employed when people did not want their association with a company to be revealed for various reasons.

The clue to ownership of the plant appears in 1946, when a chattel mortgage on the property was filed with Humboldt County, indicating the purchase and release of the company on March 10, 1944, to Max and Consuelo Hofman as Fields Landing Whaling Station. The party selling the property was Broval, Inc. The names C.G. Gratsos, George Carras, and John Carras, on the chattel mortgage, indicate the owners of the company.

Constatine Gratsos was in the Greek shipping business and was known to be buying excess ships at the end of the war and transferring them to flags of other nations. Gratsos, however, was also known as Aristotle Onassis's man in America. Indeed, he represented Onassis on his business dealings, both private and public. But why should the true owners of the company be hidden? The answer is that Onassis was very intent on keeping all information about his dealings secret. He had a lot of trouble, including being investigated by governments. Later, in his second whaling operation, in 1950, his fleet was confiscated by the Panamanian government and sold to China. At other times, he had to pay fines for his dealings. In actuality, in the United States, it was illegal for a foreign national to own a whaling company. Onassis was trying to take advantage of the benefits the whaling industry had as a wartime business.

The business did not make a lot of money in 1943, because of the low number of whales taken. It is likely that, even though the Hoffmans were released of their mortgage when the title of the factory transferred to Hunter & Foland, the debt was not paid off. Dr. Raymond Gilmore, a biologist who had accompanied Richard Byrd to the Antarctic, spent a good deal of time at Fields Landing. He was an expert on whaling and contributed business and whale-processing ideas. In his notes, at the San Diego Natural History Museum, he expressed the opinion that Hunter & Foland were probably the only managers of Fields Landing that ever paid Onassis back on his investment. Aristotle Onassis was the money man behind the creation of Maritime Industries in 1943.

An accident in May 1949 at Fields Landing Whaling Station took the life of Lester Mann, when a cable under great tension in bringing a whale up the ramp broke and struck him. According to the *Santa Cruz Sentinel-News* of Sunday, March 27, 1949, Lester Mann, 37, was killed at the Fields Landing whale station near here, when a guy-wire broke a timber to strike him on the head

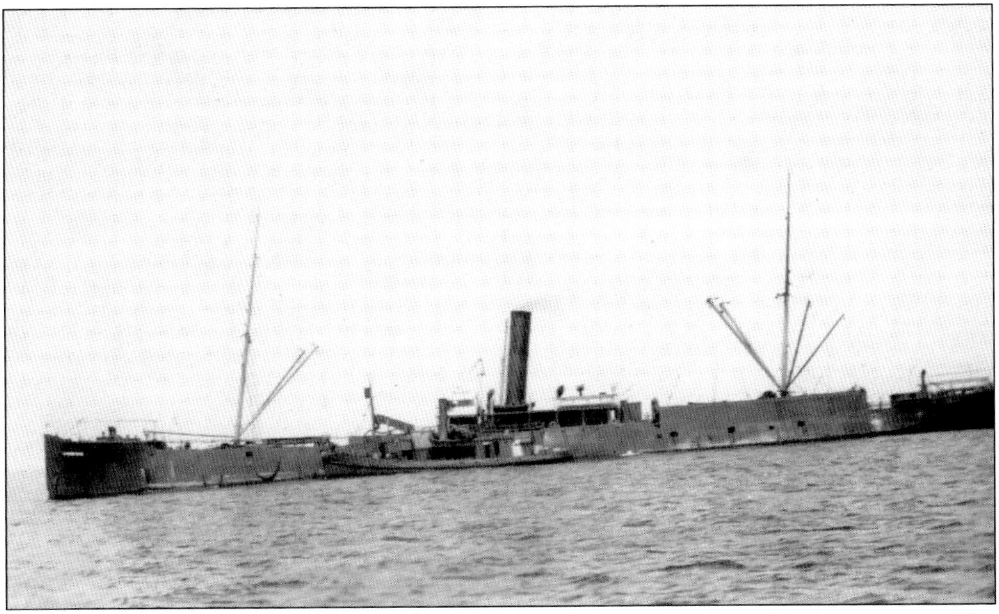

The mother ship SS *California* is at anchor, working whales in Southern California waters. The *California* usually worked from San Pedro in the channel to Catalina.

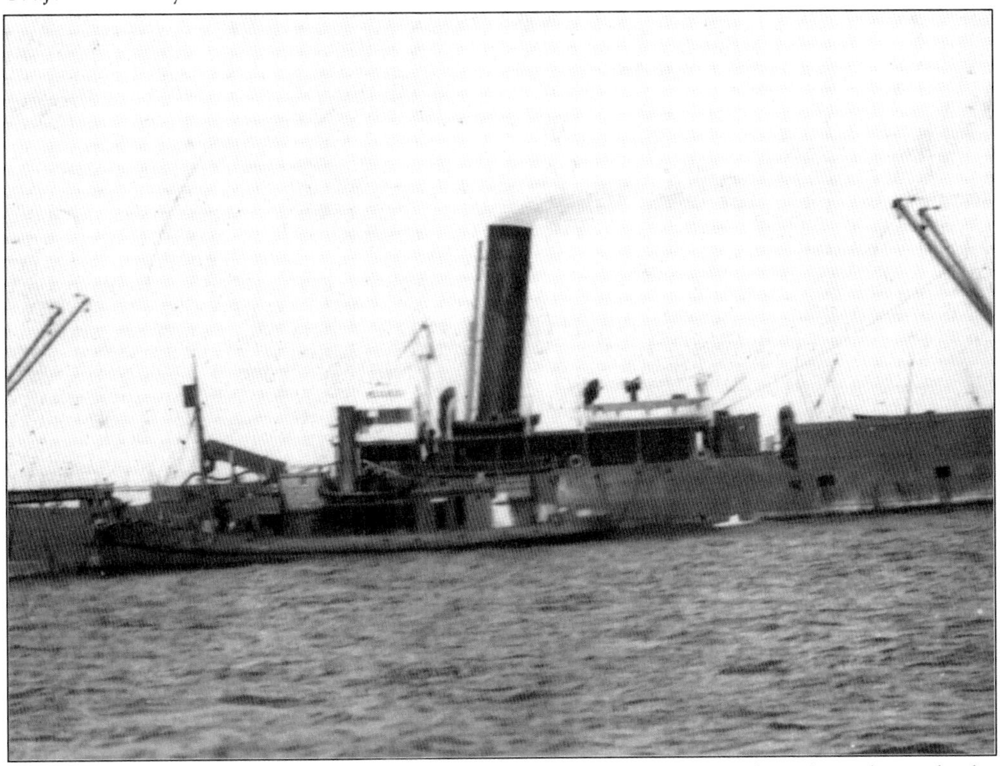

This is a close-up of the above photograph, showing the whaler *Hawk* tied up alongside the *California*, which would anchor near the whaling area. The SS *Hawk* and SS *Port Saunders* would hunt for whales and tow them back to the mother ship for processing. The *California* frequently anchored at Catalina for processing in calm waters.

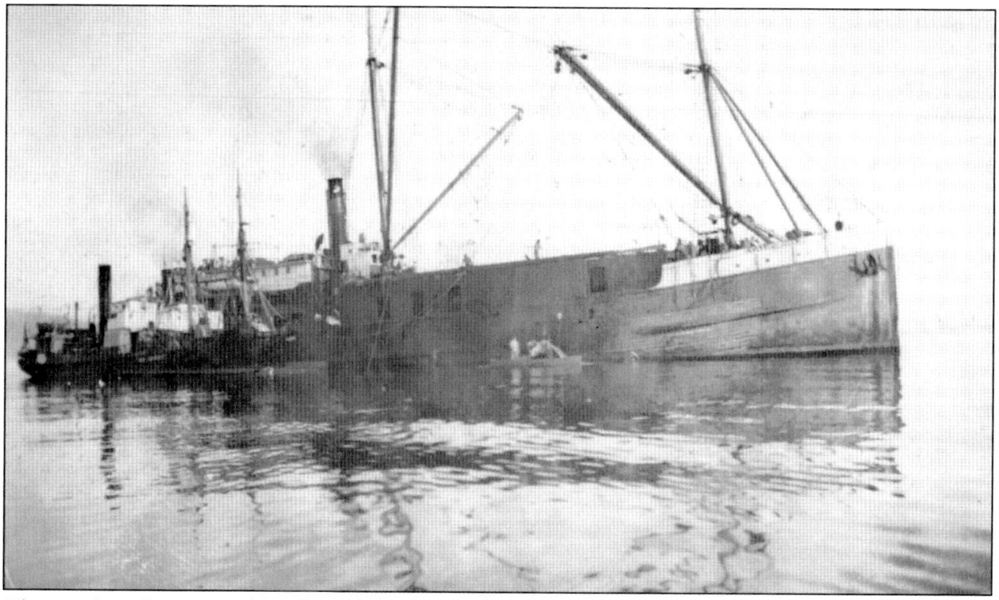

The mother ship is anchored, with both whalers, the SS *Port Saunders* and SS *Hawk*, tied up next to it. Also alongside the *California*, three men of the crew are in a small boat, flensing the whale in the water.

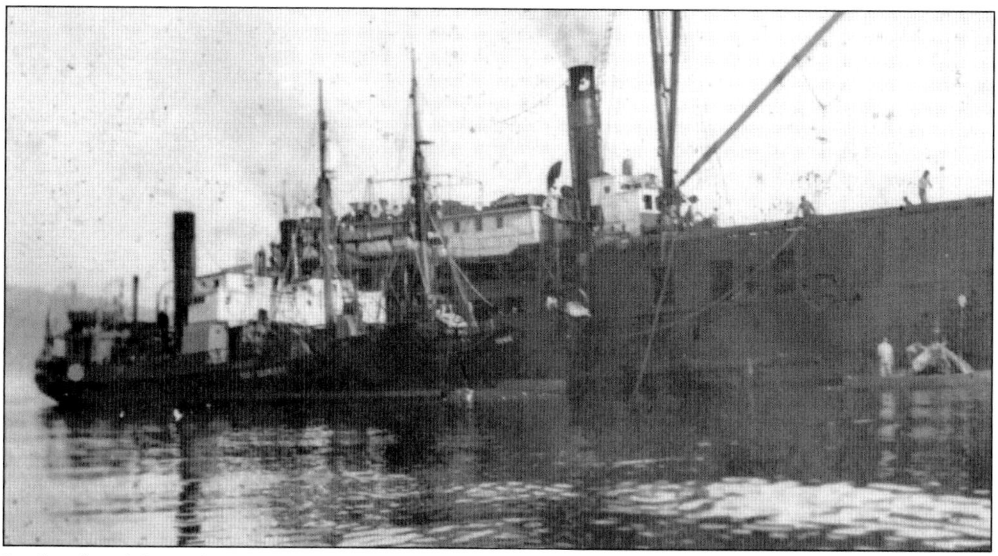

In this detail from the above photograph of the *California*, the SS *Port Saunders* is on the left, and the SS *Hawk* is on the right. Men of the crew are flensing the whale on the side of the mother ship. A tarp is draped on the side of the ship, where the parts of the whale will be hoisted aboard for final processing.

This is another view from the side of the SS *California*, with the men working on the whale. This method was used with factory ships that did not have a slipway. The pieces are hoisted aboard for final processing.

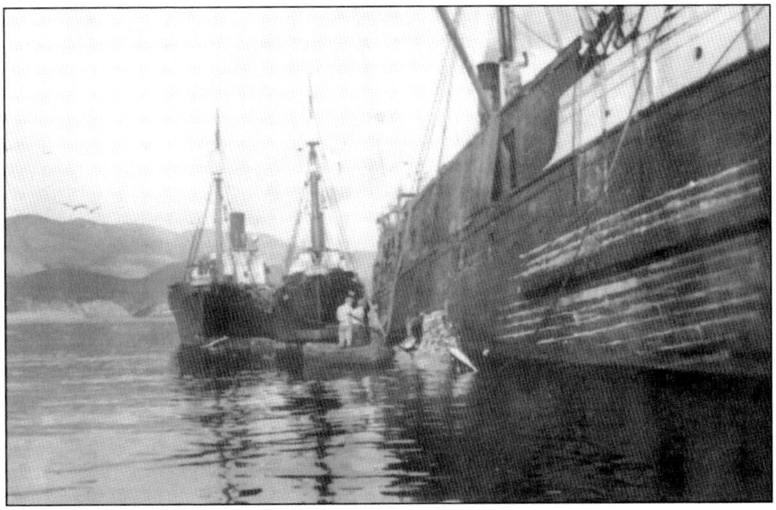

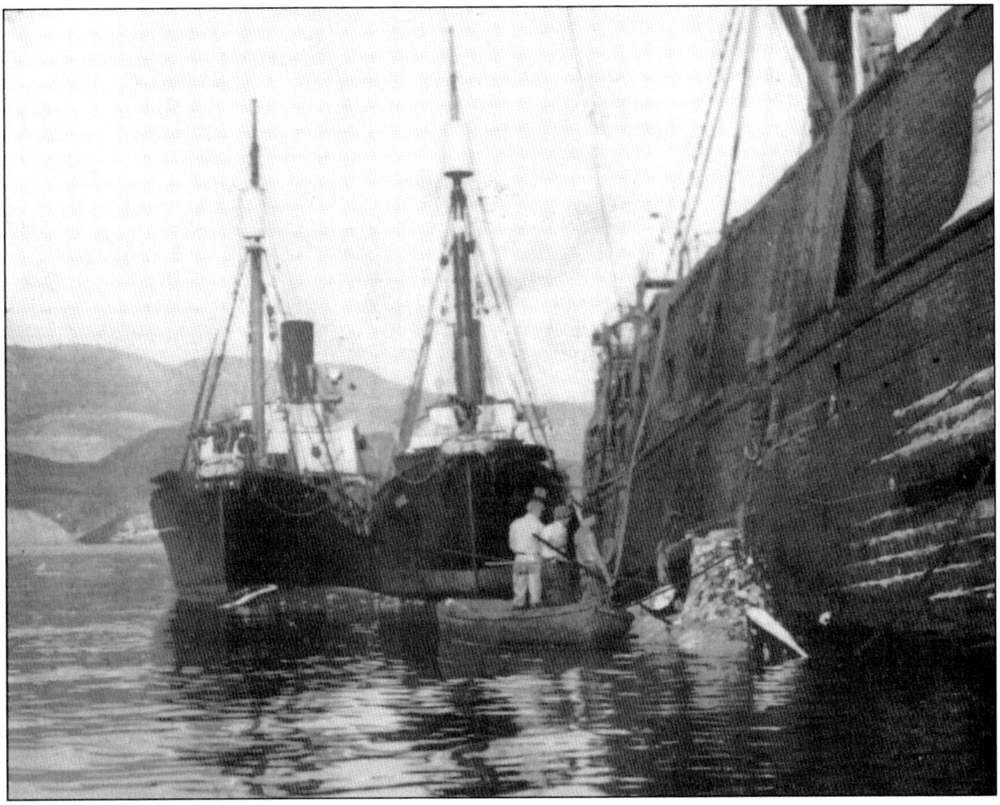

A close-up version of the above photograph shows in more detail the workers on the side of the *California*. The SS *Port Saunders* is on the left, and the SS *Hawk* is on the right. These two whalers, of Norwegian construction, were under British registry in Newfoundland when they were purchased. After they were purchased, the California Sea Products Company had to sue the Newfoundland Shipbuilding company to release the vessels. It literally took an act of Congress for the vessels to begin whaling. After the vessels were purchased, the laws were changed to no longer allow foreign-built bottoms to be used as whalers. Congress had to act to exempt the vessels before they were allowed to go whaling.

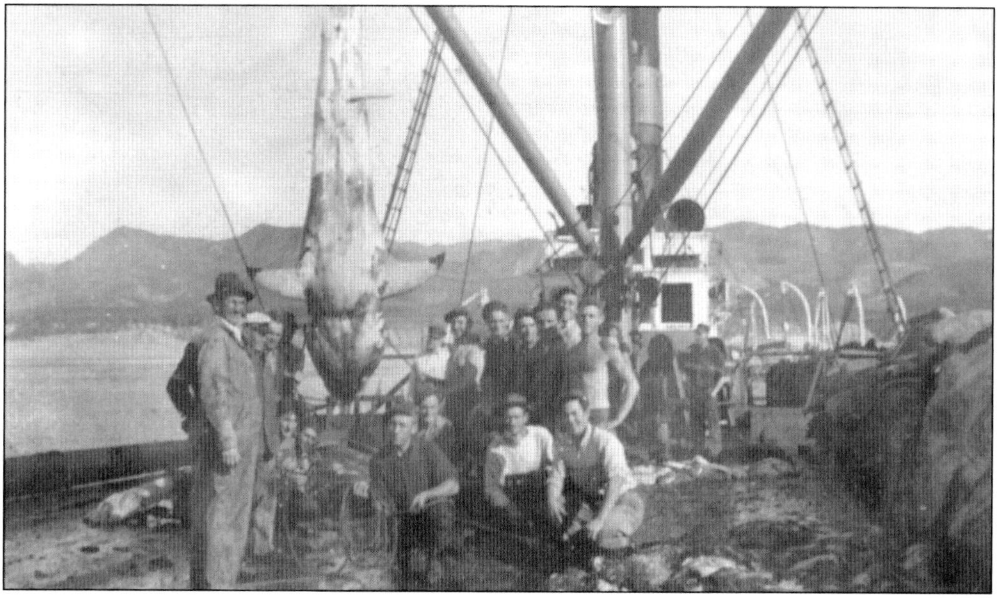

This photograph shows the flensing deck of the whaler *California*. A shark has been hoisted up by the crew. It may have been part of the contents of a whale's stomach. It certainly looks discolored or partly digested.

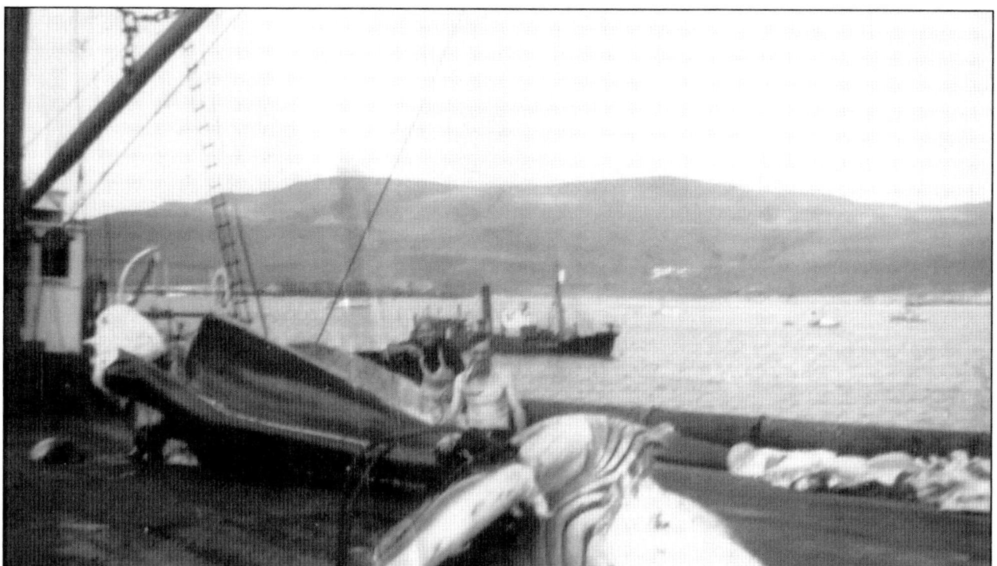

Here is a deck view of the SS *California* showing various parts of a whale. The SS *Port Saunders* is in the background.

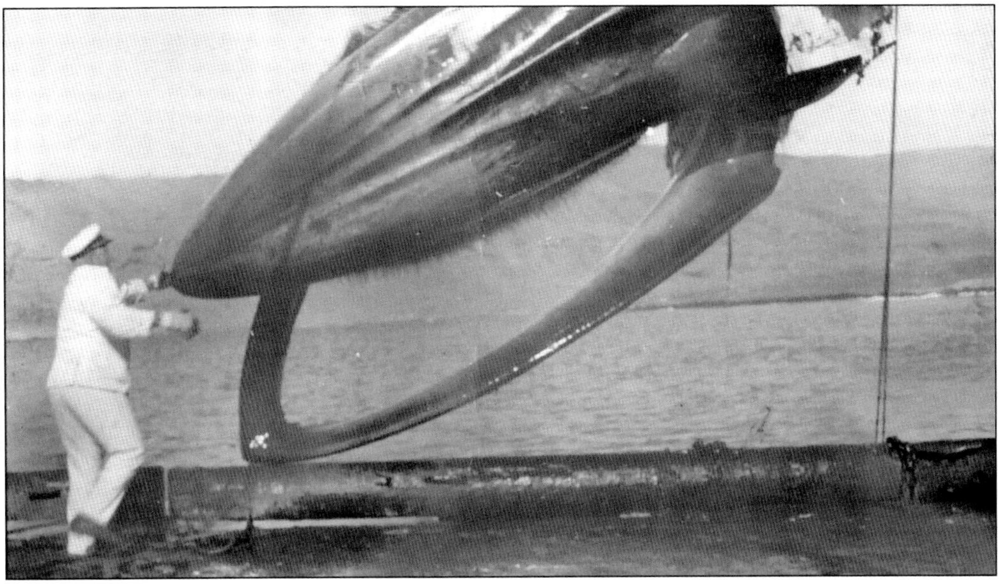

A winch is being used to move part of the head of a whale on board. Captain Dedrick has a hold on the tip of the head and is guiding the piece aboard.

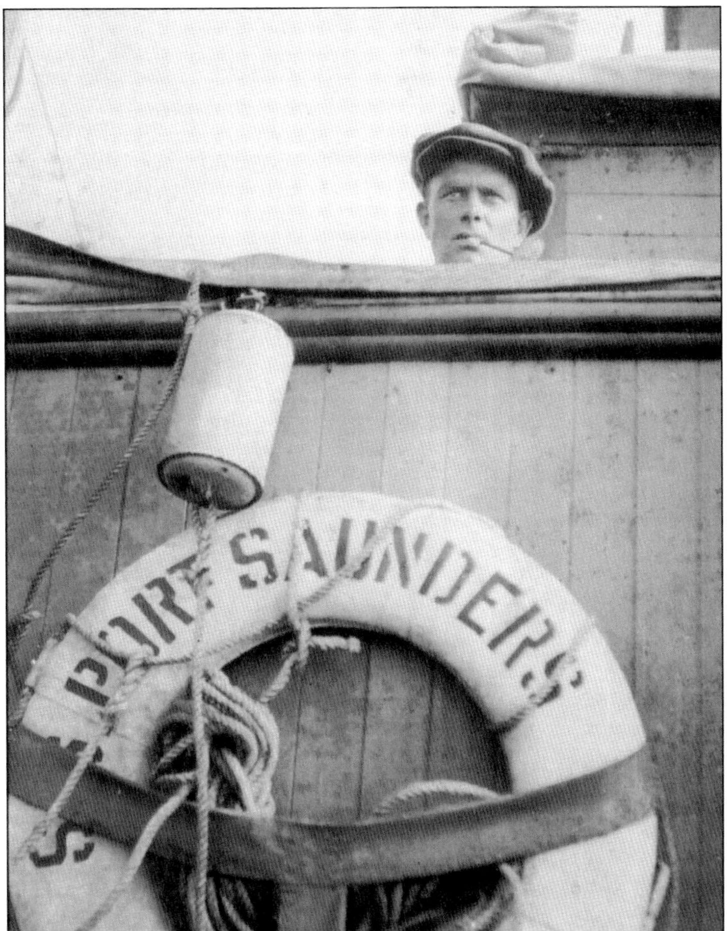

This photograph of part of the bridge of the SS *Port Saunders* shows the captain of the vessel.

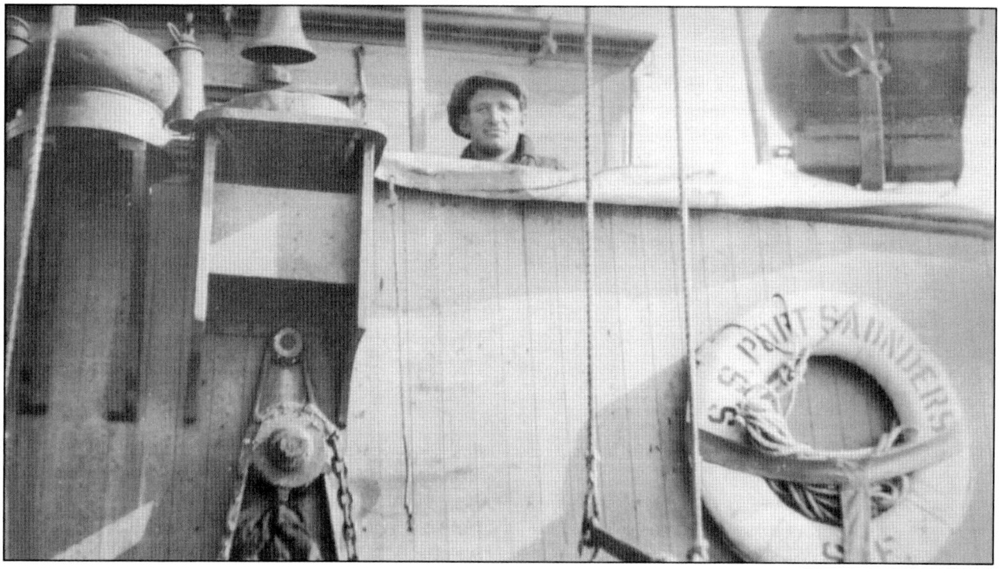

This is another view of part of the bridge of the SS *Port Saunders*. This crewman is assisting the captain of the vessel.

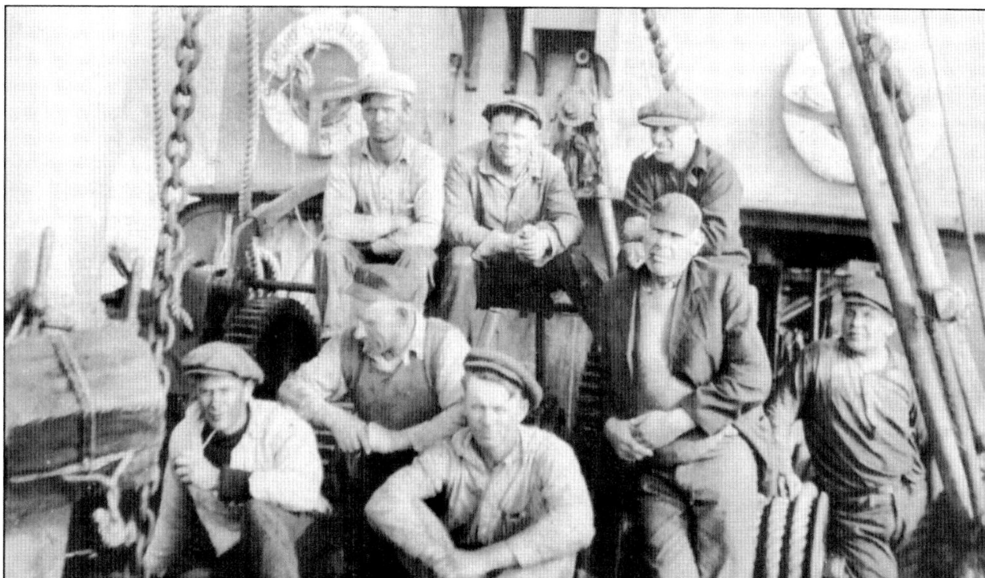

The crew of the *Port Saunders* is gathered forward of the bridge for a photograph.

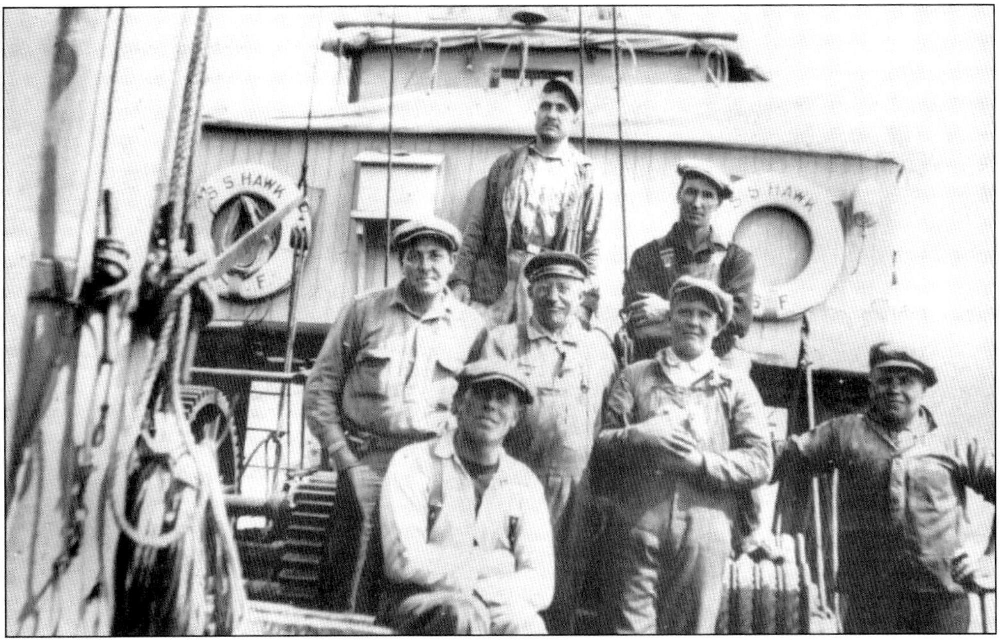

The crew of the SS *Hawk* is pictured at the winch on the bow of the whaler.

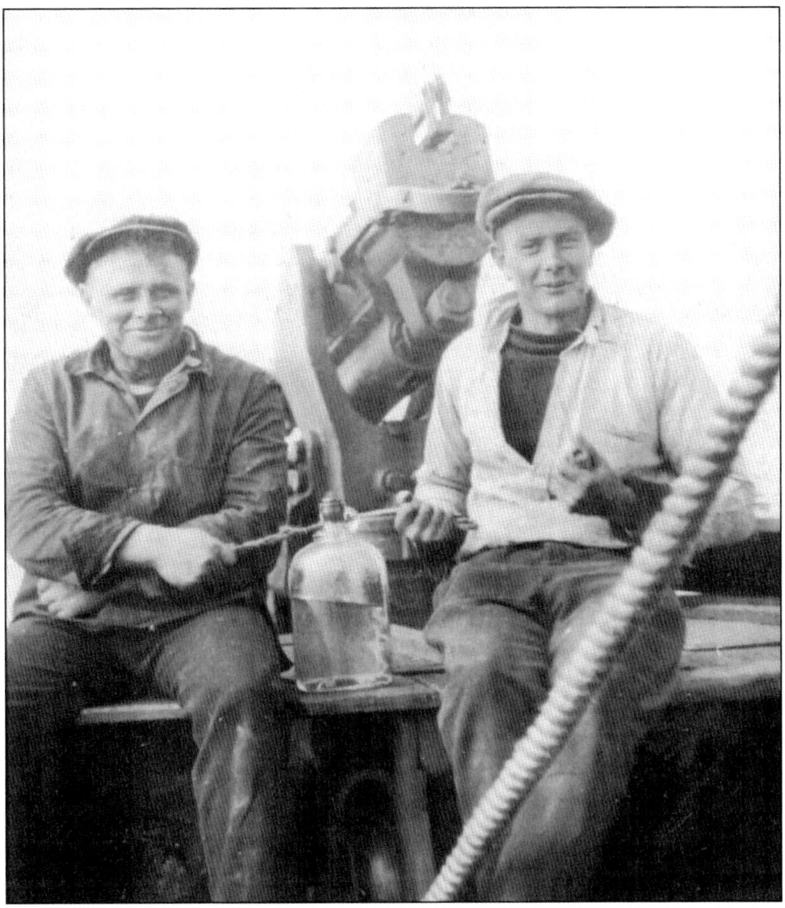

These two men of the SS *Port Saunders* are posing in front of the harpoon cannon. They also have a gallon jug, the contents of which may be alcohol.

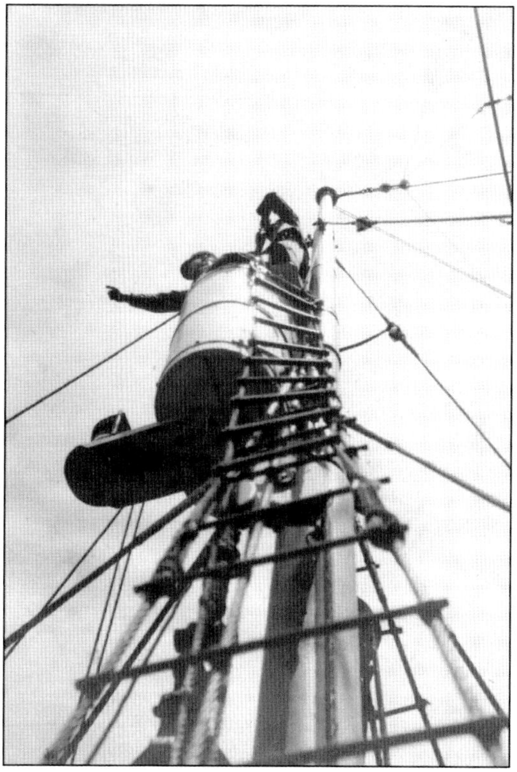

A lookout on one of the whalers is scanning the horizon for the telltale blow of a whale. The blow differs by species, and the lookouts can determine the species of whale and the direction it is going from far off.

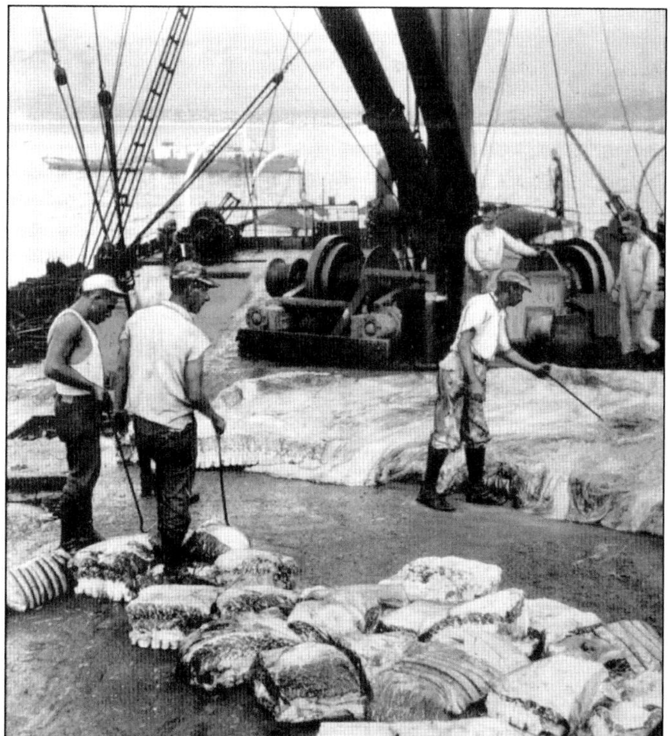

The blubber and meat are cut into small pieces that can be put through holes in the ship that lead to the cooking vats belowdecks. This photograph was taken by C.H. Townsend.

The SS *Hawk* is returning with whales to be processed on the mother ship, SS *California*. The *Hawk*, made in Norway, was purchased from a British whaling company. She whaled for the California Sea Products Company from 1919 to 1932, then California Sea Products from 1932 to 1936, then the San Francisco Sea Products Company from 1939 to 1942, and Maritime Industries from 1942 to 1945.

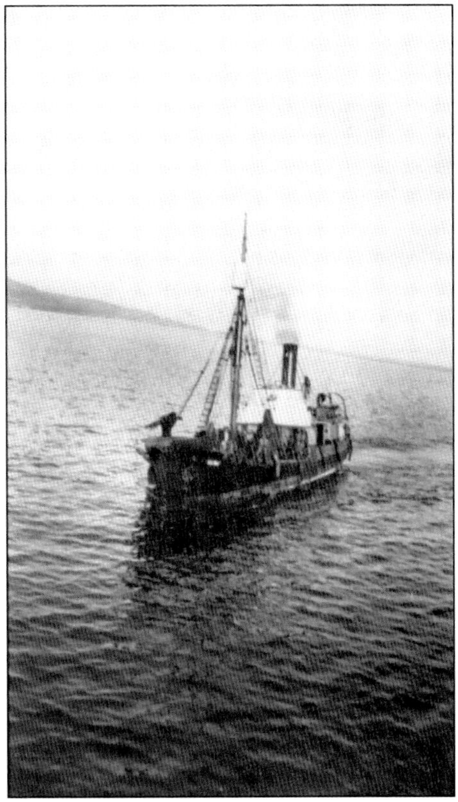

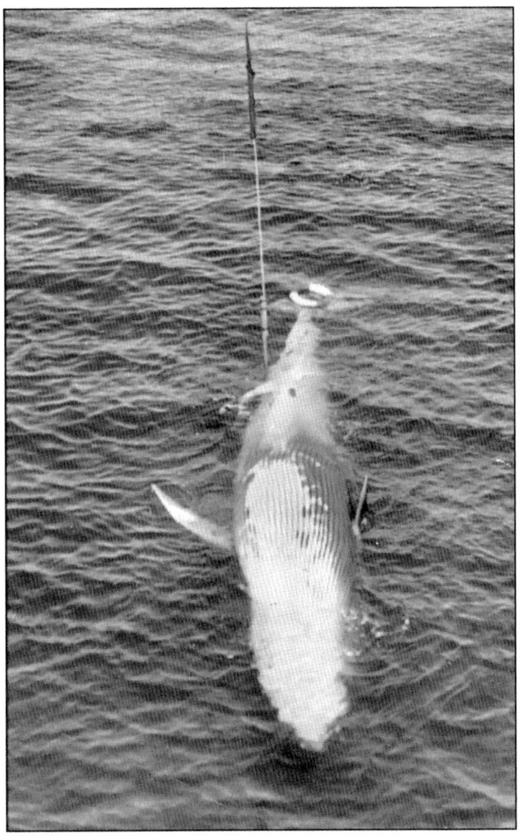

This whale is still tied out, with a flag in it. The float is attached near the tail. Regulations governed how long a whale could be kept before it was processed.

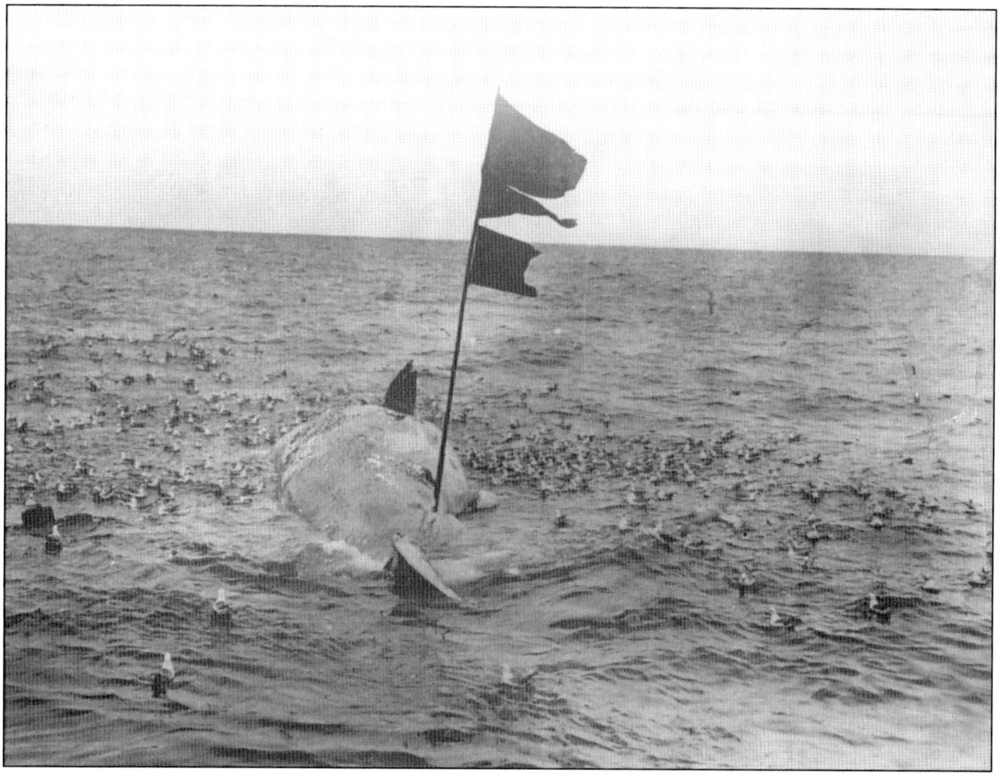

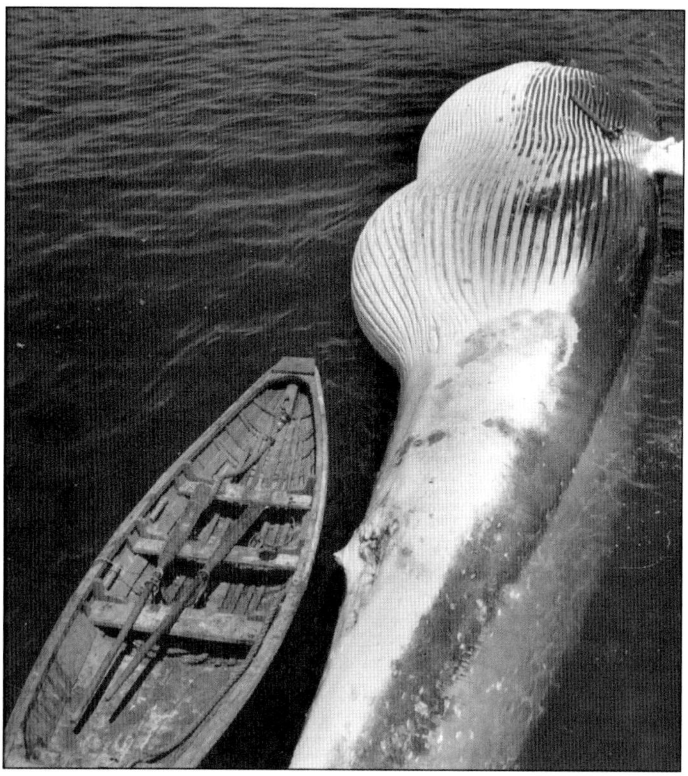

This whale has been inflated with air so it would stay afloat and then marked with a flag, which serves a couple of functions. First, it helps the whaler to relocate the whale; second, if there are other whalers in the area, it identifies the owners of the whale.

This whale is tied off at the factory ship. Soon, the crew of three men will get into the dinghy and start to remove the blubber from the whale and have it hoisted aboard. All of the whale will go onboard to be processed.

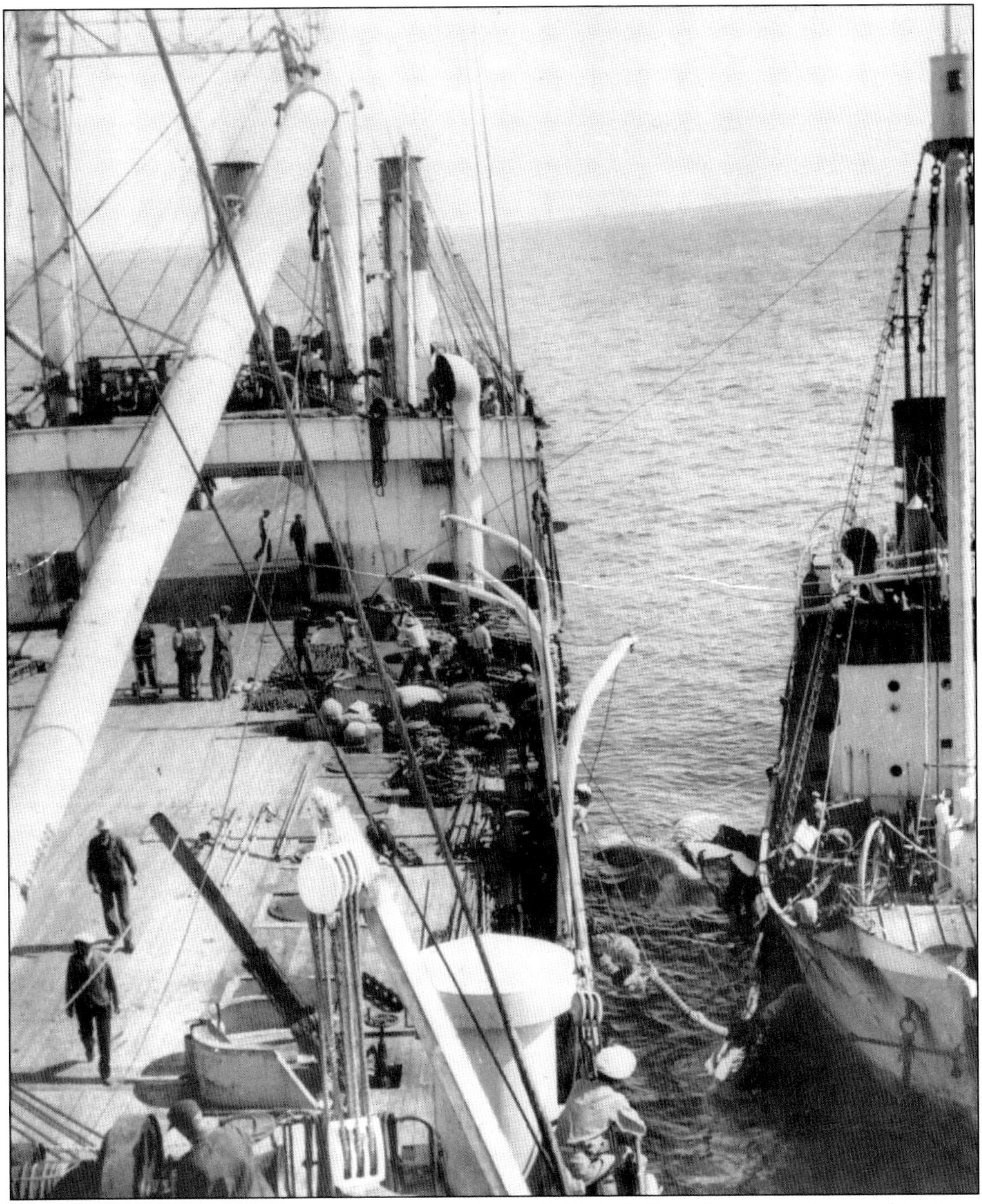

The California Whaling Company was not the only US whaling firm operating at this time. This is a photograph of the *Ulysses* and a whale killer of the American Whaling Company. The company ran into trouble for taking too many undersized whales. One account, from a whaling inspector, states, "The Ulysses Expedition of 1937–1938 was at sea ten months, cruised 30,000 miles, and obtained 191,030 barrels of oil from a kill of 3,600 whales."

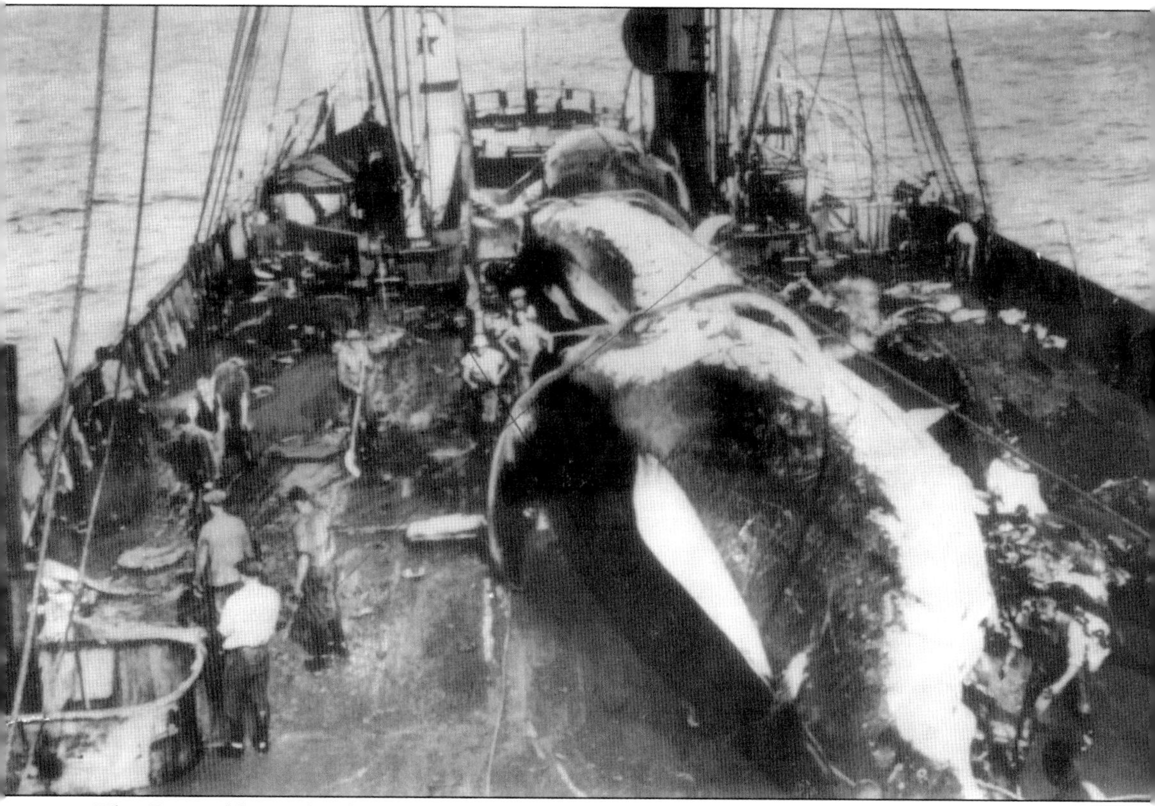

The *Frango* (shown here) and the *Ulysses* were taking undersized whales and restricted species at will, and both ships were suspected of whaling violations. The US Coast Guard inspector, Lt. Q.R. Walsh, reports: "The Frango Expedition of 1938 was at sea seven months, cruised 23,000 miles, and obtained 42,300 barrels of oil from a kill of 950 whales."

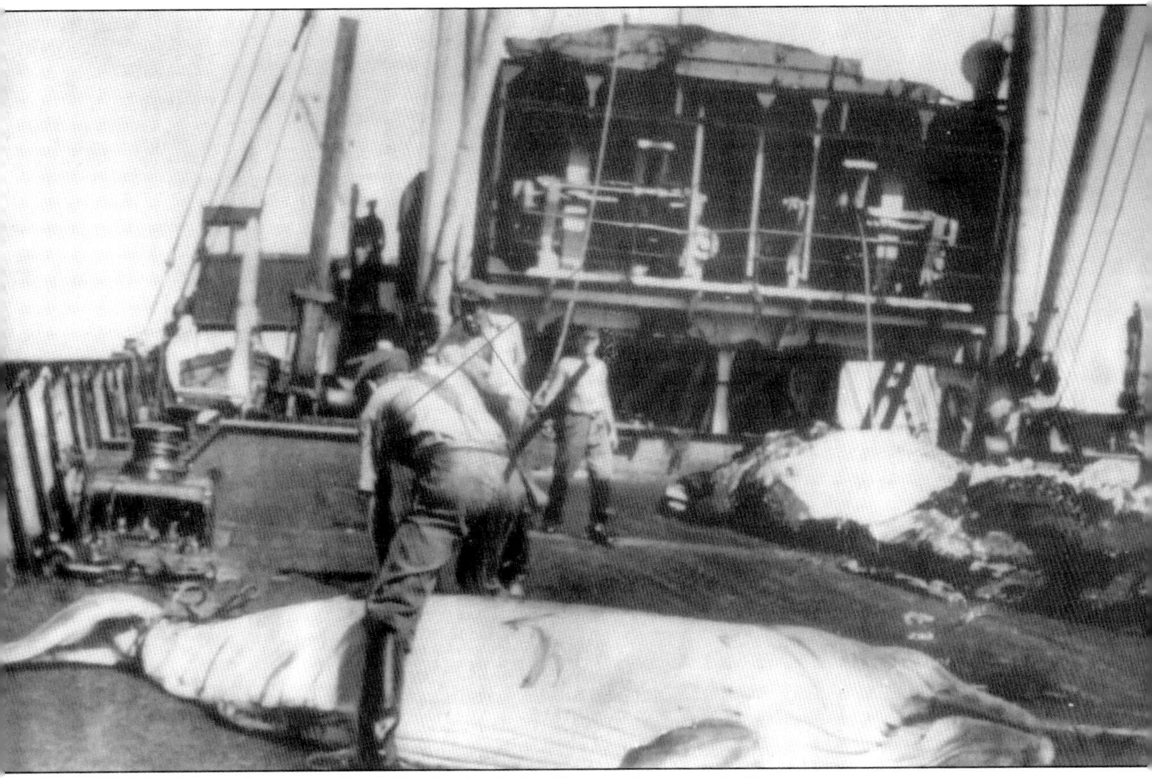

This is another photograph of the deck of the *Frango* during whaling season.

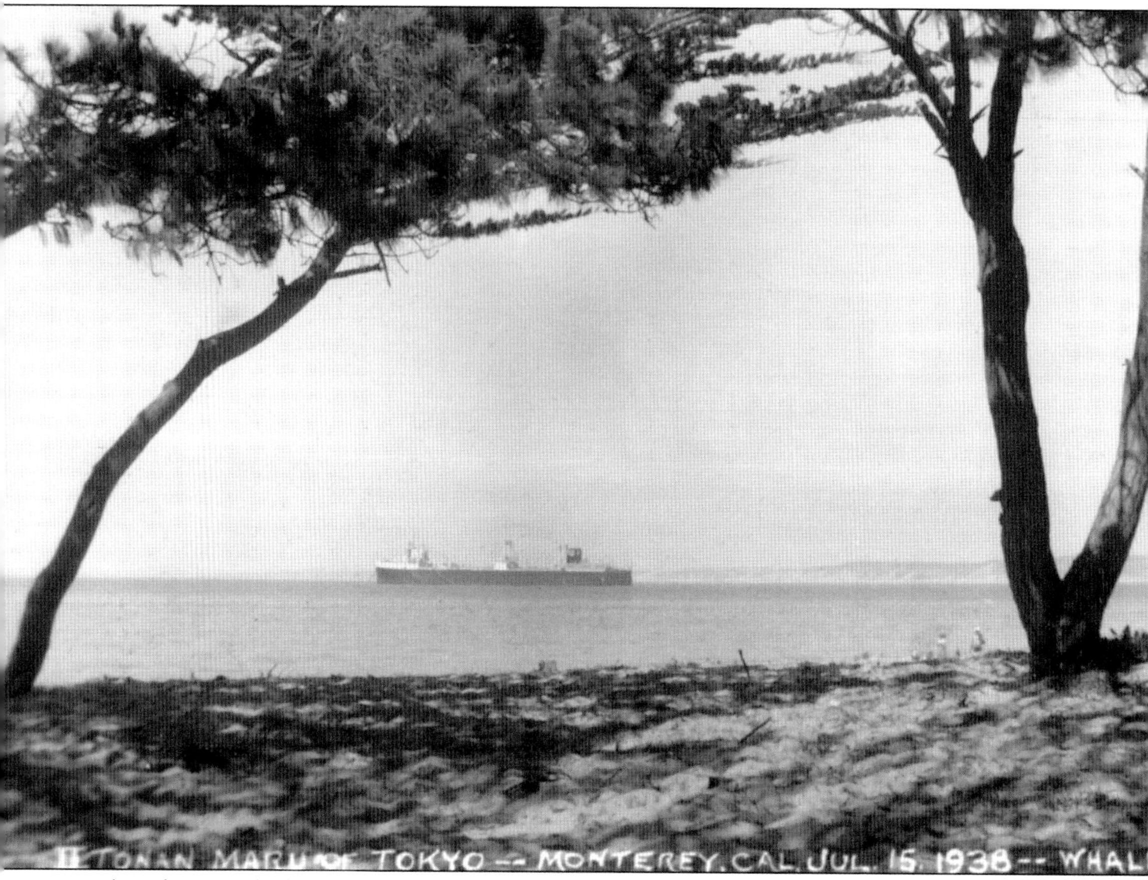

This photograph shows the *Tonan Maru II*, a Japanese ship, in waters just outside the United States' 12-mile limit. Even though the California Whaling Company was the only US company in California waters, it was not without competition. The Japanese fleet included this huge factory ship, as well as between 5 and 10 catchers in the water, too.

Seven

California Whaling from 1950 to 1971

At the end of the 1940s, the Fields Landing whaling station was managed by Gilbert "Gib" Hunter and Hermann Foland, who bought out the previous owners between the 1948 and 1949 seasons. They also owned the whale killers being used by the station.

In late 1949, the station was shut down for an indefinite period of time, a result of "controversial issues arising from the local community and involving state fish and game policies." The issue with the community was the terrible odor from the factory. The station suffered a fire, which destroyed the reduction and rendering operations of the plant in September.

The boats did not go out in mid-1950 when the plant was reopened. The company was having a record season when, in June, a second fire swept through the buildings and destroyed the equipment. The fire started in the oil-storage area and quickly spread to the entire structure. The blaze was so severe that the owners had no plan to continue the business.

After the plant shut down, the whaleboats fished locally. In early 1952, they were said to be going to the British Columbia whaling stations for the season. In mid-1953, it was announced that Hermann Foland would take the *Lynnanne* to Peru, where he managed a whaling station. At this time, Otto Weissich was negotiating with the Bay City government to reopen whaling near the location of a former whaling station from 30 years before. The Bay City station was unusable, so Weissich negotiated to use the Paragon plant.

The Del Monte Fishing Company of Richmond, California, inside San Francisco Bay, started whaling in May 1956. The plant was located across the channel from, and in view of, where whaling was carried on in 1939. Whales would be caught off the Farralones Islands and towed in the Golden Gate to Point San Pablo, to the former East Bay Fisheries sardine plant. The meat would be ground and sacked before being sold to cat-food and dog-food companies. Whale meat was marketed under the Moby Dick brand as pet food.

Converting the plant from sardine operations to a whaling facility would cost between $60,000 to $70,000. The improvements included a new 60-foot slipway for towing the whales from the water to the factory. The firm had to apply to the Army Corps of Engineers to obtain a permit to build the slipway. Other upgrades included winches for moving the whales around, and two refrigeration systems to keep the meat cold until it was transferred by truck to the National Ice and Cold Storage facility, where the sacks would be frozen.

The initial officers of the corporation were the following: A. Caito, president; Otto Weissich, vice president and assistant secretary; W.O. Weissich Jr., vice president; Antone E. Trapani, secretary-treasurer; and John Caito, superintendent of the plant (nephew of A. Caito). Otto Weissich figured prominently in the California Whaling Company, which was dissolved in 1936. Its offices were located at 356 Clay Street in San Francisco.

The bones, blubber, and anything else left over were transferred to the Independent Renderers, run by Renato E. Ricco, sole owner and manager. The whaling vessels were the *Dennis Gayle* and *Donna Mae*, former hunters for the Hunter & Foland plant in Eureka.

When whaling resumed, it accounted for a take of 145 whales in 1956. The Del Monte plant in 1956 and 1957 was devoted to cutting out prime cuts of meat, which would be ground, bagged, and frozen for sale to farms as mink food. A whale biologist named Dr. Raymond Gilmore started appearing in newspaper columns around the country, promoting the use of whale meat for human consumption. Called a whale enthusiast, he predicted that "whale meat should rank with beef and lamb as a table meat, but at the moment it is generally for animal food."

In November 1957, "Gib" Hunter of Hunter & Foland provided a recently killed whale on a flatbed truck, which was paraded down Market Street in San Francisco for the 1957 Fish Parade. The whale meat was used as pet food, due to a low supply of horsemeat at this time. The oil was sold to Europe, where it was used for margarine and cooking fats.

For the 1958 season, the Golden Gate Fishing Company began operations from Richmond. The president of the company was Leon Barlas, who had been the vice president and general manager of Hermann & Foland. He had recently returned from Peru. Robert Casebeer, who also worked in Peru, was superintendent at Golden Gate and the night superintendent for Del Monte Fishing Company.

The Golden Gate Fishing Company used the old Pittsburgh Packers building on Point San Pablo for processing. The meat was frozen and packaged and sold to mink farms. The flensing was done at this plant, with the blubber and meat going to the Independent Renderers and meat being frozen and sent to mink farmers. The operation used Hermann Foland's *Lynnanne* killer ship for catching whales.

In 1959, concern was raised about the two companies' "dumping of blubber wastes" in San Francisco Bay, along the Richmond shore.

By 1960, Del Monte Fishing Company, in its fourth year of operation, was sending out three boats for whales: *Dennis Gayle*, *Donna Mae*, and the *Allen Cody*. In the 1960 season, the catch was 169 whales: 10 sperm, 20 sei, 3 blue, 59 finback, 76 humpback, and 1 bottlenose. The Golden Gate Fishing Company, in its second year, with two boats, shipped 1.5 million pounds of frozen whale meat to Los Angeles.

These operations must have been fairly profitable, as Del Monte Fisheries purchased the sardine reduction plant, Edible Fish Meal and Oil Company, from Alex Imlach in 1960. A group from Golden Gate Fisheries, under the name of Pacific Sea Products, was again discussing reopening the Gray's Harbor, Washington, location with the Hoquiam, Washington, city government.

Whaling continued year after year, with the total catch diminishing each year. In 1967, the Golden Gate Fishing Company did not continue whaling and closed down its operation. The Del Monte Corporation continued to operate through the end of the 1971 season.

One morning, the whalers woke up to hear that their jobs had been terminated. The morning news was reporting that Maurice H. Stans, secretary of commerce in the Nixon administration, ordered a total ban on all whaling on March 1. He did this after former interior secretary Walter Hickel put all whales on the endangered species list.

The whalers agreed that some of the whales needed conservation, but there were other species that did not warrant being placed on the endangered species list. There were even a few species that had never been hunted. Del Monte Corporation requested a hearing, but the die had been cast. Stans was not going to issue a whaling license to anyone. The whalers were bitter, because the order had been handed down without any advance notice. The whalers were upset because they were out of a job, and the companies were upset because they felt their investment in the business had just vanished.

A Department of Commerce spokesman said Stans could renew Del Monte's license, "but has definitely stated he will not." Dale Rice, a federal government marine researcher, said the government wants to permit whales to replenish themselves, "and presumably the government will allow hunting again after the herds have built themselves back up to the optimum levels." He estimated this could take 50 to 100 years. Commerce Secretary Stans's ban included the importation of whale meat and oil.

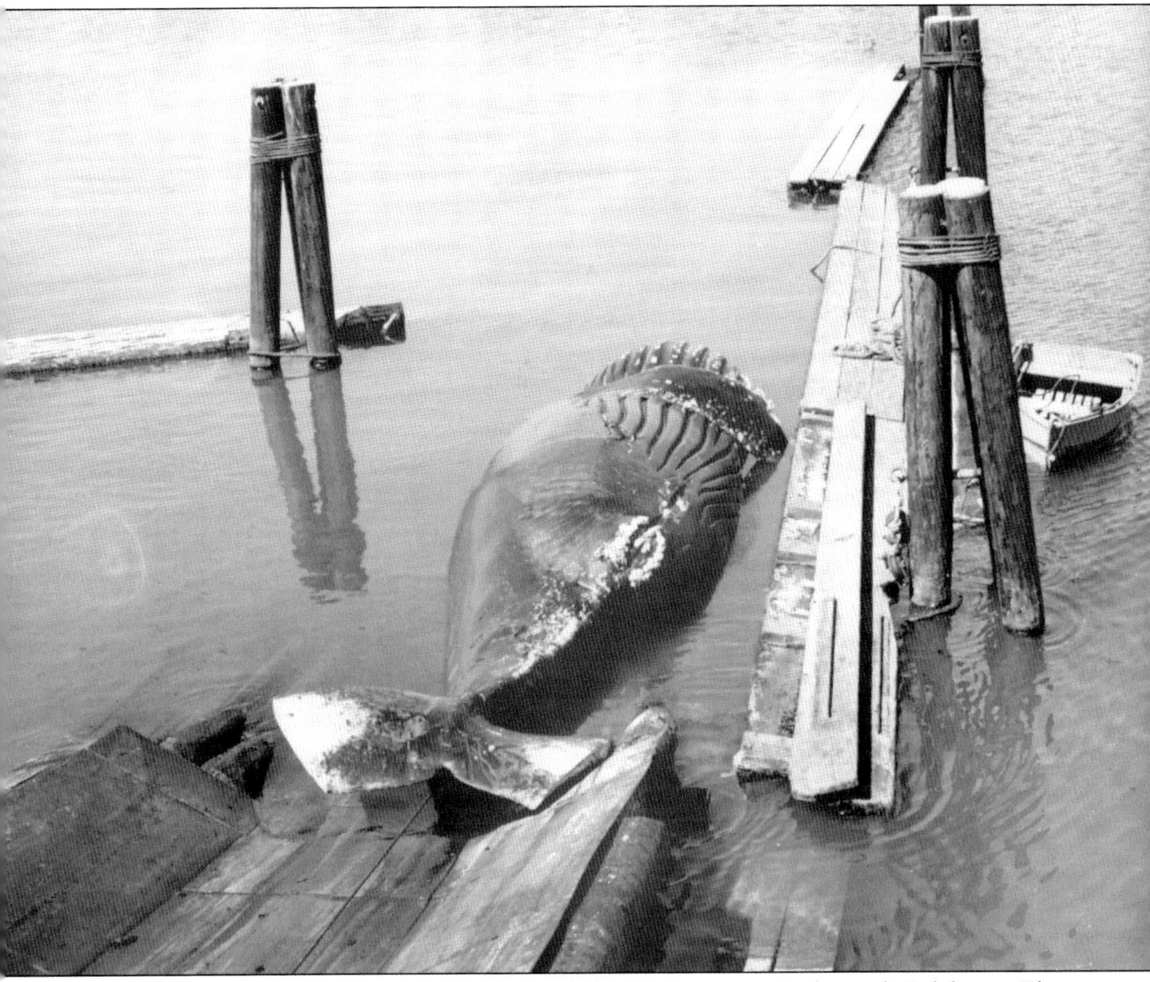

Here is a humpback whale at the Del Monte Whaling Company in Richmond, California. The company was the only firm in the United States still whaling when the hunt was shut down. It did not get a license to go whaling in 1972. In contrast, in 1971, Russia had a quota of 10,000 whales, and Japan's quota was 9,500. Del Monte's quota would have been 166. Maurice Stans made the call to not issue the US quota.

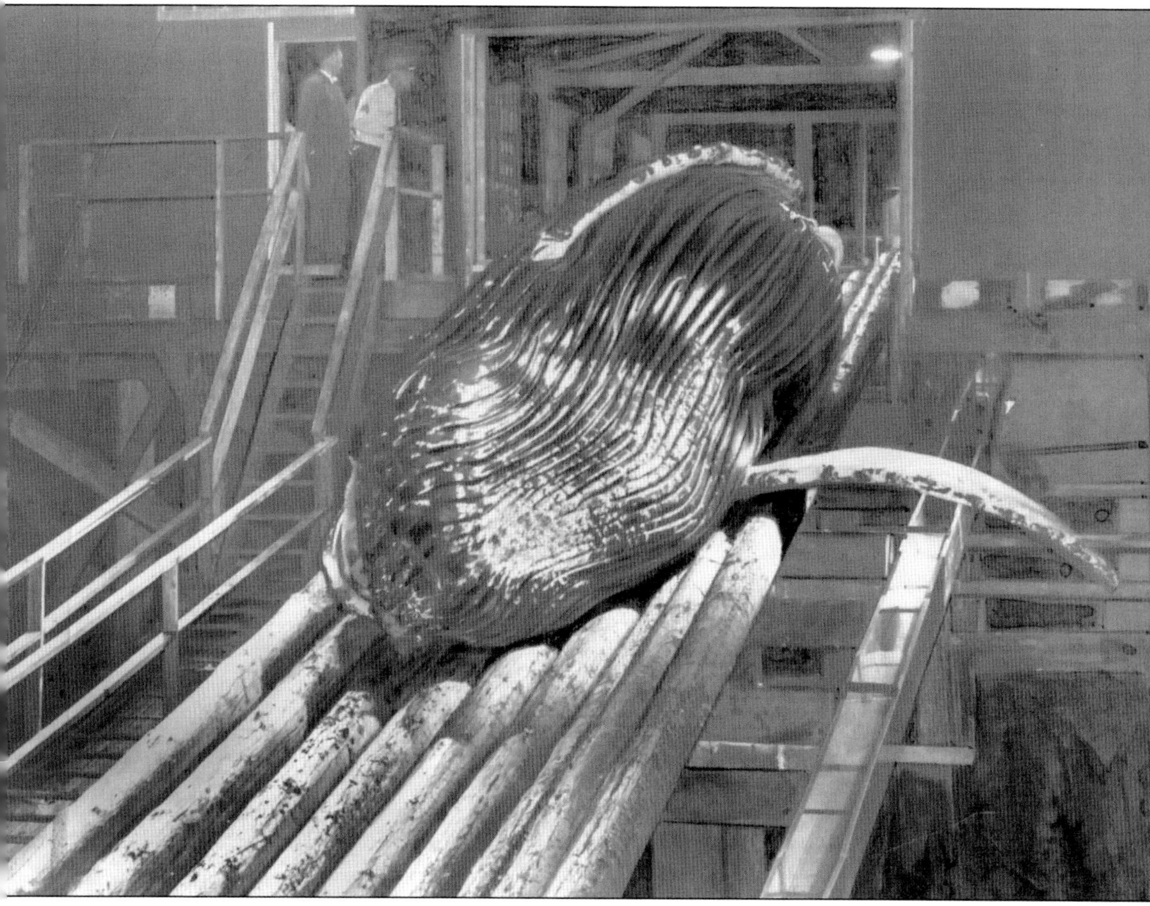

Here, the humpback whale continues up the ramp into the Del Monte plant. The factory burned down a few years later. Some pilings are what remains of the once "last whaling station in the United States."

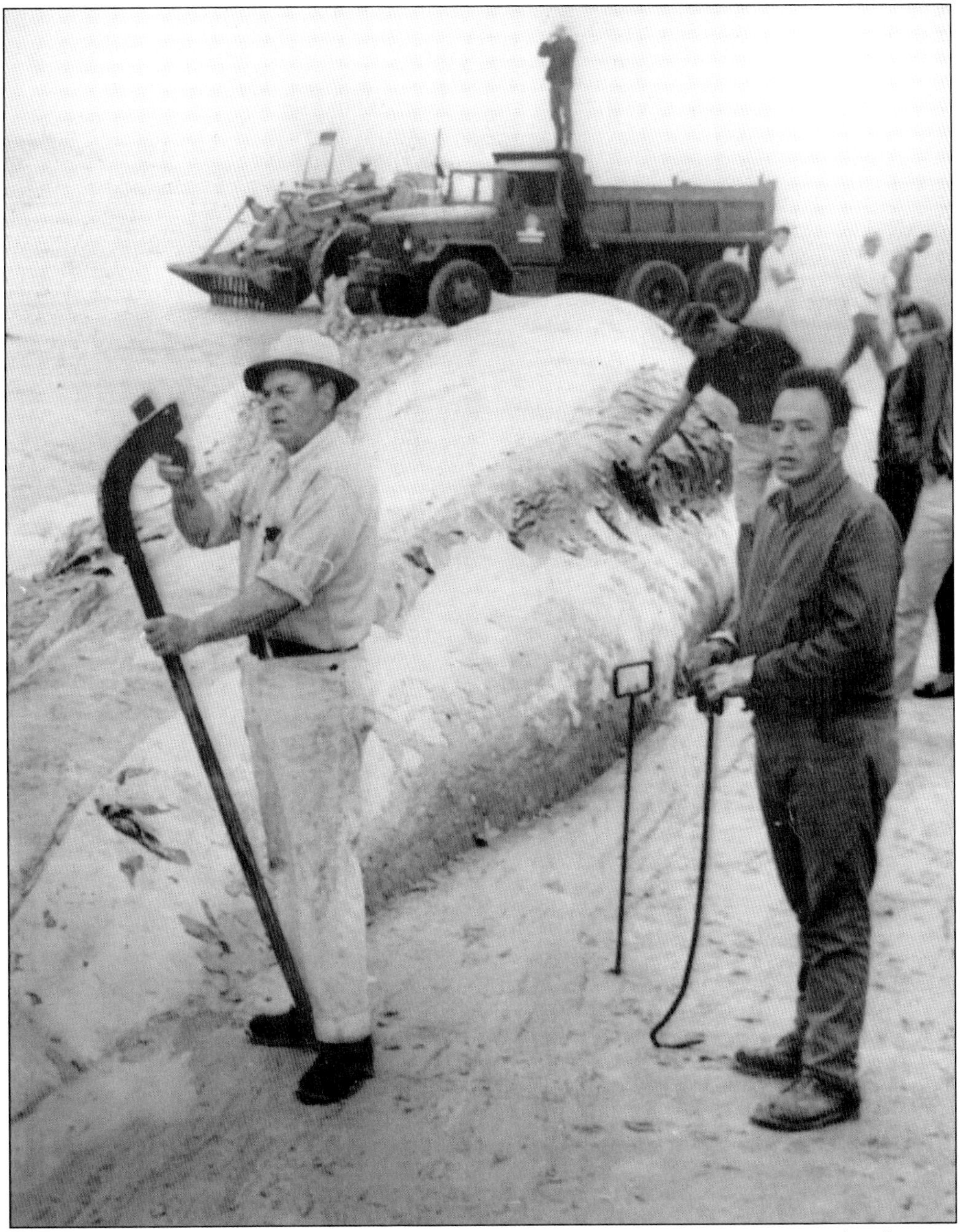

Dr. Raymond Gilmore (left) is seen here with a stranded blue whale. He is preparing his flensing knife to begin cutting the whale in order to acquire various body parts for analysis on why the whale died. He was a whale biologist and friend at the various whaling stations on the West Coast beginning in the 1940 at Fields Landing, and then at Del Monte and Golden Gate Fisheries. He visited the stations and gave advice on whales, processing, and marketing technology. Gilmore was one of the first researchers to take a census of gray whales. He was an associate curator of mammals at the National Museum in Washington and later headed whale research for the US Fish and Wildlife Service, first in San Francisco and then, in 1952 in San Diego, on the Scripps campus.

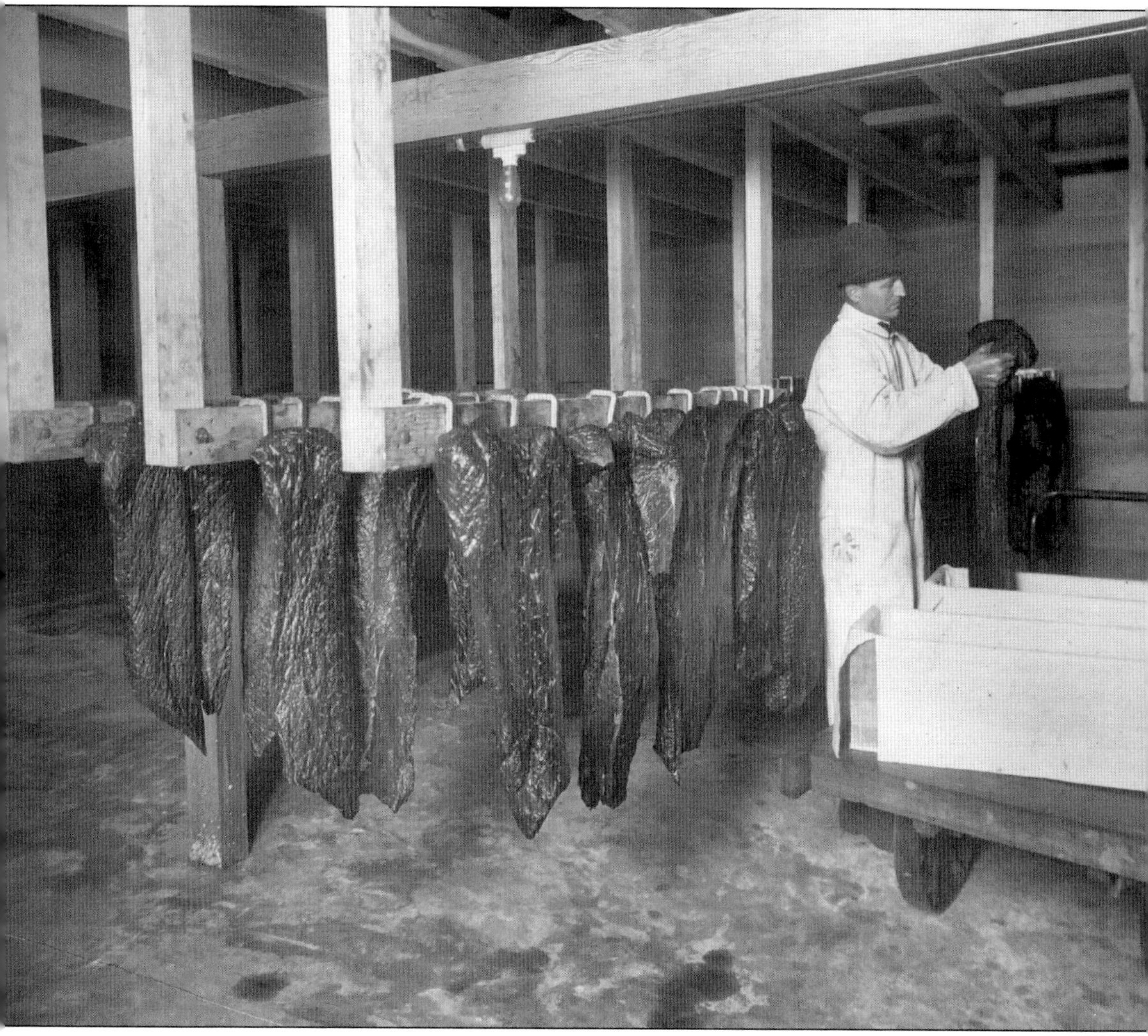

Most of the whaling stations experimented with harvesting and selling whale meat for human consumption. The US government supported the sales and distribution of whale meat during World Wars I and II. The meat had a fair consumption during the war years, when other meats were not available. The government even issued documents with whale-meat recipes and instructions for its preparation. The Catholic Church even said that whale meat was not "meat" for the purpose of Friday restrictions. After the wars were over and other meats were back on the market, interest in whale meat waned.

The Philadelphia Zoo bought whale meat in 1958 for its lion, due to a shortage of horsemeat. This lion seems to enjoy a different taste for a change.

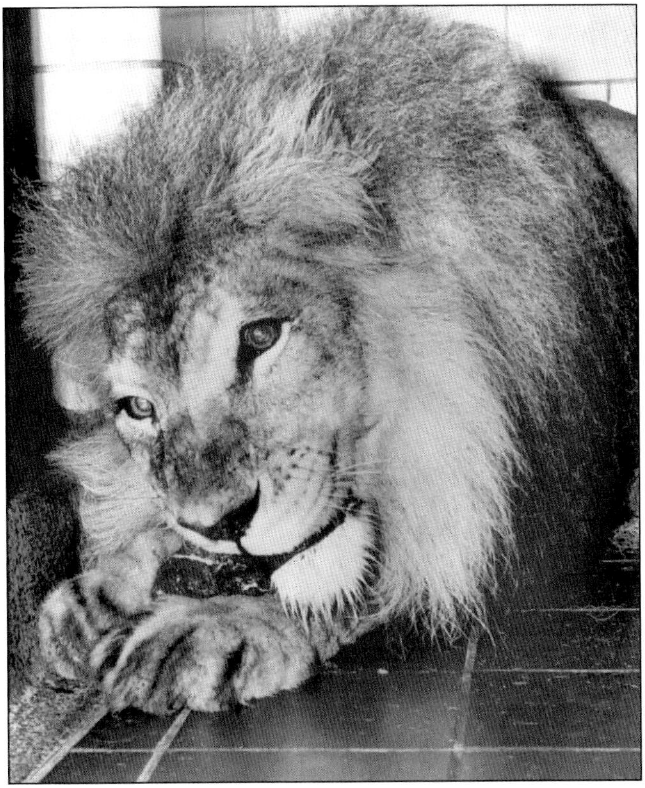

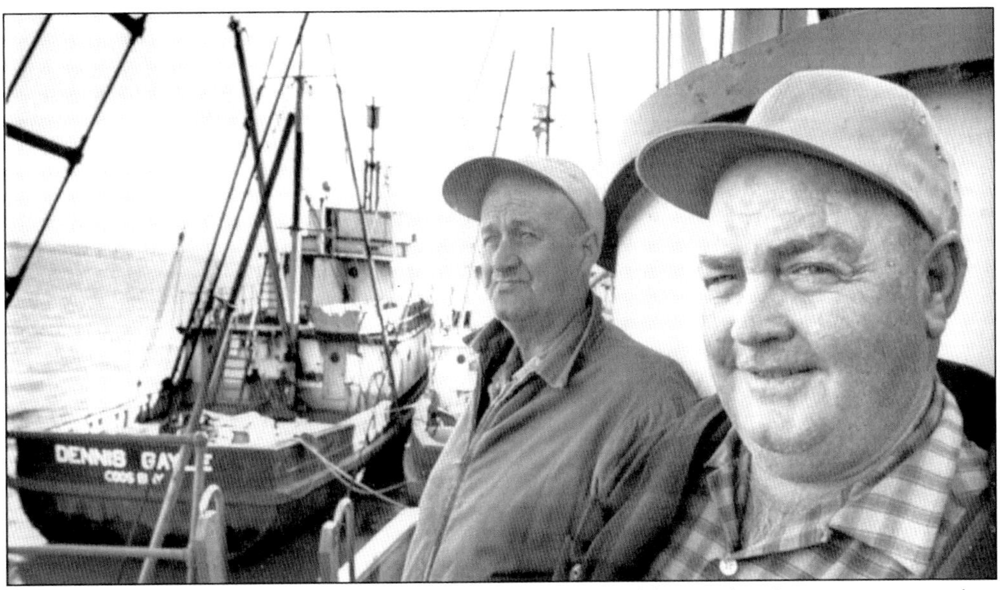

With the closing of whaling in 1972, this photograph was widely circulated in newspapers in late January 1972. The whalemen are Leo Lady (right), skipper of the vessel *Donna Mae*, and whaler Lloyd Uhl. They became poster boys for the Del Monte Whaling Company. The article in the *Daily Review* of Hayward, California, read, "America's whaling industry has sunk into the pages of history, harpooned by government edict. . . . The ending was quiet: The last harpoon has been launched, the last whale towed into the San Francisco Bay port."

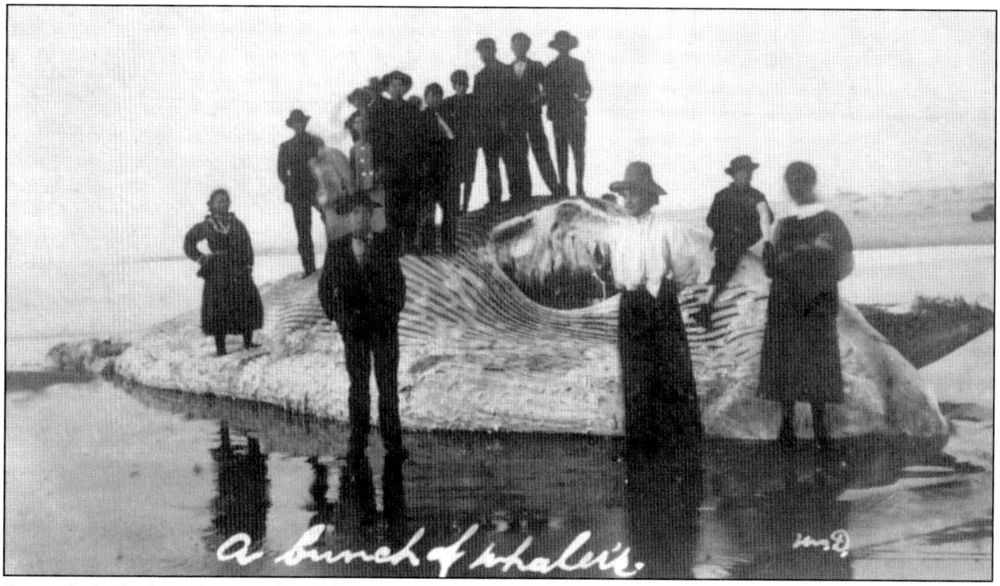

Stranded whales, alive or dead, have always been of interest to people living around or visiting the sea. This c. 1900 photograph shows the dress of the time, as well as people's desire to stand on dead whales.

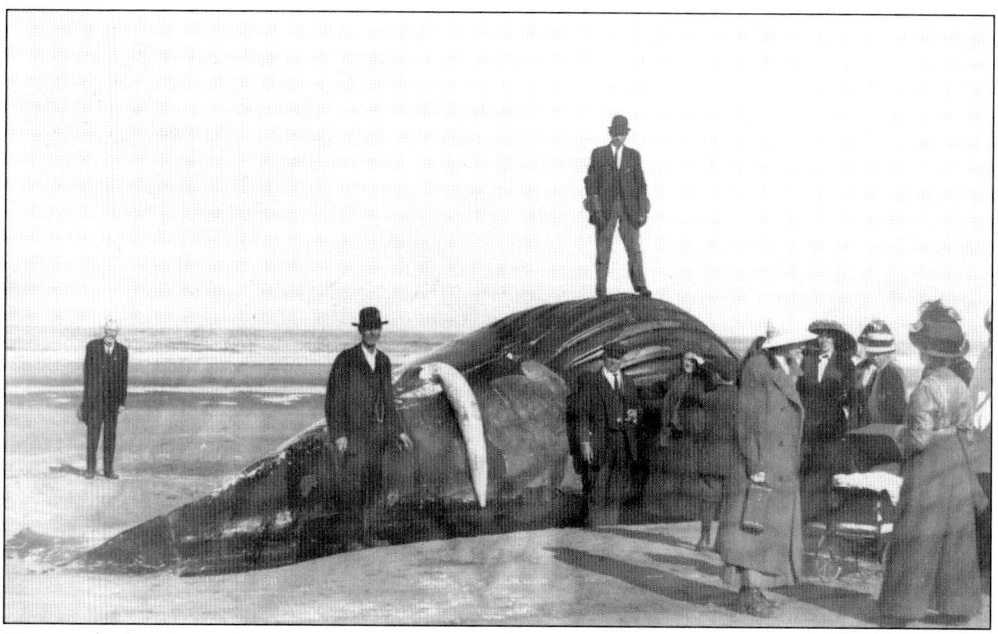

Here, onlookers have their photograph taken with a male whale.

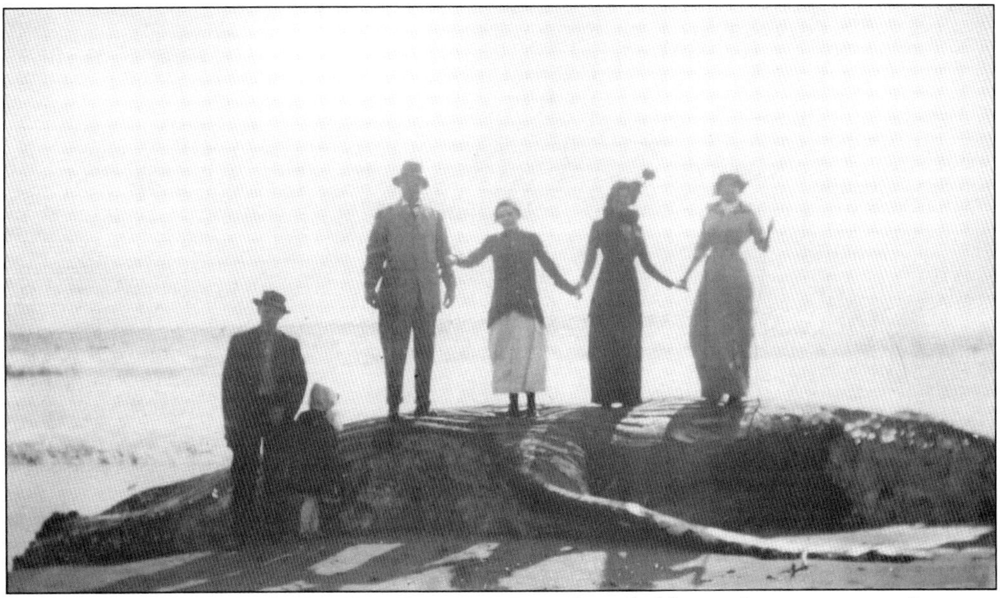

In this photograph, three women, two men, and a child stand next to—and on—a humpback whale.

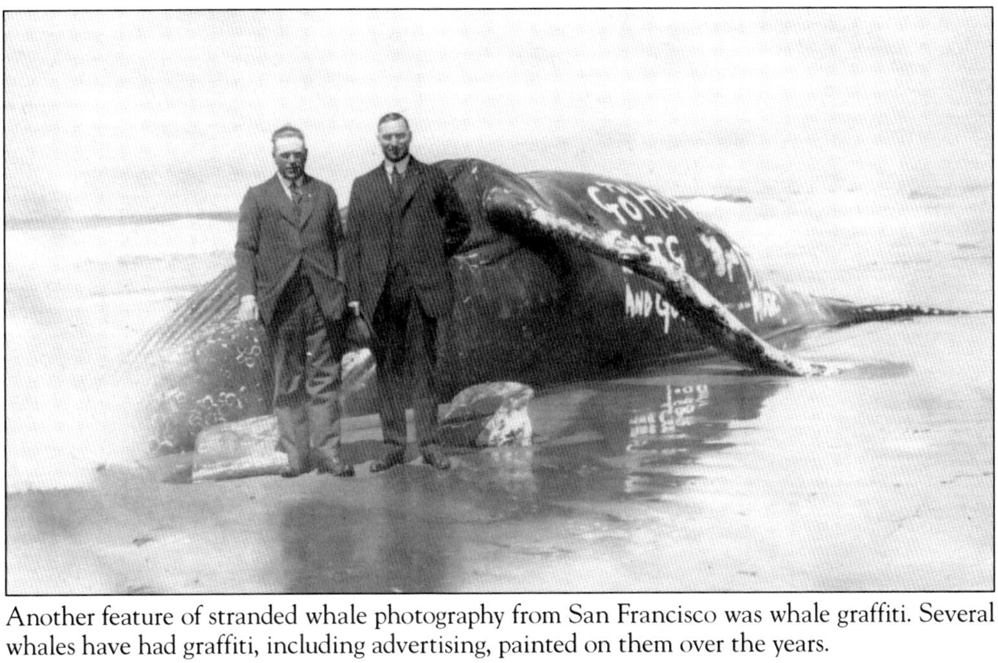

Another feature of stranded whale photography from San Francisco was whale graffiti. Several whales have had graffiti, including advertising, painted on them over the years.

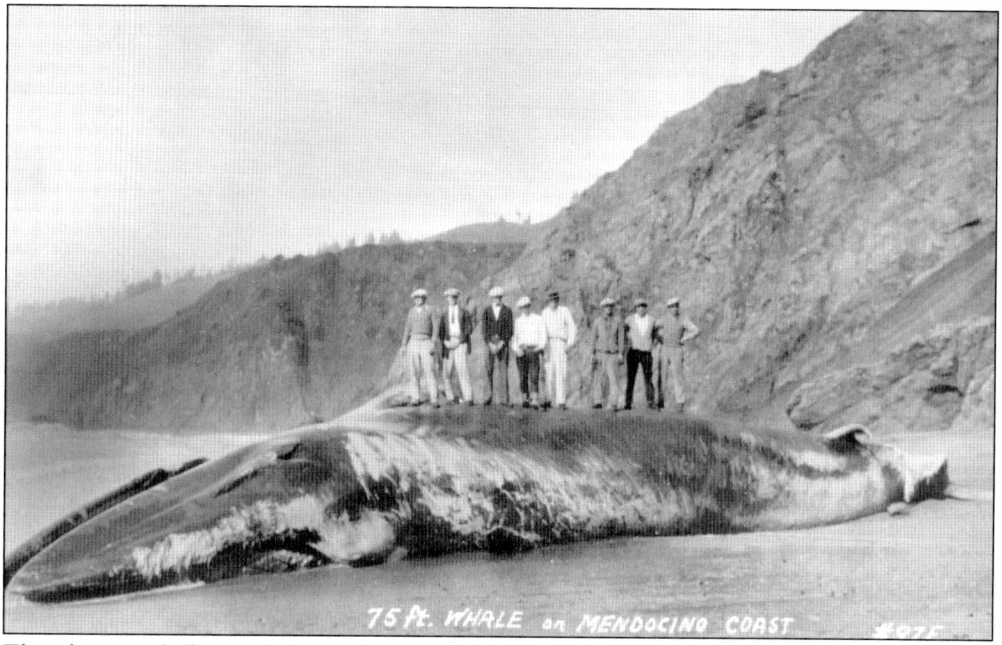

This photograph shows a 75-foot whale stranded in the Mendocino area of Northern California. There are eight men standing on the whale, looking like they just came in from a round of golf. Or perhaps they just bought their hats at the same place.

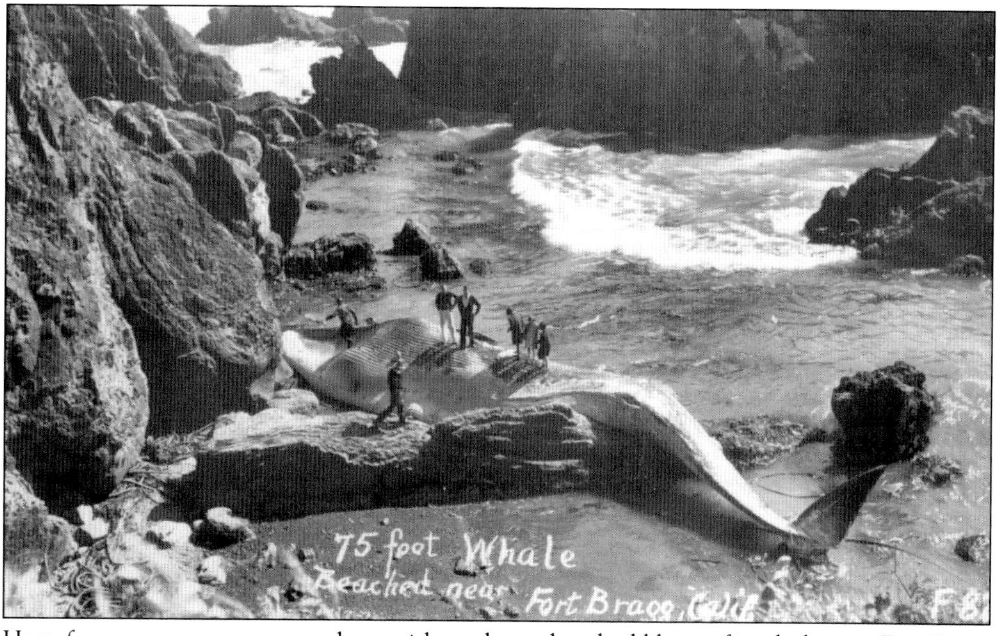

Here, four men, one woman, and two girls explore a beached blue or fin whale near Fort Bragg in Northern California.

Bibliography

Berwick, Edward. "Offshore Whaling in the Bay of Monterey." *The Cosmopolitan*. October 1900: 631.
Bertao, David E. *The Portuguese Shore Whalers of California, 1854–1904*. San Jose, CA: Portuguese Heritage Publications of California, 2006.
chartsmapsgraphics.com
Daily Review (Hayward, CA). January 10, 1957.
Dolin, Eric Jay. *Leviathan: The History of Whaling in America*. New York: W.W. Norton, 2008.
Eureka Humboldt Standard. June 3, 1960.
Independent (Pasadena, CA). November 17, 1971.
Long Beach Press. November 17, 1910.
Nevada State Journal. May 16, 1919.
Pacific Fisherman magazine, January 1914, October 1926, and July, October 1949.
Scammon, Charles Melville. *The Marine Mammals of the North-Western Coast of North America: Together with an Account of the American Whale Fishery. 1874.*
Walsh, Lt. Q.R. "Whaling Industry in Australian and Antarctic Waters," by United States Coast Guard, Inspector of Whaling.
Webb, Bob. *On the Northwest, Commercial Whaling in the Pacific Northwest 1790–1967.* Vancouver: University of British Columbia Press, 1988.
www.canneryrow.com
www.caviews.com
www.cthistoryonline.org
www.library.csustan.edu
www.mysticseaport.org
www.skinnerinc.com